Implementing RtI
With Gifted Students

Service Models, Trends, and Issues

Library of Congress Cataloging-in-Publication Data

Implementing RTI with gifted students: service models, trends, and issues / edited by Mary Ruth Coleman & Susan K. Johnsen.
    p. cm.
 ISBN 978-1-59363-950-1 (pbk.)
1. Gifted children--Education--United States. 2. Response to intervention (Learning disabled children)--United States. I. Coleman, Mary Ruth. II. Johnsen, Susan K.
 LC3993.9.I54 2013
 371.95--dc23

                          2012027443

Edited by Jennifer Robins

Cover and layout design by Raquel Trevino

ISBN-13: 978-1-59363-950-1

Printed in the United States of America.

At the time of this book's publication, all facts and figures cited are the most current available. All telephone numbers, addresses, and websites URLs are accurate and active. All publications, organizations, websites, and other resources exist as described in the book, and all have been verified. The authors and Prufrock Press Inc. make no warranty or guarantee concerning the information and materials given out by organizations or content found at websites, and we are not responsible for any changes that occur after this book's publication. If you find an error, please contact Prufrock Press Inc.

Prufrock Press Inc.
P.O. Box 8813
Waco, TX 76714-8813
Phone: (800) 998-2208
Fax: (800) 240-0333
http://www.prufrock.com

TABLE OF CONTENTS

SECTION III: GIFTED EDUCATION MODELS THAT FIT WITHIN TIERED FRAMEWORKS

SECTION IV: SPECIAL ISSUES AND CONCERNS

FOREWORD

James J. Gallagher
Kenan Professor Emeritus, UNC-Chapel Hill

It is my pleasure to provide some initial thoughts on this volume that brings together many of the most productive professionals in the field of gifted education as they explore how the Response to Intervention (RtI) model blends in with students of great intellectual potential. The RtI model has been one of the latest attempts to provide a framework for organizing assistance for students who need a different approach to meet their academic needs.

Although originally designed to meet the needs of children with learning disabilities, it soon became apparent that RtI could be used for students who were different in many dimensions, including those who are gifted. It is essentially a multi-tiered delivery model designed for students whose needs are not being met in the general education program. As it is content-free, programs with special content can be inserted into this model, as the various chapters in this volume demonstrate.

There is a great advantage to having access, in one volume, to chapters that bring together the available information on RtI and gifted education so that all of the dimensions of the relationship between the two can be explored at one time. In this way, the history of the gifted movement can be understood along with screening, monitoring, assessment, differentiated instruction, and evidence-based practices as they relate to RtI.

Particularly useful are chapters that relate RtI to existing gifted models such as the Schoolwide Enrichment Model (Reis, Gelbar, and Renzulli), the Integrated Curriculum Model (Van Tassel-Baska), the Autonomous Learner Model (Betts and Carey), and U-STARS~PLUS (Coleman and Shah-Coltrane) with discussion as to how RtI can be utilized with current approaches to gifted education. There are also chapters on gifted students from culturally different environments, collaboration with families, and twice-exceptional children.

There are several themes that run through the various chapters, suggesting that a broad agreement exists on how the RtI model should be applied with gifted students. The general consensus follows these four steps:

1. A comprehensive assessment is done using information from teachers, parents, and the students themselves. This reveals the strengths and relative weaknesses of students as well as their passions and interests.

2. Group decision making is called upon to place the assessment data into a reasonable plan of action. This includes the psychologist, gifted specialist, classroom teacher, and others as appropriate. Most plans include higher level thought processes, individual or small-group projects, and some degree of mentoring.

3. Personnel specially prepared to instruct gifted students implement the plan with the help of the team.

4. An evaluation plan is established to determine if the plan's goals and objectives are being met.

As pointed out by Ford and Scott in their chapter on culturally different gifted children, unless this RtI model takes into account the cultural differences of the students, no delivery system such as RtI will likely prosper.

Although the desirability of using evidence-based practices in determining the content is discussed (Robinson and Stein), there is a general recognition of the shortage of research to back up the plan's content—rather, there is a reliance on the judgment of experienced experts to design an operational plan.

One chapter deserves special attention, as it raises doubts and limitations about the use of RtI with gifted students. Coleman and Southern believe that the RtI model is too closely allied with its special education origins and has a remedial focus rather than stressing creativity and imaginative programming. There are a number of other chapters in this book that show this is not necessarily true, and because RtI is a service delivery model, it can deliver whatever the educator thinks is appropriate. Coleman and Southern raise a rather unusual argument that RtI applied to children with disabilities can reduce the differences between these students and average students, while RtI can actually increase the differences between gifted and average students. They seem to think that schools would not be pleased by such a result. Regardless, the editors are to be congratulated for including a chapter that discusses the possible limitations of the RtI model.

With the many chapters touching on these elements of education of the gifted, there is perhaps one chapter missing. Because the expansion of services inevitably means more personnel and more money needed, how will we convince the general public to be supportive of these ideas in an era where the predominant approach is cutting educational resources and personnel rather than expanding them? The long-term virtue of the approach of applying RtI to gifted education may well be apparent but of little help with an immediate budget crisis.

Can this approach be institutionalized through legislation, either new or amended, or some of the other engines of change that have served to establish and protect new reforms from short-term budget attacks? Can we get influential political figures and activist parents to see that we are dealing with the future leadership of the country and that this is, in fact, a national defense issue? If the battlegrounds of the 21st-century are the classrooms of the various competitive nations, then aren't the approaches mentioned in this volume more appropriate than investing in battlefield tanks and nuclear submarines?

When we are told there is no money, that isn't exactly correct, is it? There are all kinds of money available in this richest nation the world has ever seen. What we are really being told is that gifted education doesn't have priority for these funds. Unless we can change that public priority for the activities described in this volume, along with sophisticated content, we are letting down our national defense in a fundamental way.

It will be some time before we can conclude what the benefits and limitations are for the use of the RtI model in the education of gifted students. This volume, with its comprehensive coverage, can help to materially shorten that length of time. It is a useful addition to our growing library of books on educating our most talented students.

PREFACE

Mary Ruth Coleman and Susan K. Johnsen

This joint publication from The Association for the Gifted (TAG), a division of the Council of Exceptional Children (CEC), and the National Association for Gifted Children (NAGC) explores ways in which the needs of students with gifts and talents can be addressed within multi-tiered supports and services through RtI. The book is divided into four sections: an introduction, components of RtI for gifted learners, gifted education models that fit within tiered frameworks, and special issues and concerns. Additional downloadable resources to go along with the book can be found online at https://www.prufrock.com/Implementing_RtI.aspx.

In the introductory chapter, Johnsen, M. R. Coleman, and Hughes describe the characteristics of an RtI model for gifted students, which includes (a) a strong general education curriculum, (b) a system for implementing research-based interventions at all tiers prior to formal identification with fidelity checks on implementation, (c) assessments that include universal screening and progress monitoring, (d) collaborative problem solving that allows greater involvement of parents and professionals, (e) data-driven decision making, and (f) capacity building through professional development and policy.

Four components of the RtI process are examined more closely: assessment, family engagement, collaborative problem solving, and data-driven decision making. Johnsen and Sulak provide a set of questions to assist educators in selecting assessments for use within each tier of the RtI framework. Given the context of standards-based gifted education and accountability requirements, the assessments relate to academic, personal, and social gifted student outcomes. In her chapter, Davis explores the role of engaging families of gifted learners within a multileveled framework to enhance their educational experience. She specifically addresses culturally responsive practices that address the whole child, including his or her immediate and extended family, socioeconomic status, neighborhood, religious or spiritual affiliations, exceptional conditions, and language and dialects. She concludes by making recommendations that will enable schools and families to develop and maintain mutually cooperative engagement practices.

Pereles and Omdal explore the evolution of RtI and gifted education, discuss the problem-solving process as it applies to improving student outcomes, and highlight the need for the development of "problem-solving cultures" at the classroom, school, and district levels. These cultures have (a) a shared vision, (b) a belief that all students can be successful, (c) a strong culture of collaboration built on trust, (d) respect for diversity and inclusion, and (e) a continuous improvement focus that uses data to inform decisions.

In Chapter 5, M. R. Coleman and Job examine the kinds of data required for proactive data-driven decision making, look at the changing uses of data within an RtI framework from both a classroom and a systems level, and explore what data-driven decision making cultures look like. Key to the success of RtI is the proactive use of data to inform decisions at all levels.

Robinson and Stein introduce the next section by providing a context for examining models that fit within an RtI framework. They define an Evidence-Based Practice (EBP) model and show how this model has been used in analyzing research support for specific components of the RtI model. Taking a restrictive definition of EBP, they describe support services for a young, precocious child and a gifted adolescent within the RtI model.

In Chapter 7, Reis, Gelbar, and Renzulli describe how the Schoolwide Enrichment Model (SEM) might enhance Tier 1 in an RtI service delivery model where all students receive general enrichment (e.g., Type I Enrichment). Students who meet the learning objectives of Tier 1 can then qualify for Type II Enrichment or Tier 2, which consists of specific targeted enrichment or curriculum compacting. Type III Enrichment or Tier 3 might include more intense one-on-one projects and problem-based learning opportunities. Similar to RtI, the SEM focuses on the quality of the services rather than the label of the student.

In the next chapter, Betts and Carey describe the intersection between the RtI model and the Autonomous Learner Model. Both are potential-based and use a multi-tiered framework that focuses on the learners' development with intensity of support determined by the needs of an individual learner. They describe three levels of curricula for differentiating instruction and specific learning opportunities for each tier.

VanTassel-Baska also describes how RtI might be applied to features of the Integrated Curriculum Model, including advanced and accelerated content knowledge, higher order thinking and processing, product tasks, and curricular organization around major issues, themes, and ideas. She identifies the universal application of critical and creative thinking skills that result in high-level products for use at Tier 1 of the RtI model. On the other hand, Tier 2 would include activities that might be accessible to those students who are advanced in a particular domain, and Tier 3 would be reserved for students who are engaged in individual learning projects.

The final model covered is U-STARS~PLUS (Using Science, Talents, and Abilities to Recognize Students~Promoting Learning for Underserved Students). M. R. Coleman and Shah-Coltrane discuss how this approach fits within the RtI framework. The focus of U-STARS~PLUS is on nurturing potential in young children from culturally/linguistically different and/or economically disadvantaged families within the general classroom (Tier 1) and providing targeted enhancements to address students' strengths (Tier 2). Systematic observations of students help teachers recognize their strengths, the use of differentiated materials and strategies allows teachers to respond to these strengths, and partnerships with parents provide additional supports for students' success.

The final section on special issues and concerns addresses culturally different students; twice-exceptional learners; challenges, limitations, and concerns; and future opportunities and directions. Ford and Scott describe how the model applies to learning differences associated with culture. They examine RtI through three lenses: culture, giftedness, and poor achievement. They suggest RtI might prevent academic failure by providing support for culturally different students who are underachieving; however, it must be culturally responsive (e.g., have teachers who value cultural differences, a nurturing learning environment, a multicultural curriculum, instruction that considers different ways of learning, culturally fair assessments). Using the Ford-Harris Matrix of Multicultural Gifted Education, they describe how curriculum might be adapted within each of the RtI tiers.

In the next chapter within this section, Adams, Yssel, and Anwiler describe the pros and cons of identifying twice-exceptional (2e) students within an RtI framework. They recommend the use of multiple sources of information even at Tier 1, the universal level, to ensure that 2e students are recognized; progress monitoring of both strengths and weaknesses; formative, ongoing, and summative data to make decisions; and a multilevel prevention system.

In Chapter 13, L. Coleman and Southern raise concerns and challenges regarding the inclusion of gifted and talented students within an RtI framework. They describe the conceptual and philosophical differences implicit in the models underlying RtI and gifted education and argue that RtI undermines gifted education's core beliefs and its existence.

In the final chapter, Johnsen and M. R. Coleman summarize and reflect on the authors' viewpoints regarding opportunities for gifted students within an RtI framework and future directions. The authors conclude that although more study and work is needed, the RtI framework holds promise for delivering appropriate supports and services for gifted learners.

INTRODUCTION

OVERVIEW OF RESPONSE TO INTERVENTION AND ITS APPLICATION TO STUDENTS WITH GIFTS AND TALENTS

Susan K. Johnsen, Mary Ruth Coleman, and Claire E. Hughes

Response to Intervention (RtI) is a new option for examining a student's response to scientific, research-based interventions. Instead of waiting for students to fail, educators are now able to intervene earlier in the instructional process so that students may achieve at higher levels. This approach, which was introduced in 2004 within the Individuals with Disabilities Education Improvement Act (IDEA), allows each state the freedom to develop its RtI process. This chapter will provide background information for the reader by addressing the recent movement toward a developmental model in special and gifted education, definitions of RtI, standard protocol and problem-solving models, and major components of RtI.

Movement Toward a Developmental Model in Special Education

The movement toward RtI originated from special educators' concerns about the discrepancy model. In 1932, Monroe introduced the discrepancy model to operationalize unexpected underachievement. If a student performed in the above average to superior ranges on an intelligence test and was not achieving in the classroom (e.g., performing 2 years below grade level), then that student was identified as an underachiever. If the discrepancy was severe enough, the student was referred for further testing to determine eligibility for special education services. This identification approach did not focus on any factors that might contribute to the student's performance on aptitude or achievement tests (e.g., the school curriculum, instructional strategies, his or her diverse background).

Disenchantment with the effectiveness of the discrepancy model began to emerge in the late 1970s and early 1980s. Criticisms centered on the model's inability to provide sufficient information for interventions, its unreliability due to its dependence on the assessments that were being administered, its focus on deficits where students had to fail before they were referred for services, and its overidentification and labeling of students with specific learning disabilities (Bender & Shores, 2007; Fletcher et al., 1998; Vaughn, Linan-Thompson, & Hickman, 2003; Vellutino, Scanlon, & Lyon, 2000). Alternative, more developmental identification approaches were sought to identify students who needed assistance at an earlier point in their education to better guide the intervention process and to help determine the intervention's effectiveness on student performance (Deno, 1985; D. Fuchs, Mock, Morgan, & Young, 2003; L. S. Fuchs, Deno, & Mirkin, 1984; Gresham, 1989). These approaches included prereferral teams, curriculum-based measurement, and dynamic assessments, where general education teachers tried different instructional interventions to determine their effects on student progress. Although these assessments and interventions were beneficial for identifying students who needed different instructional approaches or services, they were often not valued by general education teachers because they required more work and were less efficient than traditional approaches (Gersten & Dimino, 2006).

Over the next two decades, the concept of RtI was heavily debated and researched. Numerous organizations, discussion panels, and summits brought together experts to discuss RtI's advantages and disadvantages. It was not until both the President's Commission on Excellence in Special Education (2002) and the National Research Center on Learning Disabilities (2002) supported the Response to Intervention concept that a more student-centered approach to identification became a part of IDEA in 2004. Schools would now be encouraged to develop alternative instructional approaches to identify students who were struggling. These new RtI frameworks addressed the historical criticisms and had advantages over the discrepancy model, including (a) earlier identification of learning problems, (b) the use of a developmental model rather than a deficit model, and (c) a focus on student outcomes.

Movement Toward a Developmental Model in Gifted Education

Paralleling this movement in special education, gifted educators began to examine the developmental nature of students with gifts and talents. Moving away from a singular assessment such as an intelligence test to identify gifted students, the Marland (1972) report broadened the definition of giftedness to include students from diverse domains such as the fine arts, leadership, and creativity, and the *National Excellence* (U.S. Department of Education, 1993) report emphasized the importance of developing students' strengths rather than focusing on remediating their deficiencies. *National Excellence* encouraged educators to provide challenging learning opportunities and to increase access to early childhood education, particularly for gifted students from underrepresented groups such as minorities and children in poverty. The National Research Council's (2002) report, *Minority Students in Special and Gifted Education*, echoed these concerns by calling for a focus on nurturing potential and access to challenging curricula for students from culturally or linguistically diverse and economically disadvantaged families. Theorists also offered more developmental views of giftedness. For example, Gagné (1995) proposed a Differentiated Model of Giftedness and Talent where gifts, which are natural abilities, must be developed to become talents, through the systematic learning, training, and practicing of skills that are relevant to a particular domain.

More recently, the National Association for Gifted Children (NAGC, 2011) adopted a new definition that emphasizes talent development:

> Gifted individuals are those who demonstrate outstanding levels of aptitude (defined as an exceptional ability to reason and learn) or competence (documented performance or achievement in top 10% or rarer) in one or more domains. Domains include any structured area of activity with its own symbol system (e.g., mathematics, music, language) and/or set of sensorimotor skills (e.g., painting, dance, sports).
>
> The development of ability or talent is a lifelong process. It can be evident in young children as exceptional performance on tests and/or other measures of ability or as a rapid rate of learning, compared to other students of the same age, or in actual achievement in a domain. As individuals mature through

childhood to adolescence, however, achievement and high levels of motivation in the domain become the primary characteristics of their giftedness. Various factors can either enhance or inhibit the development and expression of abilities.

A person's giftedness should not be confused with the means by which giftedness is observed or assessed. Parent, teacher, or student recommendations, a high mark on an examination, or a high IQ score are not giftedness; they may be a signal that giftedness exists. Some of these indices of giftedness are more sensitive than others to differences in the person's environment. (para. 4–6)

The NAGC definition describes ability as a "lifelong process" and emphasizes the use of assessments that examine "rapid rates of learning." Because of this emphasis on talent development in the field of gifted education, educators are encouraged to (a) identify students' strengths at an early age and provide services that address these strengths, (b) view giftedness as a developmental construct, and (c) focus on student outcomes. For students to be identified as having talents in particular domains, they need classrooms where they have opportunities to show their gifts and achieve at high levels (Coleman & Shah-Coltrane, 2010). All of these recommendations are similar to the advantages noted in the RtI model for special education. The remainder of this chapter will discuss RtI, its components, and its utility in general, gifted, and special education.

Definition of Response to Intervention

Response to Intervention is a schoolwide process that integrates curriculum and instruction with ongoing assessment and intervention (Johnson, Mellard, Fuchs, & McKnight, 2006). The purpose of RtI is for *all* students to receive high-quality, scientifically validated instructional practices in the general education classroom so that they achieve higher levels of academic and behavioral success (Campbell, Wang, & Algozzine, 2010; Kirk, Gallagher, Coleman, & Anastasiow, 2012; Mellard & Johnson, 2008). Its components include a multi-tiered or layered set of increasingly intensive interventions designed to (a) enhance the early identification of students who are struggling in basic skills so that they will not fall further behind other students (Bender & Shores,

2007; Johnson & Smith, 2008; Vaughn et al., 2003) and/or (b) nurture children's areas of strength so that they will be able to advance according to their developmental levels (Coleman & Hughes, 2009). In all cases, the purpose of RtI is to bring a child to higher levels of development by matching appropriate interventions to his or her needs.

Two approaches to designing an RtI process have been described in the literature and implemented at the state and local levels: standard protocol models and problem-solving models.

Standard Protocol Models

Standard protocol models require the use of scientifically based classroom instruction with all students, regular administration of curriculum-based assessments, and frequent comparisons of students to expected growth (D. Fuchs & Fuchs, 2005). If a student is not progressing as expected, he or she receives a well-defined and often scripted intervention. Because of the standardization of the curriculum, the standard protocol can be implemented with fidelity, which helps to ensure that a student's unresponsiveness to the curriculum is not related to poor instruction.

Most standard protocols provide support for students who are struggling in reading and math; they have not been developed for gifted students. Protocols for gifted students will look different from those in special education and will include a scientifically based curriculum that is above grade level and that supports a student's strengths and interests (VanTassel-Baska, Avery, Little, & Hughes, 2000; VanTassel-Baska, Zuo, Avery, & Little, 2002). Progress will still be monitored, but students will be expected to develop within a domain or talent area at an accelerated rate or more complex level when compared to their same-age peers. The responsiveness of the students would still be used as a guide as to the effectiveness of the intervention.

Problem-Solving Models

In problem-solving models, a student's poor classroom performance prompts a team-based examination of possible modifications, supports, or enhancements within the general education classroom (Kavale & Spaulding, 2008). The four-level problem-solving model generally involves (a) identifying the problem, (b) designing and implementing interventions, (c) monitoring the student's progress and modifying the interventions according to the student's responsiveness, and (d) planning the next steps (Bolt, 2005; Deno,

2002; Mellard, Byrd, Johnson, Tollefson, & Boesche, 2004). The model provides increasingly intensive interventions that are planned and implemented by school personnel. Referrals to special education services are made only in those cases where the suggested interventions are ineffective. The problem-solving approach is also used within a schoolwide behavioral support model (e.g., Positive Behavior Support Model; Sugai, Horner, & Gresham, 2002). In this case, the interventions address behavioral concerns in addition to academic concerns.

Some RtI problem-solving models at both the state and school district levels have included gifted and talented students (Rollins, Mursky, Shah-Coltrane, & Johnsen, 2009). For example, U-STARS~PLUS (Coleman & Shah-Coltrane, 2010) is centered in the K–3 regular education classroom with a highly engaging, science-based curriculum, whereas the Wisconsin Department of Public Instruction model has expanded upon its statewide special education model in applying Response to Intervention to include gifted students (Rollins et al., 2009). In these models, high-quality differentiated instruction is provided that engages each student in challenging, meaningful tasks. For students who have already met or exceeded the expected benchmarks, interventions occur, including acceleration, compacting, enrichment, and other forms of targeted support. Balanced assessments that incorporate formative, benchmark, and summative measures ensure that the interventions are effective with the students.

The majority of states use a combination of standard protocol and problem-solving approaches (Berkeley, Bender, Peaster, & Saunders, 2009). Each of the approaches emphasizes high-quality instruction, the use of ongoing assessments in making decisions regarding student progress, and collaboration.

Major Components of RtI

Key components of RtI include (a) a strong general education curriculum, (b) a system for implementing research-based interventions at all tiers prior to formal identification with fidelity checks on implementation, (c) assessments that include universal screening and progress monitoring, (d) collaborative problem solving that allows greater involvement of parents and professionals, (e) data-driven decision making, and (f) capacity building through professional development and policy so that practitioners can successfully implement the components of RtI (Hughes, Rollins, & Coleman, 2011; Johnson et al., 2006).

A Strong General Education Curriculum

RtI is based on the principle that all children can achieve high standards if given access to a strong core curriculum. To develop a strong core curriculum that includes gifted students, it needs to be aligned to evidence-based standards that are driven by postsecondary education and careers (e.g., PK–16 standards) and to standards in the professional fields. In implementing the standards, all educators need to be aware of research-based practices in gifted education.

Similar to general educators, gifted educators use the content standards identified by major professional associations, such as the Common Core State Standards Initiative, the National Council of Teachers of English, and the National Council of Teachers of Mathematics, as a basis for developing differentiated curriculum. In addition, the National Association for Gifted Children and the Council for Exceptional Children (NAGC, 2010 [Standard 3]; NAGC & CEC, 2006 [Standards 4 and 7]) have developed teacher preparation standards and programming standards that identify these evidence-based practices of curriculum and instruction for students with gifts and talents.

Both sets of standards emphasize that the curriculum should be:

➢ aligned to local, state, and national standards;
➢ effective for students with talents across all domains (e.g., cognitive, affective, aesthetic, social, leadership);
➢ responsive to students from diverse backgrounds;
➢ comprehensive and continuous;
➢ defined by preassessment and formative assessment so that students' needs may be identified, differentiated education plans can be developed, and plans can be adjusted based on continual progress monitoring;
➢ adapted, modified, or replacing the core or standard curriculum;
➢ advanced, conceptually challenging, in-depth, distinctive, and complex;
➢ paced, compacted, and accelerated based on the learning rates of students;
➢ individualized with technologies, including assistive technologies for twice-exceptional students; and
➢ integrated with career exploration experiences.

Along with these curriculum standards, NAGC and CEC (2006) included these specific evidence-based instructional strategies:

➢ independent research,
➢ metacognition,
➢ inquiry models,

> ➤ critical thinking,
> ➤ creative thinking, and
> ➤ problem solving.

The research base for these standards was comprised of empirical research, literature, and practice-based studies that supported each of the standards and its elements (Johnsen, VanTassel-Baska, & Robinson, 2008). More than 150 annotated summaries support the research base for the teacher preparation standards related to planning (Standard 7) and instruction (Standard 4; NAGC, 2006).

Models in gifted education incorporate many of these standards and may fit within an RtI framework, providing a strong general education curriculum for gifted and talented students.

The Tiered RtI Framework

Many of the current implementation models of RtI are graphically demonstrated by the shape of a pyramid, with multiple levels of intervention. Some states have adopted a three-tier version of the pyramid, although there are states with a four-tier version as well (Georgia Department of Education, 2011). The primary difference lies in the degree of intervention explicitly detailed between the general curriculum and very intensive, long-term, specific interventions, with the intensive intervention in the top tier serving the fewest numbers of students who are farthest away from the norm (Hughes et al., 2011). We will describe the three-tier version, as it is the one that is most widely used. Figure 1.1 provides a graphic representation of how universal, targeted, and intensive instruction is distributed across the student population.

Typically, Tiers 1 and 2 focus on small-group interventions, increasing in intensity to the individual level of Tier 3 (CEC, 2008). Each school district or state defines the indications of strengths and needs that match students with supports across the tiers.

In talent-nurturing models, student supports and enhancements will increase in depth, breadth, pacing, and/or complexity of content for students across the tiers. Students will also be provided acceleration and enrichment opportunities to develop their abilities (Coleman & Hughes, 2009). With successful achievement, gifted and talented students will move to more intensive interventions and services delivered in higher tiers. The RtI model is focused on student growth, with more intense services provided to students with more

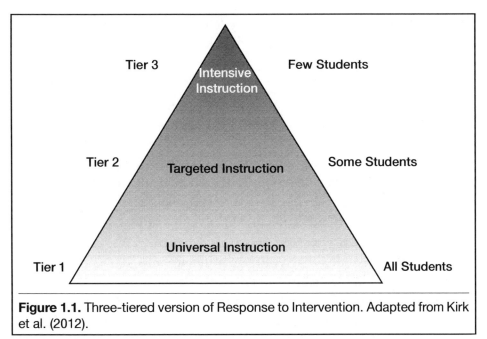

Figure 1.1. Three-tiered version of Response to Intervention. Adapted from Kirk et al. (2012).

intense needs. Essentially, as the needs of the student increase, educational responses also increase.

The use of multi-tier supports and services allows for a strategic match of students' strengths and needs with appropriate interventions. This matching process is flexible, and students often receive supports and services across all of the tiers (e.g., general education within Tier 1, additional enrichment in reading within Tier 2, and accelerated math within Tier 3). What do the tiers look like from a gifted education viewpoint?

Tier 1: Universal nurturing of potential. With the increasing acceptance of talent development as a critical part of gifted education, the importance of nurturing the potential of *all* students becomes essential. Building on a strong general education foundation, from a gifted education perspective, Tier 1 should provide enhanced learning for all students (Coleman & Shah-Coltrane, 2011). The use of universal design principles (i.e., providing multiple ways of representing, engaging, and expressing information) combined with differentiated instruction strategies allows teachers to offer enriched and challenging learning opportunities that extend the general curriculum. An enhanced curriculum within Tier 1 is key to nurturing potential in all learners and is critical for culturally/linguistically diverse and economically disadvantaged students with high potential who remain underrepresented within gifted education (Coleman & Shah Coltrane, 2010).

Tier 2: Targeted enhancements. Students who are successful in the nurturing environment provided through Tier 1 enhancements may benefit from additionally challenging learning opportunities targeted to meet their interests and strengths. Tier 2 experiences can be offered without formal identification, and these targeted enhancements may help us recognize students who need to be nominated for gifted education services. Tier 2 enhancements are often planned in collaboration with a gifted education specialist. These targeted enhancements may include a wide range of enriched and accelerated learning options that build on the students' interests and academic strengths.

Tier 3: Intensive individualized instruction. The most intensive tier focuses on the students' needs for sustainable program development. In Tier 3, a student's talent is often crystallized, and interventions can be matched with the child's areas of strength. Program implications are very specific and are driven by the individualistic nature of the talent of the child. In Tier 3, students may be identified as gifted and talented in a specific area, and long-term programming is implemented to enhance and further their specific abilities. Each state and district determines what kinds of talents and abilities are addressed and establishes the formal identification criteria for long-term programming. Ideally, gifted education specialists are deeply involved in this process. In this way, Tier 3 focuses on extending the nurturing of talents in Tiers 1 and 2 through a talent development process that is centered on specific areas of student achievement. Although there is no right or wrong way of implementing talent development, the goal is to provide instruction and learning opportunities for students so they continue to grow. Tier 3 interventions are more individualized in their planning, although not necessarily in their delivery. In other words, individual student needs must be taken into consideration when planning interventions, but this does not necessarily translate into individualized instruction.

Some students may have additional factors that impact their talent development, and Tier 3 interventions can take these into consideration. The individual planning in Tier 3 is, for example, useful for students with complex needs, such as twice-exceptional students or gifted students from special populations. A child who is gifted in math and who has a learning disability in reading, for example, may need Tier 2 remedial reading support while simultaneously needing Tier 3 talent interventions in math that also take into consideration his challenges with reading. Perhaps the most important thing to remember about the tiers is that these supports and services can be accessed as needed with flexibility across levels.

Assessments, Universal Screening, and Progress Monitoring

Assessments are incorporated throughout the tiers within the Response to Intervention framework. During Tier 1, educators administer assessments to the whole class to identify students who are progressing above or below the expected rates. These assessments may include informal teacher-made instruments, curriculum-based measurements, and/or more formal school district benchmark tests. The results are then analyzed to determine which students might need more intensive services and supports.

Students who continually exceed and/or fall below the class average may move to Tier 2 services where the frequency of progress monitoring is increased. For advanced students, this may mean changing year-end goals set by the general education curriculum so that the students may progress at an appropriate pace. Appropriate pacing involves above-grade-level preassessments to determine the need for more advanced materials and opportunities for students to delve more deeply into topics of interest that allow for innovative and more complex responses (Johnsen & Sheffield, 2013). These assessments may include above-grade-level tests and rubrics to evaluate more complex products and performances.

As data accumulate from Tier 1 and Tier 2 assessments, educators may decide that more support is needed for the student. This level of service requires clearly established protocols and may involve more comprehensive, diagnostic assessments that meet state rules and regulations in identifying students for specialized classrooms or schools. Formal identification will involve collaboration between educators, families, and other professionals, with assessments matching the student's areas of strengths and weaknesses (Johnsen, 2011a, 2011b). Assessments need to be technically adequate and include both qualitative and quantitative information so that appropriate supports can be provided.

Assessment is key in the RtI framework. It provides critical information at each tier of service to ensure that each student's strengths are developed and his or her weaknesses are addressed. Throughout the entire process, special attention needs to be paid to minimizing bias so that students from diverse backgrounds are considered for more intensive services.

Collaborative Problem Solving and Parent Engagement

The fourth major component of RtI is the collaborative problem-solving process, which brings together professionals and parents. As noted earlier in the chapter, problem-solving models for planning curriculum interventions were essential to the development of RtI. Building on this, the use of collaborative problem solving with teams of professionals and parents is now a central feature of most RtI frameworks. The collaborative process is essential to creating the conditions for synergy needed to address the complex needs of students (Pereles, Baldwin, & Omdal, 2011). Families are key partners in shaping and supporting the education of each learner, and their participation is what makes the collaborative problem-solving process successful (Colorado Department of Education, 2009). The success of the collaborative problem-solving process hinges on the use of data to inform and support decisions. This data-driven decision-making approach allows all members of the problem-solving team to see the student's strengths and needs and to reflect on outcomes of the supports and services provided.

Data-Driven Decision Making

Data-driven decision making is the use of pertinent information to support the decision-making process (Ysseldyke, Burns, Scholin, & Parker, 2010). What is considered pertinent depends, of course, on the decision to be made. Data can take many forms and may include numerical summaries, narrative descriptions, and even pictorial or graphic representations of information. Data can also come from multiple sources, including students and their families. Data can be tracked and monitored overtime to help identify meaningful trends, patterns, and changes.

The data-driven decision-making process can be used for instructional and planning decisions for individual students, classes, schools, and school districts. Within the RtI process, data help us determine the intensity of the student's strengths and needs so that we can match these with appropriate supports and services (Allain & Eberhardt, 2011). Data also help us gauge schoolwide success and identify challenge areas that need systemic attention (e.g., attendance, family participation in school activities, student outcomes). Finally, data can be used at the school district level to guide policy decisions regarding the allocation of resources and personnel. The key is that the data *inform* the decision process. If the data we use are informative, valid, and comprehensive, we have greater confidence that the decisions we make will be good ones.

Capacity Building: Professional Development and Policy

Building the infrastructure needed to support change is key to its success (Fixsen, Naoom, Blasé, Friedman, & Wallace, 2005). The infrastructure needed to support RtI implementation includes policies at the school, district, and state levels and professional development (Brown & Abernethy, 2009, 2011; Johnsen, 2011b). Policy and professional development combine to provide support for high-quality implementation.

Policies that guide practice. Policies shape, define, and standardize practice in a way that hopefully leads to consistency and quality assurance (Coleman, Gallagher, & Job, 2012). Gallagher (1994) noted that:

> policy creates the rules and standards by which scarce resources are allocated to meet almost unlimited social needs. An effective social policy should answer the following questions:
> 1. Who shall receive the resources?
> 2. Who shall deliver the resources?
> 3. What are the resources to be delivered?
> 4. What are the conditions under which the resources are delivered? (p. 337)

When we think about gifted education and RtI, policies addressing these questions are usually found at the state level (Brown & Abernethy, 2011). However, although many states have developed policies related to RtI, gifted education has not always been included. As states move forward with implementation, it is essential that gifted education become an active partner with RtI initiatives to ensure that the needs of all students can be addressed (Brown & Abernethy, 2011).

Professional development and technical assistance. The second element of infrastructure needed to support RtI implementation is professional development (both preservice and in-service). Professional development is essential because it addresses the knowledge and skills needed for success. The Association for the Gifted (TAG), a division of the Council of Exceptional Children (CEC), in collaboration with the National Association for Gifted Children, defined the body of knowledge needed to be a teacher of students with gifts and talents (NAGC, 2006). These teacher preparation standards fit well with the RtI framework and offer a solid foundation for professional development designed to support its implementation.

Concluding Thoughts

RtI approaches that address the needs of students with gifts and talents are emerging in many states and districts. These approaches draw on a strong foundation of talent development within gifted education. Throughout the remaining chapters, we will explore ways in which the needs of students with gifts and talents can be addressed within multi-tiered supports and services through RtI.

References

Allain, J. K., & Eberhardt, N. C. (2011). *RtI: The forgotten tier: A practical guide for building a data-driven Tier I instructional process.* Stockton, KS: Rowe.

Bender, W., & Shores, C. (2007). *Response to Intervention: A practical guide for every teacher.* Arlington, VA: Council for Exceptional Children.

Berkeley, S., Bender, W. N., Peaster, L. G., & Saunders, L. (2009). Implementation of Response to Intervention: A snapshot of progress. *Journal of Learning Disabilities, 42,* 85–95.

Bolt, S. E. (2005). Reflections on practice within the Heartland Problem-Solving Model: The perceived value of direct assessment of student needs. *The California School Psychologist, 10,* 65–79.

Brown, E. F., & Abernethy, S. H. (2009). Policy implications at the state and district level with RtI for gifted students. *Gifted Child Today, 32*(3), 52–57.

Brown, E. F., & Abernethy, S. H. (2011). RtI for gifted students: Policy implications. In M. R. Coleman & S. K. Johnsen (Eds.), *RtI for gifted students* (pp. 87–102). Waco, TX: Prufrock Press.

Campbell, P., Wang, A., & Algozzine, B. (2010). *55 tactics for implementing RtI in inclusive settings.* Thousand Oaks, CA: Corwin Press.

Coleman, M. R., Gallagher, J. J., & Job, J. (2012). Developing and sustaining professionalism within gifted education. *Gifted Child Today, 35*(1), 27–36.

Coleman, M. R., & Hughes, C. (2009). Meeting the needs of gifted students within an RtI framework. *Gifted Child Today, 32*(3), 14–17.

Coleman, M. R., & Shah-Coltrane, S. (2010). *U-STARS~PLUS professional development kit.* Arlington, VA: Council for Exceptional Children.

Coleman, M. R., & Shah-Coltrane, S. (2011). Remembering the importance of potential: Tiers 1 and 2. In M. R. Coleman & S. K. Johnsen (Eds.), *RtI for gifted students* (pp. 43–61). Waco, TX: Prufrock Press.

Colorado Department of Education. (2009). *Response to Intervention (RtI) family and community partnering: "On the team and at the table" toolkit.* Denver, CO: Author.

Council for Exceptional Children. (2008). *CEC's position on Response to Intervention (RTI): The unique role of special education and special educators.* Retrieved from http://www.cec.sped.org/AM/Template.cfm?Section= Response_to_Intervention&Template=/TaggedPage/TaggedPageDisplay. cfm&TPLID=37&ContentID=8363

Deno, S. L. (1985). Curriculum-based measurement: The emerging alternative. *Exceptional Children, 52,* 219–232.

Deno, S. L. (2002). Problem solving as "best practice." In A. Thomas & J. Grimes (Eds.), *Best practices in school psychology IV* (pp. 37–56). Bethesda, MD: NASP.

Fixsen, D. L., Naoom, S. F., Blasé, K. A., Friedman, R. M., & Wallace, F. (2005). *Implementation research: A synthesis of the literature.* Tampa, FL: University of South Florida.

Fletcher, J. M., Francis, D. J., Shaywitz, S. E., Lyon, G. R., Foorman, B. R., Stuebing, K. K., & Shaywitz, B. A. (1998). Intelligent testing and the discrepancy model for children with learning disabilities. *Learning Disabilities Research and Practice, 13,* 186–203.

Fuchs, D., & Fuchs, L. S. (2005). Responsiveness-to-Intervention: A blueprint for practitioners, policymakers, and parents. *Teaching Exceptional Children, 38,* 57–61.

Fuchs, D., Mock, D., Morgan, P. L., & Young, C. L. (2003). Responsiveness-to-Intervention: Definitions, evidence, and implications for learning disabilities construct. *Learning Disabilities Research and Practice, 18,* 157–171.

Fuchs, L. S., Deno, S. L., & Mirkin, P. (1984). Effects of frequent curriculum-based measurement and evaluation on pedagogy, student achievement, and student awareness of learning. *American Educational Research Journal, 21,* 449–460.

Gagné, F. (1995). From giftedness to talent: A developmental model and its impact on the language of the field. *Roeper Review, 18,* 103–111.

Gallagher, J. J. (1994). Policy design for diversity. In D. M. Bryant & M. A. Graham (Eds.), *Implementing early intervention: From research to effective practice* (pp. 336–350). New York, NY: Guilford Press.

Georgia Department of Education. (2011). *Pyramid of interventions.* Retrieved from http://www.doe.k12.ga.us/Curriculum-Instruction-and-Assessment/

Curriculum-and-Instruction/Documents/RTI%20document%20Full%20Text.pdf

Gersten, R., & Dimino, J. (2006). RtI (Response to Intervention): Rethinking special education for students with reading difficulties (yet again). *Reading Research Quarterly, 41,* 99–107.

Gresham, F. M. (1989). Assessment of treatment integrity in school consultation and prereferral intervention. *School Psychology Review, 18,* 37–50.

Hughes, C. E., Rollins, K., & Coleman, M. R. (2011). Response to Intervention for gifted learners. In M. R. Coleman & S. K. Johnsen (Eds.), *RtI for gifted students* (pp. 1–20). Waco, TX: Prufrock Press.

Individuals with Disabilities Education Improvement Act, Pub. Law 108-446 (December 3, 2004).

Johnsen, S., VanTassel-Baska, J., & Robinson, A. (2008). *Using the national gifted education standards for university teacher preparation programs.* Thousand Oaks, CA: Corwin Press.

Johnsen, S. K. (Ed.). (2011a). *Identifying gifted students: A practical guide* (2nd ed.). Waco, TX: Prufrock Press.

Johnsen, S. K. (2011b). Assessing your school's RtI model in serving gifted students. In M. R. Coleman & S. K. Johnsen (Eds.), *RtI for gifted students* (pp. 103–118). Waco, TX: Prufrock Press.

Johnsen, S. K., & Sheffield, L. S. (Eds.). (2013). *Using the Common Core State Standards for Mathematics with gifted and advanced learners.* Waco, TX: Prufrock Press.

Johnson, E., Mellard, D. F., Fuchs, D., & McKnight, M. A. (2006). *Responsiveness to Intervention (RtI): How to do it.* Lawrence, KS: National Research Center.

Johnson, E. S., & Smith, L. (2008). Implementation of Response to Intervention at middle school: Challenges and potential benefits. *TEACHING Exceptional Children, 40*(3), 46–52.

Kavale, K. A., & Spaulding, L. S. (2008). Is Response to Intervention good policy for specific learning disability? *Learning Disabilities Research and Practice, 23,* 168–179.

Kirk, S., Gallagher, J., Coleman, M. R., & Anastasiow, N. (2012). *Educating exceptional children* (13th ed.). Belmont, CA: Cengage Learning.

Marland, S. P., Jr. (1972). Education of the gifted and talented: Report to the Congress of the United States by the U.S. Commissioner of Education and background papers submitted to the U.S. Office of Education, 2 vols. Washington, DC: U.S. Government Printing Office. (Government Documents, Y4.L 11/2: G36)

Mellard, D., Byrd, S. E., Johnson, E., Tollefson, J. M., & Boesche, L. (2004). Foundations and research on identifying model Responsiveness-to-Intervention sites. *Learning Disability Quarterly, 27,* 243–256.

Mellard, D. F., & Johnson, E. S. (2008). *RtI: A practitioner's guide to implementing Response-to-Intervention.* Thousand Oaks, CA: Corwin Press.

Monroe, M. (1932). *Children who cannot read.* Chicago, IL: The University of Chicago Press.

National Association for Gifted Children. (2006). *Teacher Knowledge and Skill Standards for Gifted and Talented Education.* Retrieved from http://www.nagc.org/uploadedFiles/Information_and_Resources/NCATE_standards/final%20standards%20(2006).pdf

National Association for Gifted Children. (2010). *Pre-K–Grade 12 Gifted Education Programming Standards.* Retrieved from http://www.nagc.org/index.aspx?id=546

National Association for Gifted Children. (2011). *What is giftedness?* Retrieved from http://www.nagc.org/WhatisGiftedness.aspx

National Association for Gifted Children, & Council for Exceptional Children. (2006). *Initial Knowledge and Skill Standards for Gifted Education.* Retrieved from http://www.cectag.org

National Research Center on Learning Disabilities. (2002). *Achieving better outcomes—maintaining rights: An approach to identifying and serving students with specific learning disabilities.* New York, NY: Author.

National Research Council. (2002). *Minority students in special and gifted education.* Washington, DC: National Academy Press.

Pereles, D., Baldwin, L., & Omdal, S. (2011). Addressing the needs of students who are twice-exceptional. In M. R. Coleman & S. K. Johnsen (Eds.), *RtI for gifted students* (pp. 63–86). Waco, TX: Prufrock Press.

President's Commission on Excellence in Special Education. (2002). *A new era: Revitalizing special education for children and their families.* Washington, DC: U.S. Department of Education.

Rollins, K., Mursky, C.V., Shah-Coltrane, S., & Johnsen, S. K. (2009). RtI models for gifted children. *Gifted Child Today, 32*(3), 20–30.

Sugai, G., Horner, R., & Gresham, F. (2002). Behaviorally effective school environments. In M. Shinn, H. Walker, & G. Stoner (Eds.), *Interventions for academic and behavior problems II: Preventive and remedial approach* (pp. 315–350). Bethesda, MD: Bethesda School of Psychologists.

U.S. Department of Education, Office of Educational Research. (1993). *National excellence: A case for developing America's talent.* Washington, DC: U.S. Government Printing Office.

VanTassel-Baska, J., Avery, L. D., Little, C. A., & Hughes, C. E. (2000). An evaluation of the implementation: The impact of the William and Mary units on schools. *Journal for the Education of the Gifted, 23,* 244–272.

VanTassel-Baska, J., Zuo, L., Avery, L. D., & Little, C. A. (2002). A curriculum study of gifted student learning in the language arts. *Gifted Child Quarterly, 46,* 30–44.

Vaughn, S., Linan-Thompson, S., & Hickman, P. (2003). Response to instruction as a means of identifying students with reading/learning disabilities. *Exceptional Children, 69,* 391–409.

Vellutino, F., Scanlon, D., & Lyon, G. R. (2000). Differentiating between difficult-to-remediate and readily remediated poor readers: More evidence against the achievement discrepancy definition of reading disability. *Journal of Learning Disabilities, 33,* 223–238.

Ysseldyke, J., Burns, M. K., Scholin, S. E., & Parker, D. C. (2010). Instructionally valid assessment within Response to Intervention. *TEACHING Exceptional Children, 42*(4), 54–61.

COMPONENTS OF RTI FOR GIFTED LEARNERS

CHAPTER TWO

SCREENING, ASSESSMENT, AND PROGRESS MONITORING

Susan K. Johnsen and Tracey N. Sulak

Assessments are integrated within the Response to Intervention (RtI) framework. They are used to determine if students are making expected progress and to examine the effectiveness of the curriculum and instruction. This chapter will focus on different types of assessments that are used within RtI (i.e., universal screening, progress monitoring, and identification), their relationship to gifted education programming standards, and ways they might be used to identify gifted students' strengths and weaknesses. Across all situations, the assessments and procedures need to minimize bias and be fair to each and every student.

Universal Screening

Universal screening involves administering assessments to the whole class at set times to identify students who are not progressing at the expected rate and, in the case of gifted students, to identify those who are progressing at a more advanced rate. For example, at the beginning of the school year, the teacher might administer curriculum-based measurement (CBM) instruments to examine basic skill proficiency or other teacher-made, informal assessments to determine the students' knowledge and skills. All of the students in the class might be asked to respond to a writing prompt and an informal reading inventory to determine their current fluency levels, decoding and comprehension skills, and organization of thoughts. The assessment results would be analyzed to determine which students are progressing at the expected rate and which might need to be closely monitored to determine if they need more intensive services. Intensive services are offered to students who are struggling or performing below grade level, as well as those who are advanced and performing above grade level. Other universal screeners might include standardized diagnostic instruments such as the Test of Written Language (TOWL-4; Hammill & Larsen, 2009) or school district benchmark tests that are aligned with the curriculum. The intention of all universal screeners is to identify students who need additional supports or individual interventions in order to make progress.

Progress Monitoring

Progress monitoring, or the use of formative and interim assessments, informs the practice of teaching and learning (Heritage, 2010). Direct and frequent samples of student performance before, during, and after instruction provide the most meaningful information to teachers. Teachers are able to use this information in determining how a student is responding and whether or not to make any changes. For struggling students, these assessments need to be precise regarding the mastery of specific knowledge or skills, frequent, and sensitive to small changes (Ysseldyke, Burns, Scholin, & Parker, 2010). For students who are advanced, they need to incorporate above-grade-level knowledge and skills.

Sato, Wei, and Darling-Hammond (2008) provided a set of questions that educators might want to consider when selecting formative or progress monitoring assessments:

> ➢ *Do I use a variety of quality assessment methods that are consistent with learning goals and further each student's learning?* A variety of data (e.g., qualitative and quantitative) are important in monitoring students' strengths and weaknesses, because a single assessment samples only a limited set of behaviors. The progress monitoring assessments need to engage the learner and be aligned with the full range of knowledge and skills within a domain. For an advanced student, the range might include above-grade-level curricula; for a struggling learner, the range may be below grade level. The range might include measures of

knowledge acquisition, depth of problem representation, mental models, efficiency of procedures, metacognitive skills, and automaticity of performance (Anderson, 1982).

➤ *Have I clearly articulated learning goals and success criteria that are conceptually important and developmentally appropriate for each student?* Assessment criteria that determine advancement or the need for intervention must be challenging yet attainable and understood by both the teacher and the student (Moon, Brighton, Callahan, & Robinson, 2005). Clarity provides opportunities for student self-monitoring and improved assessment design. To be developmentally appropriate, the selection of assessments needs to be based on the learner's prior knowledge so that they are sensitive to identifying each student's strengths and weaknesses (Dochy, Segers, & Buehl, 1999).

➤ *Do I provide opportunities for student self-monitoring?* For self-monitoring to occur, students need to understand the standard, recognize what the teacher views as quality work, compare their actual level of performance with the standard, and engage in learning that helps them achieve the standard (Sadler, 1989). Teachers, in turn, need to help students in developing the skills to make judgments about their learning, help them organize new knowledge, and eventually reduce support so that learners become more independent in the process of self-monitoring. Self-monitoring furthers student achievement (Phillips, Hamlett, Fuchs, & Fuchs, 1993) and helps the learner progress from a novice to an expert within a domain of study (Donovan & Bransford, 2005; Ericsson, 1993).

➤ *Do I consider the student's prior knowledge and demonstrate flexibility and responsiveness to the student's needs and interests in making future instructional decisions?* Modifications that are made during the learning process are sometimes described as dynamic assessments, where the teacher focuses on the interaction between the student and the learning activity, providing assistance as needed to understand the student's strengths and weaknesses (Swanson & Lussier, 2001). For a teacher to discover potential, the progress monitoring assessments must be novel, problem-based, and require complex strategies (Geary & Brown, 1991; Kurtz & Weinert, 1989; Scruggs & Mastropieri, 1985). Researchers have reported that dynamic assessment and other progress monitoring and formative assessment procedures, such as curriculum compacting, improve students' performance substantially (Dochy et al., 1999; Reis, Burns, & Renzulli, 1992; Swanson & Lussier, 2001).

> ➤ *Do I provide feedback to the student that is specific to the task, prompts him or her to take further action, and is tailored to each student's needs?* Feedback is the information communicated to the learner that is intended to modify his or her thinking or behavior to improve learning (Shute, 2008). Quality feedback is timely and frequent, specific, well formatted, and constructive (Black, Harrison, Lee, Marshall, & Wiliam, 2003; Brunner et al., 2005; Clymer & Wiliam, 2007; Schunk & Swartz, 1992; Shute, 2008; Shepard, 1995). It focuses on the task, not the learner, and considers errors as opportunities for learning (Dweck, 1999). For high-achieving students, delayed feedback, verification of their responses, and hints or prompts seem to be most effective (Hattie & Timperley, 2007). Tools that help students learn from feedback include templates for listing strengths and weaknesses and areas to focus on (Stiggins, 2007), lists of questions for students to respond to (Phillips et al., 1993), worksheets to facilitate reflection (Stiggins, 2007), graphs that track students over time (Clymer & Wiliam, 2007), and grids on which students can record baseline and interim scores to track gains over time in specific dimensions (Lane, Marquardt, Meyer, & Murray, 1997).

Progress monitoring tools might include informal reading inventories, running records, observations, checklists, teacher-created probes, products, performances, portfolios, and conference interviews. For advanced students, it's important that the progress monitoring tools sample behavior that is above grade level to address ceiling concerns. All assessments need to be documented to examine their effectiveness, note how often they are used, and ensure fidelity. In this way, current and future decisions are based on standardized approaches that can examine whether or not one set of intervention conditions are better than another for a particular student.

Standards in Gifted Education Regarding Assessment

The use of assessments for universal screening and progress monitoring within a Response to Intervention framework are closely aligned to the National Association for Gifted Children's (NAGC, 2010) Pre-K–Grade 12

Gifted Programming Standards. The NAGC assessment standards, which address identification and the assessment of learning progress, emphasize the importance of students having "equal access to a comprehensive assessment system that allows them to demonstrate diverse characteristics and behaviors" (Student Outcome 2.1; NAGC, 2010, p. 9) and opportunities for each student to reveal "his or her exceptionalities or potential so that instructional accommodations and modifications can be provided" (Student Outcome 2.2; NAGC, 2010, p. 9).

Best practices therefore require that educators develop classroom environments where advanced students are able to show their strengths and weaknesses. For students to show their strengths, the teacher needs to implement a curriculum that challenges each student with personally meaningful learning experiences, is broad enough to cover a vast array of talents, and provides opportunities to go beyond the curriculum (Dai & Coleman, 2005; Davalos & Haensly, 1997; Hébert & Olenchak, 2000; Subotnik & Coleman, 1996). Universal and progress monitoring assessments are then aligned to a curriculum that is sufficiently advanced and tailored to the student's interest so that he or she is able to show progress. On the other hand, for students to show their weaknesses, assessments need to be sensitive enough so that students who are twice-exceptional (i.e., have both a gift and a disability) reveal the areas where they are struggling. For example, Assouline, Foley Nicpon, and Whiteman (2010) found that gifted students with a disability in written language often performed at or above grade level in math and had verbal abilities that were stronger than nonverbal abilities. Because unintentional masking of both ability and disability are found within this twice-exceptional population, it's extremely important to vary assessments so that students are recognized and interventions can be customized. In addition to highlighting the importance of designing classroom environments that recognize students with gifts and talents, standards in gifted education address not only academic progress but also personal and social development. These student outcomes also need to be assessed and monitored (see Table 2.1).

Examples of Universal Screening Assessments

This section will describe specific universal screening assessments that address the student outcomes within the NAGC Pre-K–Grade 12 Gifted

Table 2.1
Student Outcomes in the NAGC Pre-K–Grade 12 Gifted Programming Standards

Academic Outcomes	Social Outcomes	Personal Outcomes
Demonstrate growth commensurate with ability.	Possess skills in communicating, teaming, and collaborating with diverse individuals and across diverse groups.	Demonstrate self-knowledge.
Become more competent in multiple talent areas.	Develop social competence manifested in positive peer relationships and social interactions.	Understand how they learn and grow.
Demonstrate advanced oral and written skills, balanced biliteracy or multiliteracy, and creative expression.	Use positive strategies to address social issues, including discrimination and stereotyping.	Recognize preferred approaches to learning.
Display fluency and technologies that support effective communication.	Demonstrate personal and social responsibility and leadership skills.	Recognize influences on development.
Become independent investigators.	Develop competence in interpersonal and technical communication skills.	Demonstrate understanding of differences.
Identify career goals and pathways for developing talents.		Develop knowledge and skills for a diverse society.
Access resources to develop talents.		Value their own and others' language, heritage, and circumstance.
		Demonstrate growth in personal competence and dispositions for academic and creative productivity.

Programming Standards and that might be used within an RtI framework for distinguishing advanced students who need more intensive interventions.

Academic Outcomes

Universal screening instruments that measure academic student outcomes need to allow gifted students to demonstrate an advanced level of skills within a curricular framework. Universal screening instruments are typically used as whole-class assessments and should be aligned with the general education curriculum. At the same time, they should also allow for demonstration of ability above grade level. It can be difficult to find an instrument designed for students who struggle as well as students who excel in a domain, but by incorporating some of the elements of differentiated instruction into assessment, it is possible to find an instrument that offers data at several different levels of ability.

One commonly used type of universal screening instrument is a curriculum-based measurement (CBM). A CBM covers the same curriculum taught in the general education classroom and can be useful for identifying students who are struggling with a specific concept; however, using a CBM for screening students with needs beyond the scope of the graded general education curriculum may require an adjustment of content. One example is the use of a grade-level oral reading passage to calculate the number of words per minute a student is able to read. The score gives a measure of reading fluency, and this type of assessment has been shown to be predictive of reading comprehension ability and general reading achievement (Fuchs, Fuchs, Hosp, & Jenkins, 2001). Graded passages are available for purchase through websites such as http://www.aimsweb.com and are also included in many leveled, commercially available reading programs. The scores on reading CBMs are typically used to identify flexible grouping of students within a general education classroom, but the scores could be used to screen for academically advanced reading performance. To do this, an average performance on the CBM should be determined and students scoring above the average could be grouped for more advanced work under a Tier 2 system. Once a student receives the Tier 2 enrichment, performance at that level of intervention should help clarify the identification of a need for further talent development in the area of reading.

Although research about the use of CBMs in reading has been extensive, less work has been conducted on the use of CBMs in math in an RtI framework. The idea behind a math CBM is the same as the reading fluency CBM with some exceptions. Oral reading speed is continuous, but many scores on math measures represent several discrete skills gathered into a total score. For example, if a CBM with 100 multiplication facts was used to test for multiplication fluency, then students could reach the ceiling of 100 facts at the initial testing. The other difference between this type of measure and the reading fluency measure is that the multiplication represents the memorization of discrete bits of information, whereas the oral reading speed is less a measure of memorization and more a measure of performance. When choosing an instrument to screen for math abilities, CBMs using discrete skills like fact fluency may not be useful for identifying advanced students. To meet this goal, a math universal screening instrument needs to measure more than simple fluency and include math processes outlined in the state standards for a particular grade level. Websites like http://www.rti4success.org/screeningTools provide information on many different types of universal screening instruments that may be adapted to identify above-average math performance (National Center on Response to Intervention, 2010). An RtI framework allows flexibility in identification of student needs, which may also increase the number of students who have access to advanced instruction content.

Personal Outcomes

Universal screening instruments that assess personal outcomes can help students recognize diversity, approaches to learning, and the value of self-knowledge (NAGC, 2010). As universal screening instruments are meant to be brief, checklists and reflections may be the most useful types of screening assessments for social outcomes. Teaching students to self-assess growth in the social domains allows gifted learners to develop an individualized approach to learning. Self-report instruments are useful for identifying students with unique interests and perspectives related to personal outcomes and also may allow for identification of students who are typically missed through teacher or parent report forms. These students may have potential for leadership or display talents in other domains as well. For example, the North Little Rock School District (Curlin & Kirspel, 2011) prepared a handbook that contains links to student interest inventories for elementary and secondary students (see http://gifted--talented.nlrsd.org/modules/locker/files/get_group_file.phtml?fid=14028600&gid=2250306). The sample interest inventories include questions related to areas of study, types of learning preferred, learning settings, and student disposition. By removing items not contributing to the current assessment goal, the teacher might reduce the length of the inventory. Although no technical information is available for this instrument, the teacher might be able to use the inventory throughout the year to identify students who show unusual interests and preferences and to target specific enrichment activities.

For secondary students, universal screening instruments may be used to help stimulate group discussions and as a way to promote identification of students demonstrating superior self-knowledge. The Cultural Diversity Self-Assessment (Indiana University, 2010) is used with college students to identify levels of multicultural awareness, but is also appropriate for use with high school students (see http://www.cue.indiana.edu/activitymanual/activities/Cultural%20diversity%20self%20assessment.pdf). It is a self-report instrument with statements related to cultural and interpersonal awareness. Students assign a level of agreement to each statement and tabulate a score of multicultural awareness. According to the scale on the bottom of the form, the score indicates a categorical level of awareness, but students are also encouraged to develop goals based on the results. For example, if a student shows a low level of agreement with statements about judging others based on dialect or accents, then the student is encouraged to explore this aspect of multicultural and self-awareness. If used as a screening instrument with secondary students, results from this form could be used as a formative assessment and tied to instructional objectives for progress monitoring, or the results could be used to identify students who show an unusual level of cultural and interpersonal awareness.

Another facet of personal outcomes for gifted students includes self-understanding, such as preferred approaches to learning and topics of intense interest. Including these in a universal screening instrument demonstrates an understanding that these personal outcomes evolve over time. A brief and useful tool for screening interests and approaches to learning in middle school and high school is the If I Ran the School instrument (Reis & Siegle, 2002). A copy of the instrument may be found at http://www.gifted.uconn.edu/siegle/CurriculumCompacting/SEC-IMAG/ranschol.pdf. The instrument is self-report, so it allows identification of students who may not be recognized as gifted under other methods, and covers science, technology, social studies, language arts, and fine arts. Students are instructed to circle the 10 items they would choose to learn about if they had control of the curriculum. Some items are content representative, such as "The Human Body," but other items are more process oriented, like "Designing a Web Page." Although no technical information is available on the instrument, knowledge gained from it could be used for grouping students in Tier 2 enrichment.

Social Outcomes

A universal screening instrument for social outcomes needs to evaluate communication, collaboration, and leadership skills. An instrument for this purpose needs to address social outcomes in a brief and reliable form, but should also allow for a variety of interpretations. Definitions of social competence change according to the developmental level of the student and, as such, it may be difficult to find instruments that are valid for both primary and secondary students.

Rubrics often allow for multiple, flexible interpretations, which contribute to their usefulness in measuring social outcomes. The rubric for assessing communication skills and competencies provides feedback on collaboration and written, spoken, and visual communication. A copy of the rubric may be found at http://www.uwgb.edu/clampitp/Communication%20skills.htm (Clampitt, 2007). It is a self-report rubric and is best suited for secondary-level students; however, parts of the instrument may be adaptable for use with younger students. Students use the rubric to rate each competency and then identify strengths and weaknesses according to the ratings. Although no technical information is currently available for the instrument, the rubric could provide valuable information for identifying students gifted in communication skills or debate.

For screening leadership skills, the National Association of Student Councils (n.d.) provides an instrument that may be accessed from http://www.nasc.us/portals/5/content/56458.pdf. The initial document was published as the T-P Leadership Questionnaire (Sergiovanni, Metzcus, & Burden, 1969) and permission should be requested prior to use. Technical information on reliability and validity may be found in Sergiovanni et al. (1969). The questionnaire was also reprinted in Pfeiffer and Jones (1984). The 34-item questionnaire is used as a part of gifted teacher education, but the items are relevant for students in middle school and above. Each item is rated according to frequency of the behavior, and the scoring indicates where the individual falls along a continuum of a task-oriented to a people-oriented style of leadership. As a screening instrument, the leadership profile could help identify students who are gifted at both kinds of leadership as well as students who have combined both styles into a shared type of leadership.

Whereas the previously mentioned universal screening instruments are more appropriate for secondary students, the Social Attributes Checklist is appropriate for early childhood through elementary levels and may be accessed at http://ceep.crc.uiuc.edu/pubs/ivpaguide/appendix/mcclellan-assessing.pdf (McClellan & Katz, 2001). The 24-item checklist assesses individual, social, and peer relation attributes in young children and should be completed by a teacher or caregiver who has prolonged contact with the child. The instructions specify information gathered from the checklist should be supplemented with additional observations and interviews. As a universal screening instrument, the checklist could help identify young children who excel at interpersonal relations. No technical information is available on the instrument.

The Teacher's Observation of Potential in Students (TOPS; Coleman & Shah-Coltrane, 2010) is another tool to help teachers recognize signs of high potential in young children (ages 5–9) across nine developmental domains (learns easily, shows advanced skills, displays curiosity and creativity, has strong interests, shows advanced reasoning and problem solving, displays special abilities, shows motivation, shows social perceptiveness, displays leadership). (Information about the TOPS may be accessed through http://www.cec.sped.org/ustars.) Systematic and intentional documentation of observations of strengths with the TOPS allows educators to see patterns of student behavior. They can use this information to plan intellectually and emotionally nurturing learning opportunities for their students. The TOPS is specifically designed to be used with other formal and informal assessments to help recognize potential in young children from culturally/linguistically different and/or economically disadvantaged families. Technical data on the TOPS is limited to construct and content validity.

Examples of Progress Monitoring Assessments

This section will describe progress monitoring assessments that address the student outcomes within the NAGC Pre-K–Grade 12 Gifted Programming Standards and that might be used within an RtI framework for distinguishing advanced students who may need Tier 2 instruction.

Academic Outcomes

The results of a CBM as a universal screening instrument may help identify students who need additional instruction beyond the general education curriculum. Students with scores on the universal screening instrument that continually exceed the average should be considered for advanced-level instruction. If this involves moving a student to Tier 2 instruction, then the frequency of progress monitoring needs to be increased and records of the progress toward the end-of-year goals need to be maintained. Computer programs offer a simple method for tracking progress over time, and tracking progress in this manner may offer gifted students a real-world application for self-monitoring.

Along with a library of universal screening instruments, AIMSweb (http://www.aimsweb.com) has progress monitoring tools for math and literacy for grades K–8. For gifted students, year-end goals may not be the same as the goals set by the general education curriculum, a situation making tracking of progress difficult. The website allows tracking of individual progress through graphs and also maintains a record of the student's performance and current placement.

The program, including its web-based tracking software, CBMs, and administration instructions, can be purchased online. In addition, technical information can be found at http://www.rti4success.org/progressMonitoringTools (National Center on Response to Intervention, 2010).

For early literacy progress monitoring, the Dynamic Indicators of Basic Early Literacy Skills (DIBELS) are free, downloadable standardized measures for grades K–6. The measures are free to use, but teachers may purchase access to the online data system, which then generates reports based the assessment scores. The reports track current performance and maintain records of past performance through graphs. Students working at levels beyond the current curriculum can be progress monitored through off-level assessments. The DIBELS system can be accessed at http://dibels.uoregon.edu (University of Oregon Center on Teaching and Learning, n.d.). Technical information related to the DIBELS systems can be accessed at http://www.rti4success.org/progressMonitoringTools (National Center on Response to Intervention, 2010).

Another website with free progress monitoring CBMs in literacy and early math is Intervention Central (http://www.interventioncentral.com). Unlike DIBELS or AIMSweb, Intervention Central warehouses CBM manuals, norms, technical information, graphing options, and measures for math, reading, and writing. The Maze Passage Generator allows users to create off-level reading assessments for tracking progress of students who are currently above grade level. The math and written expression CBM sites also allow the creation of a specialized progress monitoring tool based on input from the user. The information collected from the CBMs can be graphed on Intervention Central through the ChartDog Graphmaker or entered into a predesigned Excel spreadsheet that can be downloaded. Intervention Central also provides links to other websites with CBM materials for purchase. Technical information is available for many of the progress monitoring tools found in the warehouse at Intervention Central.

Personal Outcomes

Progress monitoring personal outcomes of gifted education includes tracking growth in communication, creativity, and self-understanding. For written communication, rubrics like the Primary Continuum for Beginning Writers (Spandel, 1996) allow for tracking student growth through ideas, organization, word choices, fluency, and conventions. The rubric may be accessed at http://apps.educationnorthwest.org/toolkit98/six.html#primary. To use the rubric as a progress monitoring tool, the teacher may want to focus on a specific aspect of writing and use scores from the rubric to direct Tier 2 advanced writing with students demonstrating exceptional skills in written expression. The rubric is designed to highlight a student's strengths and may be a useful tool for helping young, talented writers develop and self-monitor. No technical data are available on the instrument.

Rubrics to evaluate thinking may provide information for progress monitoring the development of creative and critical thinking. Lake Oswego School District's Thinking Assessment Traits rubric (Bond-Esser & Korach, 1990) uses differentiating, distancing, and designing to assess products and performances of students; it can be accessed at http://apps.educationnorthwest.org/toolkit98/thinking.html. The rubric can be used for any grade level because the language allows for adaptation to fit the needs of the student. For instance, the highest level of "thinking as differentiating" describes a student as having accurate and complete knowledge of the topic. The statement can be interpreted differently depending on the developmental level of the student, such that a kindergarten student may demonstrate a qualitatively different type of "complete" knowledge when compared to an older student. For progress monitoring, the rubric could be applied to complex tasks in any subject area. No technical information is available for the instrument.

Evaluation and progress monitoring of metacognitive skills of students in grades 3–9 is possible with the Jr. Metacognitive Awareness Inventory (Jr. MAI; Sperling, Howard, Miller, & Murphey, 2002). The Jr. MAI is an adaptation of the Metacognitive Awareness Inventory and is available as an appendix in the above-cited article. The scale has also been used in dissertation research on gifted African American populations (Kearney, 2010). Validity studies indicate the Jr. MAI may be measuring a construct separate from general achievement and items on the scale may represent knowledge of cognition and regulation of cognition. As a progress monitoring tool, the Jr. MAI could be helpful for tracking growth in these two key areas of metacognition.

Social Outcomes

Social outcomes focus on leadership, communication, and social interaction skills. Students with strengths in this area may recognize and be concerned about injustices in any field, typically posses excellent written and verbal communication skills, and may demonstrate a tendency toward leadership. Progress monitoring growth in social outcomes should be focused on helping the student develop strengths in these areas.

For students to develop leadership gifts into talents, Roberts (2004) suggested focusing on the relationship between planning, decision making, and leadership in the classroom. Progress monitoring tools for measuring the development of leadership skills in students may be self-report instruments or teacher rating scales. Shaunessy and Karnes (2004) provided an overview of leadership instruments for children and youth. Some of the leadership instruments designed for identification of talents may also be used as a tool to progress monitor development of these skills. The Gifted and Talented Evaluation Scale (GATES; Gilliam, Carpenter, & Christensen, 1996) contains a 10-item scale for measuring leadership. For the GATES, test-retest reliability ranges from $r = .42$ to $.97$ with an internal consistency of $\alpha > .90$ for each subscale (Jarosewich, Pfeiffer, & Morris, 2002). In addition to teacher-report instruments like the GATES, self-report instruments could be used as progress monitoring tools. The Leadership Skills Inventory (LSI; Karnes & Chauvin, 2000) measures leadership across nine domains, including group dynamics and communication. It is self-report and includes information on planning for leadership development. Information on purchasing the instrument may be found at http://www.greatpotentialpress.com.

Collaboration and communication skills represent a facet of social development that may contribute to leadership development. Progress monitoring of collaboration and communication skills could enhance group projects undertaken as part of a Tier 2 intervention. Checklists, like the Elements of Small Group Communication (Engleberg & Wynn, 2003, p. 23), provide a method for categorically tracking group communication and collaboration skills. In addition to checklists, rubrics for performance assessment allow the tracking of growth and progress. A simple list of proficiencies for communication and collaboration skills rated according to a predefined scale, such as the Example Proficiencies in Non-Content Categories (Marzano, 1994), can be used to progress monitor development by assigning a score to the behaviors exhibited in a real-world problem-solving activity. The list of proficiencies also includes descriptors for complex thinking, cultural diversity, and self-regulation. No technical information is available on the list of proficiencies.

Identification of Gifted Students

As data accumulate from universal and progress monitoring assessments, it becomes clearer to educators that more intensive services are needed to support advanced learners, such as radical acceleration, telescoping more than one year's curriculum into a single instructional year, small-group instruction with other gifted students, long-term mentorships, individualized programming, specialized classrooms or schools, and/or early admission to college (Colangelo, Assouline, & Gross, 2004; Treffinger, 1986; VanTassel-Baska & Little, 2011). This level of service should require clearly established protocols with specific criteria for areas such as radical acceleration (Colangelo et al., 2004) and may involve more comprehensive, diagnostic assessments that meet state rules and regulations in identifying students for specialized classrooms or schools.

When formally identifying students, assessments need to include special educators, gifted educators, and other professionals in the school as well as families and other individuals within the community who may be involved with the student's education (e.g., mentors, internship supervisors). According to the Pre-K–Grade 12 Gifted Education Programming Standards (NAGC, 2010), educators need to provide families with information that is culturally sensitive regarding diverse characteristics, inform them about the formal identification procedures, and elicit evidence regarding the child's interests and potential outside of the classroom setting (see Evidence-Based Practices 2.1.2, 2.2.6, and 2.3.3). If the school has been involving families throughout the RtI process, this collection of further assessment information would simply be the next logical step in the collaboration process to ensure adequate services.

Although 30 states require specific criteria and/or methods to identify gifted and talented students for special services, the remaining states leave some or all of the specifics to local education agencies (NAGC, 2011). Therefore, it's important that educators be aware of the technical qualities of instruments and seek information from test publishers, test reviewers such as the *Mental Measurements Yearbook*, and publications such as *Identifying Gifted Students* (Johnsen, 2011) before selecting assessments to use in the identification process. Robins and Jolly (2011) have provided these questions to use in the technical review process (pp. 75–76):

1. What is the assessment's purpose?
2. Is the assessment valid for this purpose?
3. Is the test reliable?
4. When was the test last normed?
5. Does the sample used to norm the test reflect current national census data and the school district's population?
6. What type of scores does the instrument provide?
7. How is the test administered?

8. Are there qualified personnel available to administer the instrument?
9. What is the cost of the instrument?

Besides meeting technical standards, the assessments need to be matched to the student's areas of strengths, provide both qualitative and quantitative information from a variety of sources, and be nonbiased and equitable (NAGC, 2010; see Evidence-Based Practices 2.2.2, 2.2.3, 2.2.4, and 2.3.1).

In matching assessments to the student's strengths, educators need to identify tests that will be able to discriminate across the full range of abilities in a particular domain. For example, if a student is advanced in English language arts, product- and performance-based assessments that require problem solving and other forms of higher level thinking, such as discerning themes, explaining meaning, and discussing big ideas, might be used. In addition to these types of assessments, an above-grade-level standardized achievement test might be administered to examine the student's proficiency in specific knowledge and skills. On the other hand, if a student shows an interest or promise in science, the student's projects might require higher level thinking in a specific scientific area. In both cases, educators might collect information from teachers, families, and peers and also use other measures to determine the student's overall aptitude such as an intelligence test, particularly if such a score is required to enter the specialized program.

The assessments in the above examples offer both qualitative (e.g., interviews, products, performances, checklists) and quantitative information (e.g., intelligence and achievement tests) for educators who are making decisions about appropriate interventions for the student. In selecting multiple assessments, educators are able to sample a wider range of behaviors across multiple settings to ensure an approach that is more valid for identifying students who have gifts in specific domains. Some behaviors are simply not demonstrated at school because students don't have the opportunity or others such as peers, parents, or teachers might not approve (Coleman & Cross, 2005).

Across all situations, the assessments and the procedures need to minimize bias and be fair to each and every student. English language learners need to be tested in their native language or with nonverbal assessments. Students who are struggling in reading and/or writing need assessments that are not heavily weighted toward language skills. Young children from poverty who may not have had many opportunities for learning academic knowledge outside of school need assessments that do not focus on acquired knowledge but instead on ways that they use problem solving, acquire new knowledge, or reason analogically. For students who educators suspect have both a gift and a disability, a school psychologist or certified diagnostician may need to conduct case histories and administer comprehensive, individualized assessments that create a learning profile to uncover the variations in performance that are often indicative of twice-exceptional students (Al-Hroub, 2010; Foley Nicpon, Allmon, Sieck, & Stinson, 2011).

To illustrate how a child might be referred for more intensive services within an RtI framework, consider a student, Annie, whose strength is in math. After monitoring Annie's progress, the teacher has noted that she is consistently three to four grade levels above the expected school district standards and that the gap is increasing as she progresses in her educational program. Her general education teacher is struggling to keep her engaged during math time and is concerned that she is becoming more and more isolated because no other children are at her ability level. Her teacher meets with the School Intervention Team to discuss her referral to the specialized school for students who are advanced in science, technology, engineering, and math (STEM) areas. As a team, they decide to begin the formal identification process. They contact Annie's parents to ask permission for further testing and collect information from them as well as from a standardized above-grade-level achievement test, an intelligence test (as required by the state and the school for formal admission into the program), a student interview, and a portfolio of her mathematics work. Following the collection of the data, the team meets together with the student and her family to discuss the need for more intensive services. In Annie's case, they notice that she is not only advancing at a more rapid pace but that she also demonstrates many of the characteristics associated with mathematically talented learners such as strong number and computation sense, the ability to see relationships and recognize patterns, and originality in solving complex problems. Along with the family (and Annie!), the team decides to recommend her for placement in the STEM school.

Summary

A variety of assessments are integrated within the Response to Intervention framework: universal screening, progress monitoring, and identification. Universal screening involves administering assessments to the whole class at set times to identify students who are progressing at a more advanced rate as well as those who are not progressing at the expected rate. Progress monitoring involves more direct and frequent samples of student performance before, during, and after instruction and informs teaching and learning. More formal identification for gifted education programming occurs as the data indicate the need for more intensive services to support the advanced learner.

The NAGC Pre-K–Grade 12 Gifted Programming Standards support these types of assessments. The standards address the creation of learning environments where (a) students can demonstrate both their strengths and weaknesses, (b) learning progress is assessed, and (c) comprehensive, cohesive, and nonbiased identification occurs. The NAGC standards are linked to specific student outcomes in academic, social, and personal domains. This chapter described some examples of assessments that might be used to measure progress in these domains at both the universal screening and progress monitoring levels.

Educators need to pay particular attention to special populations of students with gifts and talents who are most vulnerable to inappropriate services, including low-income, ELL, minority, and twice-exceptional students. All assessments and procedures need to be nonbiased and fair so that each and every student's progress is adequately monitored. When the implementation of RtI is successful, assessments match each student's strengths and weaknesses, examine the effectiveness of the curriculum and instruction, and provide useful information for the quality and intensity of services.

References

Al-Hroub, A. (2010). Developing assessment profiles for mathematically gifted children with learning difficulties at three schools in Cambridgeshire, England. *Journal for the Education of the Gifted, 34,* 7–44.

Anderson, J. R. (1982). Acquisition of cognitive skill. *Psychological Review, 89,* 369–406.

Assouline, S. G., Foley Nicpon, M., & Whiteman, C. (2010). Cognitive and psychosocial characteristics of gifted students with written language disability. *Gifted Child Quarterly, 54,* 102–115.

Black, P., Harrison, C., Lee, C., Marshall, B., & Wiliam, D. (2003). *Assessment for learning: Putting it into practice.* Maidenhead, UK: Open University Press.

Bond-Esser, J., & Korach, R. M. (1990). *Thinking skills assessment.* Retrieved from http://apps.educationnorthwest.org/toolkit98/thinking.html

Brunner, C., Fasca, C., Heinze, J., Honey, M., Light, D., Mandinach, E., & Wexler, D. (2005). Linking data and learning: The grow network study. *Journal of Education for Students Placed At Risk, 10,* 241–267.

Clampitt, P. G. (2007). *Communication skills and competencies.* Retrieved from http://www.uwgb.edu/clampitp/Communication%20skills.htm

Clymer, J. B., & Wiliam, D. (2007). Improving the way we grade science. *Educational Leadership, 64,* 36–42.

Colangelo, N., Assouline, S. G., & Gross, M. U. M. (2004). *A nation deceived: How schools hold back America's brightest students* (Vol. 1). Iowa City: The University of Iowa, The Connie Belin & Jacqueline N. Blank International Center for Gifted Education and Talent Development.

Coleman, L. J., & Cross, T. L. (2005). *Being gifted in school* (2nd ed.). Waco, TX: Prufrock Press.

Coleman, M. R., & Shah-Coltrane, S. (2010). *U-STARS~PLUS professional development kit.* Arlington, VA: Council for Exceptional Children.

Curlin, B. D., & Kirspel, K. (2011). *Handbook for North Little Rock School District gifted programs.* Retrieved from http://gifted--talented.nlrsd.org/modules/locker/files/get_group_file.phtml?fid=14028600&gid=2250306

Dai, D. Y., & Coleman, L. J. (2005). Epilogue: Conclusions and implications for gifted education. *Journal for the Education of the Gifted, 28,* 374–388.

Davalos, R., & Haensly, P. (1997). After the dust has settled: Youth reflect on their high school mentored research experience. *Roeper Review, 19,* 204–207.

Dochy, F., Segers, M., & Buehl, M. M. (1999). The relation between assessment practices and outcomes of studies: The case of research on prior knowledge. *Review of Educational Research, 69,* 145–186.

Donovan, M. S., & Bransford, J. D. (2005). Introduction. In M. S. Donovan & J. D. Bransford (Eds.), *How students learn: History, mathematics, and science in the classroom* (pp. 1–28). Washington, DC: National Academic Press.

Dweck, C. S. (1999). *Self-theories: Their role in motivation, personality and development.* Philadelphia, PA: Psychology Press.

Engleberg, I. N., & Wynn, D. R. (2003). *Working in groups: Communication principles and strategies* (3rd ed.). Boston, MA: Houghton Mifflin.

Ericsson, K. A. (1993). The role of deliberate practice in the acquisition of expert performance. *Psychological Review, 100,* 363–406.

Foley Nicpon, M., Allmon, A., Sieck, B., & Stinson, R. D. (2011). Empirical investigation of twice-exceptionality: Where have we been and where are we going? *Gifted Child Quarterly, 55,* 3–17.

Fuchs, L. S., Fuchs, D., Hosp, M. K., & Jenkins, J. R. (2001). Oral reading fluency as an indicator of reading competence: A theoretical, empirical, and historical analysis. *Scientific Studies of Reading, 5,* 241–258.

Geary, D. C., & Brown, S. C. (1991). Cognitive addition: Strategy choice and speed-of-processing difference in gifted, normal, and mathematically disabled children. *Developmental Psychology, 27,* 398–406.

Gilliam, J. E., Carpenter, B. O., & Christensen, J. R. (1996). *Gifted and Talented Evaluation Scales.* Austin, TX: Pro-Ed.

Hattie, J., & Timperley, H. (2007). The power of feedback. *Review of Educational Research, 77*, 81–112.

Hébert, T. P., & Olenchak, F. R. (2000). Mentors for gifted underachieving males: Developing potential and realizing promise. *Gifted Child Quarterly, 44,* 196–207.

Heritage, M. (2010). *Formative assessment and next-generation assessment systems: Are we losing an opportunity?* Washington, DC: Council of Chief State School Officers.

Hammill, D. D., & Larsen, S. L. (2009). *Test of Written Language—Fourth edition.* Austin, TX: Pro-Ed.

Indiana University. (2010). *Cultural diversity self-assessment.* Retrieved from http://www.cue.indiana.edu/activitymanual/activities/Cultural%20diversity%20self%20assessment.pdf

Jarosewich, T., Pfeiffer, S. I., & Morris, J. (2002). Identifying gifted students using teacher rating scales: A review of existing instruments. *Journal of Psychoeducational Assessment, 20,* 322–336.

Johnsen, S. K. (Ed.). (2011). *Identifying gifted students: A practical guide* (2nd ed.). Waco, TX: Prufrock Press.

Kearney, L. J. (2010). *Differences in self-concept, racial identity, self-efficacy, resilience, and achievement among African-American gifted and non-gifted students: Implications for retention and persistence of African Americans in gifted programs* (Doctoral dissertation). Available from ProQuest Dissertations and Theses database. (UMI3404513)

Karnes, F., & Chauvin, J. (2000). *Leadership Development Program.* Scottsdale, AZ: Gifted Psychology Press.

Kurtz, B. E., & Weinert, F. E. (1989). Metacognition, memory performance, and causal attributions in gifted and average children. *Journal of Experimental Child Psychology, 48,* 45–61.

Lane, C., Marquardt, J., Meyer, M. A., & Murray, W. (1997). *Addressing the lack of motivation in the middle school setting* (Master's action research project). St. Xavier University, Chicago, IL.

Marzano, R. J. (1994). Lessons from the field about outcome-based performance assessments. *Educational Leadership, 51*(6), 44–50.

McClellan, D. E., & Katz, L. G. (2001). *Assessing young children's social competence.* Retrieved from http://ceep.crc.uiuc.edu/pubs/ivpaguide/appendix/mcclellan-assessing.pdf

Moon, T. R., Brighton, C. M., Callahan, C. M., & Robinson, A. (2005). Development of authentic assessments for the middle school classroom. *The Journal of Secondary Gifted Education, 16,* 119–133.

National Association for Gifted Children. (2010). *NAGC Pre-K–Grade 12 Gifted Programming Standards: A blueprint for quality gifted education programs.* Washington, DC: Author.

National Association for Gifted Children. (2011). *2010–2011 state of the nation in gifted education: A lack of commitment to talent development.* Washington, DC: Author.

National Association of Student Councils. (n.d.). *T-P leadership questionnaire.* Retrieved from http://www.nasc.us/portals/5/content/56458.pdf

National Center on Response to Intervention. (2010). *Progress monitoring tools.* Retrieved from http://www.rti4success.org/progressMonitoringTools

Pfeiffer, W. J., & Jones, J. E. (Eds.). (1984). *A handbook of structured experiences for human relations training* (Vol. 1). San Diego, CA: Pfeiffer.

Phillips, N. B., Hamlett, C. L., Fuchs, L. S., & Fuchs, D. (1993). Combining classwide curriculum-based measurement and peer tutoring to help general educators provide adaptive education. *Learning Disabilities Research & Practice, 8,* 148–156.

Reis, S. M., Burns, D. E., & Renzulli, J. S. (1992). *Curriculum compacting: The complete guide to modifying the regular curriculum for high ability students.* Mansfield Center, CT: Creative Learning Press.

Reis, S. M., & Siegle, D. (2002). *If I ran the school: An interest inventory.* Retrieved from http://www.gifted.uconn.edu/siegle/CurriculumCompacting/SEC-IMAG/ranschol.pdf

Roberts, J. L. (2004). Leadership is a "must" for children who are gifted and talented. *Gifted Child Today, 27*(1), 5.

Robins, J. H., & Jolly, J. L. (2011). Technical information regarding assessment. In S. K. Johnsen (Ed.), *Identifying gifted students: A practical guide* (2nd ed., pp. 75–118). Waco, TX: Prufrock Press.

Sadler, D. R. (1989). Formative assessment and the design of instructional systems. *Instructional Science, 18,* 119–140.

Sato, M., Wei, R. C., & Darling-Hammond, L. (2008). Improving teachers' assessment practices through professional development: The case of National Board Certification. *American Educational Research Journal, 45,* 669–700.

Sergiovanni, T. J., Metzcus, R., & Burden, L. (1969). Toward a particularistic approach to leadership style: Some findings. *American Educational Research Journal, 6,* 62–79.

Schunk, D. H., & Swartz, C. W. (1992, April). *Goals and feedback during writing strategy instruction with gifted students.* Paper presented at the annual meeting of the American Educational Research Association, San Francisco, CA.

Scruggs, T., & Mastropieri, M. (1985). Spontaneous verbal elaborations in gifted and nongifted youths. *Journal for the Education of the Gifted, 9,* 1–10.

Shaunessy, E., & Karnes, F. A. (2004). Instruments for measuring leadership in children and youth. *Gifted Child Today, 27*(1), 42–47.

Shepard, L. A. (1995). Using assessment to improve learning. *Educational Leadership, 52*(5), 38–43.

Shute, V. J. (2008). Focus on formative feedback. *Review of Educational Research, 78,* 153–189.

Spandel, V. (1996). *Primary continuum for beginning writers.* Retrieved from http://apps.educationnorthwest.org/toolkit98/six.html#primary

Sperling, R. A., Howard, B. C., Miller, L. A., & Murphey, C. (2002). Measures of children's knowledge and regulation of cognition. *Contemporary Educational Psychology, 27,* 51–79.

Stiggins, R. (2007). Assessment through the student's eyes. *Educational Leadership, 64*(8), 22–26.

Subotnik, R. F., & Coleman, L. J. (1996). Establishing the foundations for a talent development school: Applying principles to creating an ideal. *Journal for the Education of the Gifted, 20,* 175–189.

Swanson, H. L., & Lussier, C. M. (2001). A selective synthesis of the experimental literature on dynamic assessment. *Review of Educational Research, 71,* 321–363.

Treffinger, D. (1986). Fostering effective, independent learning through individualized programming. In J. S. Renzulli (Ed.), *Systems and models for developing programs for the gifted and talented* (pp. 429–468). Mansfield, CT: Creative Learning Press.

University of Oregon Center on Teaching and Learning. (n.d.). *DIBELS data system.* Retrieved from https://dibels.uoregon.edu

VanTassel-Baska, J., & Little, C. A. (2011). *Content-based curriculum for high-ability learners* (2nd ed.). Waco, TX: Prufrock Press.

Ysseldyke, J., Burns, M. K., Scholin, S. E., & Parker, D. C. (2010). Instructionally valid assessment within Response to Intervention. *TEACHING Exceptional Children, 42*(4), 54–61.

CHAPTER THREE

THE IMPORTANCE OF FAMILY ENGAGEMENT

Joy Lawson Davis

The family is a universal social institution (Kottak & Kozaitis, 2012). Educators and other child development practitioners generally agree that parent and family involvement lend crucial support to the success of children in schools (Epstein, 2001). The family construct is the primary source of learning and experience for most students, as the family is where they learn their first language, traditions, values, and the most essential characteristics that make them who they are.

Today's families are unique configurations. It is not uncommon for children in our schools to live in households that consist of multigenerational families (where three or more generations live in the same household) or come from households with single mothers; unmarried, same-sex, or multiracial couples; and other nontraditional family types. According to the U.S. Census Bureau, nontraditional family types are beginning to outnumber nuclear families across the nation (Cohn, 2011). Regardless of the family type, one of the critical responsibilities of educational institutions is to engage families in the educational process of all children on a regular basis.

The links between family involvement, student achievement, and better outcomes in school is clear (Henderson & Mapp, 2002).

> The evidence is consistent, positive, and convincing: families have a major influence on their children's achievement in school and through life. . . . When schools, families, and community groups work together to support learning, children tend to do better in school, stay in school longer, and like school more. (Henderson & Mapp, 2002, p. 7)

The impact of families on student achievement and the changing trends of our nation's families provide strong support for a more comprehensive look at how family engagement is critical both now and in the future, as it enables success for all learners, including high-ability and gifted learners from a range of backgrounds and communities. Family engagement is also a central tenant of the RtI process (Byrd, 2011). This chapter explores the role of engaging families of gifted learners with schools for the purpose of enhancing the educational experience of all learners. It specifically addresses culturally responsive practices and the importance of family engagement within a multi-tiered framework.

The Role of the Family in Talent Development

Parents of gifted children, particularly at the elementary level, are usually very involved in their children's academic and social lives (Colangelo, Assouline, Chen, & Tsai, 1999). In Gagné's (2000) talent development model, parents and community members are described as catalysts who nurture and stimulate the high aptitudes of gifted learners across multiple domains over time. These catalysts, along with those of school environments, chance circumstances, and the individual's character traits, set the pace for talent development. Nurturance, support, and stimulation of gifts by motivation, developmental processes, and environmental catalysts are critical to the manifestation of talent in Gagné's theory.

Family encouragement and specific family dynamics are also specified in talent development literature (Hrabowski, Maton, & Greif, 1998; Olszewski-Kubilius, 2002). On a more subtle level, praise and encouragement have been noted to impact student success (Davis, 2008; Jeynes, 2010). In a study of the impact of family on the lives of African American learners from low-income environments, praise, encouragement, and development of resiliency were evident from student and parent responses (Davis, 2008). When these students' lives are examined more closely, there are expressions of encouragement and praise that they remember as being of great support to them during their developmental years. Parents of gifted learners—in particular, those who are traditionally underrepresented in gifted programs nationwide (e.g., children from culturally different, linguistically diverse, and economically disadvantaged families)—suggest that they may often be the child's sole source of praise and encouragement (Davis, 2008).

As Olszewski-Kubilius (2002) noted in a review of previously conducted research, high achievers generally originate from families that are cohesive and child-centered, where parent-child identification is stronger. In an earlier study, Sloane (1985) provided interview responses from parents and other family members (e.g., extended family and older siblings) related to talent development and family values. She described how parents of gifted and talented students shared their values and work ethic and modeled behaviors that eventually led to high achievement and school success.

Culturally and Linguistically Diverse Family Engagement

In studies examining the home environment of high-achieving Black and Hispanic students, similar family traits emerge. Students and family members note that encouragement of mothers, parental presence in school, consistent discussions at home about the value of education, and parent encouragement for children to use challenges as opportunities to prove their ability to be successful and dispel stereotypes are among common family traits of high achievers from diverse cultures (Davis, 2008; Garrett, Antrop-Gonzalez, & Velez, 2010; Hrabowski et al., 1998).

Singly and collectively, mothers, extended family members, and school personnel influence the child's attainment of an appropriate education. In many communities, church leaders, extended family members, neighbors, and even older siblings are also among the persons who serve in crucial roles, assisting parents with what can sometimes be a daunting task—the development of talent potential. To effectively engage with the high-ability child, schools will need to position themselves to address a wide range of catalysts that, along with families, may impact the intellectual and social-emotional development of the child. It is clear from the research that families of high-achieving, high-ability, and gifted learners from varied backgrounds have established traditions and values that influence their child's success in the educational arena.

Family participation in school-related activities may vary, however, based on the level of understanding school personnel have about the factors that impact a child's daily experience. These family factors may differ from that of a traditional school's experience with highly involved families. Providing guidance to diverse families to access services and to improve their level of understanding of the field of gifted education is one critical engagement strategy. Briggs, Reis, and Sullivan (2008) investigated methods to increase successful participation of gifted culturally and linguistically diverse (CLD) students in programs around the country. Their findings suggested that bridging the connection with students' families significantly contributed to successful identification and participation for gifted CLD students.

In a guidebook for African American families of gifted learners, Davis (2010) offered numerous resources, including an advocate's glossary that shares specific language related to the identification of gifted children, assessment procedures, programming options, and other important terminologies that are often held exclusively by educators trained in the field of gifted education. Additional resources that can be accessed online, in schools, and in libraries list specialized programming, scholarship opportunities, and college planning resources that are available to families of gifted learners. Experience with accessing resources is an important skill families need to acquire to improve their engagement role. Grantham and Henfield (2011) provided specific guidance on how parents of high-ability and gifted minority youth can directly access specific programmatic material. Their instructive article discussed the need for minority families to be more involved in increasing their children's engagement in science, technology, engineering, and mathematics (STEM) instruction and special activities.

Attendance at school conferences, PTA meetings, and other school-related affairs often varies for parents based on their cultural differences with school personnel. Oftentimes, when cultures of school personnel differ from that of their students, problems in communication arise. In these cases, it is wise to reexamine the cultural mismatch theory for deeper understandings and solutions (Villegas, 1988). This theory describes the impact of teacher effectiveness or lack thereof based on the mismatch between classroom teachers, who are predominately middle-class White females, and their students, many of whom originate from culturally and linguistically diverse backgrounds and nontraditional family types. This mismatch manifests itself when teachers have little or no personal and professional experience with the cultural background of their students and, thus, students' needs are misunderstood, which negatively affects the teaching and learning environment. When this mismatch occurs, teachers and school personnel are not as cognizant of the best strategies for engaging all students or for fully engaging their families.

In order for teachers and personnel to develop a full engagement mentality with families of all gifted learners, they must consider the whole child and be able to connect with the child as a holistic being. The gifted learner, with his or her high intellectual and psychological capacities, is part of a larger configuration. This configuration includes the child's immediate and extended family, socioeconomic status, neighborhood, religious or spiritual affiliations, exceptional conditions, and language and dialects.

Figure 3.1 shows the child at the center of this holistic configuration. All of these variables are important to the child, and thus should be important to the school in developing a model of family engagement that caters to the needs of individual gifted children and youth from a variety of experiences. For teachers of gifted children to design appropriate instructional challenges for their students, they must have a respectful understanding of the differences and similarities that exist within their classrooms. This same understanding holds true when establishing relationships with families and communities. Meeting individual needs of families requires teachers who are sensitive to students' needs and who are willing to make efforts to familiarize themselves with the strengths and limitations of all communities.

As noted earlier in this chapter, to understand how best to engage all families, culturally responsive strategies are critically important with children from culturally and linguistically diverse backgrounds, just as they are in the classroom. These strategies demand an integration of family traditions, values, and level of experience with gifted education. Developing collaborative partnerships models for family engagement will enable school personnel to become more familiar with the traditions, values, and strengths of their students' families and communities.

Delpit (1992) recommended that schools use parents as "cultural informants." As informants, parents and families can help schools learn about diverse families and communities, thus enhancing educators' understanding of differences, traditions, and learning preferences specific to culturally diverse groups. Encouraging families to take the lead in sharing cultural legacies and using culture as a bridge or conduit for reciprocal understanding strengthens bonds between school personnel and families and enriches understandings that teachers have of the complexities of the varied cultures of their students, many of whom originate from cultures quite different from their own (Espinosa,

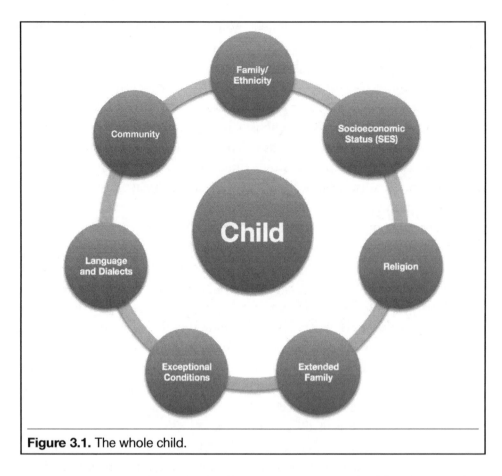

Figure 3.1. The whole child.

2005; Gay, 2010). The goal of such engagement is to build and strengthen cultural competencies of school personnel, so that they learn to think, feel, and act in ways that demonstrate respect for and trust of the cultural, linguistic, and educational diversity of all student populations.

Connecting With Family Strengths

Increasingly, families are working with schools to address the needs of their children. In a study of 280 families in two Midwestern districts, Hertzog and Bennett (2004) acknowledged the important role of parents in making decisions about the complex matter of educational programming for gifted learners. They suggested that a better educational outcome for students could be obtained if the match between a student's strengths and the learning environment was more closely aligned (Hertzog & Bennett, 2004). Schools must be encouraged to engage with parents and others with direct contact with gifted children outside of the school (Coleman & Shah-Coltrane, 2010). Dunst and Trivette (1987) shared a family empowerment philosophy based on acknowl-edgement of the strengths and needs of families and their children. To empower families, school personnel must gain a better understanding of the strengths and resources families have available to them that contribute to their ability to nurture their children, including those who are gifted.

All families, even those with limited economic resources, have strengths that should be considered as important and valid (Dunst & Trivette, 1987). Resources generally provided by parents and families to supervise, moni-tor, advise, and provide leadership for the child are considered *social capital* (Coleman, 1988; Wegmann & Bowen, 2010). Using data from the National Educational Longitudinal Study of 1988 (NELS:88), Yan (1999) examined the relationship between the family's social capital and the child's academic achievement. Study participants were in the eighth grade when first surveyed. The data collected in Yan's study specifically requested responses to patterns of interaction between parents and students originating from Anglo American, African American, and Hispanic American ethnic groups.

Yan's analysis captured four interactive social capital constructs: (a) parent-teen interactions, (b) parent-school interactions, (c) interactions with other parents, and (d) family norms. The analysis concluded that African American parents' social capital in the areas of home discussion and school contact were significantly higher than those of Anglo American students' families. In the category of family norms, African American families were found to have higher levels of family rules than White families. After a complete analysis of all of the data, the researcher concluded that despite their economically disadvantaged status, academically successful Black high school students had higher levels of social capital when compared to successful White students and to their unsuc-cessful equally disadvantaged Black peers (Yan, 1999).

Using social capital as a framework, Davis (2008) examined the impact of families on the academic success of high-achieving, low-income gifted African American learners. The study revealed a full range of social and cultural capital that participants believed were instrumental in the gifted learner's sustained school success (Davis, 2008). Among the resources were the ability to engage students in regular discussions regarding education and its importance to their future, ability to maintain orderly and cohesive home environments, having access to resources of extended family members, and positive achievement orientation.

Research has also documented additional strengths of families from economically disadvantaged environments, which include the ability to teach their children to negotiate between two worlds—being Black and living in their own communities and living within the context of the majority culture and functioning within the intellectual and social demands of accelerated school programs. Skills emphasized by families included instilling in students the value of personal effort, determination, perseverance, and the ability to set goals beyond one's current circumstances (Ford, 2011; Patton & Baytops, 1995). Combining an understanding of family dynamics and the cultural and social impact on academic achievement with family involvement in talent development enables educators to see a new holistic construct of giftedness that involves all of the influences impacting a child's learning on a day-to-day basis.

Mutual Collaboration: Families Reaching in, Schools Reaching Out

In the past, parent or family engagement models have been based primarily on a unidirectional framework developed by Epstein (2001) that spoke more to the influence of parents and families on the academic success of children. Similarly, the talent development literature focused primarily on families and communities as catalysts that have an important role as a nurturer of talent. What has been less clearly defined is a multidimensional or multidirectional framework of schools *and* families mutually interacting to benefit the needs of students, families, and schools simultaneously. What follows is an exploration of a new model for family engagement—one that is more interactive and mutually respectful, enabling families and schools to engage in the process of talent development together.

Baytops (1994) delineated a mutual interactions systems model for the engagement of African American families with schools as a result of data gathered from a set of 140 families originating from a variety of urban, suburban, and rural school districts. This early collaborative model was designed to have families and community members aptly trained to better understand the needs of their gifted learners and subsequently engage more proactively with school personnel. As with the empowerment model discussed earlier (Dunst & Trivette, 1987), such a model is also suggested to improve engagement in gifted education to a traditionally underrepresented population group and their families (Patton & Baytops, 1995).

Table 3.1 outlines the differences between the traditional gifted education parent involvement program and one that is more empowering for African American families. This new model has implications for improving family engagement overall, as increased interest and involvement are sought by both families and by school personnel. Important to the delivery of a more empowering model is a collaborative training plan designed to make the best use of resources in the home, community, and school.

It is important to be mindful that recent efforts to promote more inclusionary practices in identification and services relative to learners with superior potential will result in increasing numbers of gifted learners who are culturally diverse and economically disadvantaged on the rosters of school programs for the gifted. Consequently, the increased numbers of learners will compete for individual attention from educators who may already be overtaxed and not always understand a learner's cultural background and the impact that ethnicity has on learning preferences, motivation, and self-concept. Conversely, family members who themselves may not have experienced schooling in advanced instructional settings nor the demands of working on an equal level with mainstream groups may not understand the difficulties faced by learners who are confronted daily with the complexities of being a culturally diverse gifted learner. Such an existence will require these learners to possess coping skills that will enable them to withstand pressures and develop the self-sufficiency necessary to survive and thrive both within their own communities and in the mainstream culture.

In 2009, Price-Mitchell suggested that combining research from complexity theory, systems theory, and organizational science would enable the creation of a new paradigm for parent involvement, one that is multidimensional in nature and benefits all constituents equally. With schools and parents crossing boundaries and sharing resources, both are poised to benefit from these new collaborations. A new framework for collaborative engagement has the potential for refocusing priorities on the needs and potential of the individual learner, regardless of class or ethnicity, allowing families and educators to cooperatively work to change the course of the future while making use of all available resources in schools and communities to provide for every learner who comes across the doorsteps of schools each day.

Collaboration of resources between families, communities, and schools will not only enhance educational opportunities, but it also has the potential to create new understandings and, thus, respect for the core of American society, its families, and communities. Providing more information to cross the

Table 3.1
Approaches to Involving Families in the Education of Their Gifted Children

Traditional Approach	Empowering Approach
• Initial contact with parents is primarily to obtain permission to test.	• Initial contact with family and community leaders should be to provide information about gifted education services and the benefits to students and schools. • Subsequent contact with family and community leaders should be to obtain data for referral and description of gifted behaviors as expressed in the home and/or community.
• Letter is sent to notify parents of child's eligibility to participate in program.	• Educators should share the results of assessment with family members and clarify their meaning and their implications for the child's future.

• Parent sessions are held to provide information about program offerings and to solicit support for advocacy with policy makers.	• Family sessions are held to:
	  o provide training regarding characteristics of giftedness and concomitant behaviors to expect in home and school.
	  o provide information regarding social-emotional needs of all gifted learners, with particular attention to the needs of culturally and linguistically diverse learners.
	  o provide ways that families can help the child counteract negative pressures of being gifted and begin the process of planning for the future.
	  o train families to develop advocacy skills and understand the educational policy-making process.
	  o solicit input from parents to share their expertise relative to program offerings.

• An Individualized Education Program (IEP) may be developed that focuses on the child's academic needs.	• An Individualized Family Service Plan (IFSP) is developed to document learner and family strengths, resources, areas needing enhancement, and support needs of family (e.g., psychosocial, economic, educational).
• Parent education services are provided only to parents of gifted learners.	• Services are provided to parents, extended family, church and community leaders, and agency personnel, using a collaborative support model to enhance services for all gifted learners.

Note. Adapted from the work of Baytops (1994), Damiani (1996), and Patton and Baytops (1995).

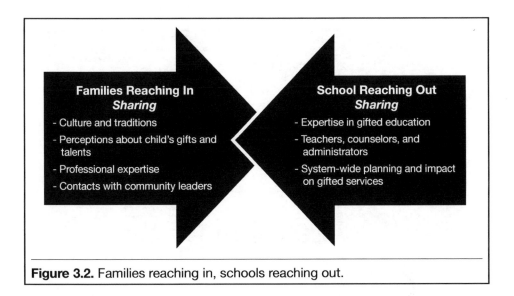

Figure 3.2. Families reaching in, schools reaching out.

cultural bridges, more active outreach to families, and more active inreach on the part of families can create a more congruent and positive learning environment. Figure 3.2 demonstrates this framework for collaborative engagement.

Alignment of Family Engagement With the Response to Intervention Framework

Response to Intervention (RtI) is a fluid and flexible framework for providing services based on needs of the recipients (Coleman & Hughes, 2009). The model requires a collaborative approach to thinking about these needs. In the family engagement process, the recipients and participants are students, families, *and* school personnel (Byrd, 2011). As such, the research and programming reviewed in this chapter suggest that RtI may be an ideal framework to use when designing family engagement programs for schools to work collaboratively with the multiple and varied types of families of gifted learners. As with the RtI framework for designing instructional services for students based on specific needs for many, some, and a few (Coleman & Hughes, 2009), family engagement services may also be designed based on needs of most families, some families, and a smaller group of families that align with their experience with gifted and advanced learner programming. Figure 3.3 shows a tiered approach to family engagement.

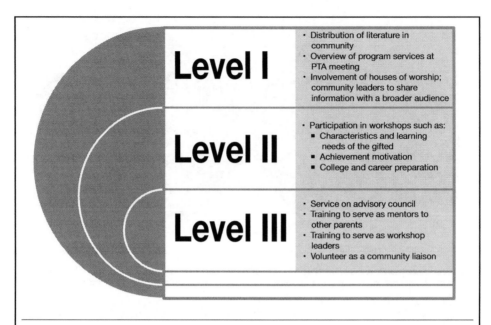

Figure 3.3. Levels of family engagement based on need and experience with gifted education.

The Colorado Department of Education (2009) has developed a very comprehensive guide for schools and families called *Response to Intervention Family and Community Partnering: "On the Team and at the Table" Toolkit* (see http://www.cde.state.co.us/RtI/downloads/PDF/FamilyCommunityToolkit.pdf). The toolkit provides guidance for school districts to establish active family engagement programs based on the RtI model. Structured around three tiers of services—universal, targeted, and intensive—the toolkit shares examples of presentations, activities, and stakeholder materials that schools may use to design their own programs. The underlying premise of the toolkit is that there is a place at the table for all key stakeholders—families, schools, and communities—and without the presence of all, family engagement and involvement will have only limited effectiveness. The importance of all stakeholders is noted in this statement:

> In forming partnerships, it is important to nurture the collaborative process. To develop true collaboration, parents and families must be fundamentally involved in the entire educational experience. Parents should be recognized as having important information and expertise that they can contribute to the partnership. It is important for school personnel to provide the

parents with information and empower them as equal partners in supporting their children's learning. (Colorado Department of Education, 2009, p. 9)

Some communities are quite homogenous and share similar traits (e.g., those who share a primary language, such as intergenerational households and immigrant families; those with similar income status), while other communities may be more heterogeneous and share only some traits (e.g., mixed-income communities, those with two or more ethnic groups living in the same neighborhood). However, all communities do have one thing in common: gifted learners who demonstrate specific intellectual and affective traits. Bianco's (2010) strength-based RtI model enables educators of the gifted to use the framework as services for gifted learners are developed, regardless of student background. Table 3.2 provides a proposed framework for developing family engagement programs that meet the needs of a variety of families of gifted students.

At Engagement Level I, the school reaches out to all families and the community by sharing introductory information about gifted education services. This outreach can take the form of awareness workshops in schools; distribution of literature throughout the community in electronic and hard copy versions as well as notices in local newspapers; and special notices at PTA meetings. This awareness level outreach will provide families and the community at large with information about the benefits of gifted and advanced learner programs, how students are identified for services, and who to contact for more information.

Engagement Level II activities offer more targeted activities for families of students newly identified. However, families of students receiving services for 2 or more years should also take advantage of the workshops and committee service opportunities made available at this level. Indeed, families of students not yet receiving services may also be interested in workshop topics that are offered in this stage of service.

Engagement Level III activities provide more experienced families opportunities to become leaders as trainers of other families and to serve on the advisory council. This level is also well suited for community leaders who have access to a larger group of families and can serve as liaisons between the community and gifted and advanced learner programs. These types of family "reaching in" activities are very beneficial and inclusive.

Table 3.2
Proposed Framework for Family Engagement: Targeting Services Based on Family Need and Level of Experience With Gifted Education Programs

Level of Engagement	Level of Experience	Types of Engagement	Key Role of Families
Engagement Level I: Initial contact and introduction to gifted education	No prior involvement	• Awareness workshops • Literature on identification and benefits of services distributed in all schools and throughout the community (e.g., electronic copies, hard copies, local news media)	• Families as informants of student traits/ manifestations of giftedness in home and community contexts • Families and communities as receivers of general information about gifted and advanced educational programs
Engagement Level II: Upon identification	New to gifted education	• Educator- and parent-led workshops • Potential workshop topics include: benefits of gifted education programming, underachievement in gifted learners, social-emotional needs of the gifted, unique challenges of culturally and linguistically diverse gifted students, twice-exceptional students and the role of parents in advocacy and education, gender identity and the gifted, and college and career counseling	• Families as informants of student traits • Families as collaborators • Families as cultural agents connecting schools with community, spiritual, and civic leadership
Engagement Level III: Families in leadership roles	Prior experience in gifted education	• Active participation in an advisory council • Training to lead parent/family workshops (e.g., nature and needs of the gifted, unique challenges of giftedness, accessing services, advocacy tips)	• Families as decision makers • Families as leaders/ trainers of other families

Conclusion

It is important to note that although this chapter has provided a wide range of theoretical models supported by some empirical research in family involvement in general education, there is a paucity of empirical research on family engagement and schools specifically related to gifted learners. There is insufficient parent involvement research of any kind to validate much of what has been developed in the name of parent engagement in schools today (Caspe, 2008; Ferguson, Ramos, Rudo, & Wood, 2008). It is therefore acknowledged that more research is needed to validate family and school engagement frameworks within the construct of gifted education. The research recommended would examine how schools and families work together in a proactive, multidimensional manner to enhance services for a wide range of high-ability learners across cultures, income groups, and varied geographical settings. In the meantime, however, utilizing the frameworks presented as models for family engagement in gifted education is a positive step in the right direction.

It is critical for educators to recognize that not all parents and families of gifted and potentially gifted students are the same, therefore they should be treated and respected as individually unique families with one specific trait in common: the presence of an exceptional child with specific intellectual, academic, and psychosocial talents. Developing family engagement programs that are mutually respectful of the strengths, capital, expertise, and needs of schools, communities, and families provides the best chance to help each student reach his or her highest potential.

Finally, based on prior experience, available research, and a review of pragmatic theoretical models from other fields, the following recommendations are made that can enable schools and families to develop and maintain mutually cooperative engagement for the benefit of all gifted learners:

> ➤ Make available to all families the broad repertoire of expertise that schools and gifted education experts have regarding the intellectual, academic, and psychosocial needs of high-ability learners.

> ➤ Engage families in sharing their strengths and a reservoir of cultural capital, including their traditions and legacies for supporting their own communities across generations. Take advantage of opportunities to train and deploy families as expert trainers in an effort to increase the involvement of other families traditionally not as comfortable or engaged in the school setting.

➤ Design flexible family engagement models that offer activities to meet the needs of families who differ in terms of their experience with gifted services, neighborhood and community resources, familial ties to enrichment, cultural capital, and students' level of ability.

➤ Assign a community liaison as the go-between to communities, families, and schools to troubleshoot, share information, engage with families within the community outside of school locations, and continuously build partnerships.

➤ Ensure that your family engagement model allows for regular, consistent, and frequent meetings between all stakeholders, including family members, gifted education personnel, community leaders, teachers, and school administrators. Frequent meetings demonstrate the importance of family engagement and keep everyone focused on the task: improving educational services for high-potential and gifted learners.

The goal for our educational systems should be full engagement of all families to enable more gifted and high-ability learners to reach their full potential. When schools reach out to families and families reach in—and both are working collaboratively, respectfully, and cooperatively—what will result is the most effective stream of support needed to enhance the present educational environment and future success of high-ability learners from all backgrounds.

References

Baytops, J. L. (1994). At-risk African American gifted learners: Enhancing their education. In J. S. Stanfield (Ed.), *Research in social policy* (Vol. 3, pp. 1–32). Greenwich, CT: JAI Press.

Bianco, M. N. (2010). Strength-based RtI: Conceptualizing a multi-tiered system for developing gifted potential. *Theory Into Practice, 49,* 323–330.

Briggs, C. J., Reis, S. M., & Sullivan, E. E. (2008). A national view of promising programs and practices for culturally, linguistically, and ethnically diverse gifted and talented students. *Gifted Child Quarterly, 52,* 131–145. doi:10.1177/0016986208316037

Byrd, E. S. (2011). Educating and involving parents in the Response to Intervention process. *TEACHING Exceptional Children, 43*(3), 32–39.

Caspe, M. (2008). Ask the expert: Building the field. *The Evaluation Exchange, 14*(1–2), 1–5. Retrieved from http://www.hfrp.org/evaluation/

the-evaluation-exchange/issue-archive/current-issue-building-the-future-of-family-involvement/building-the-field

Cohn, D. (2011). *Census 2010 news stories: The changing family.* Retrieved from http://www.pewsocialtrends.org/2011/06/23/census-2010-news-stories-the-changing-family

Colangelo, N., Assouline, S., Chen, I., & Tsai, T. (1999). Parental involvement in the academic and social lives of academically talented elementary school students. In N. Colangelo, S. G. Assouline, & I. Chen (Eds.), *Talent development: Proceedings from the 1995 H. B. and Jocelyn Wallace National Research Symposium on Talent Development* (pp. 307–311). Scottsdale, AZ: Great Potential Press.

Coleman, J. (1988). Social capital in the creation of human capital [Supplement]. *American Journal of Sociology, 94,* 95–120.

Coleman, M. R., & Hughes, C. E. (2009). Meeting the needs of the gifted students within an RtI framework. *Gifted Child Today, 33*(2), 14–17.

Coleman, M. R., & Shah-Coltrane, S. (2010). *U-STARS~PLUS family involvement packets.* Alexandria, VA: Council for Exceptional Children.

Colorado Department of Education. (2009). *Response to Intervention (RtI) family and community partnering: "On the team and at the table" toolkit.* Denver, CO: Author.

Damiani, V. B. (1996). The individual family service plan: A tool for special populations of gifted learners. *Roeper Review, 18,* 293–297.

Davis, J. L. (2008). *An exploration of the impact of family on the achievement of African American gifted learners originating from low-income environments* (Unpublished doctoral dissertation). The College of William and Mary, Williamsburg, VA.

Davis, J. L. (2010). *Bright, talented & Black: A guide for families of African American gifted learners.* Scottsdale, AZ: Great Potential Press.

Delpit, L. D. (1992). Education in a multicultural society: Our future's greatest challenge. *The Journal of Negro Education, 61,* 237–249.

Dunst, C. J., & Trivette, C. M. (1987). Enabling and empowering families: Conceptual and intervention issues. *School Psychology Review, 16,* 443–456.

Epstein, J. L. (2001). *School, family, and community partnerships: Preparing educators and improving schools.* Boulder, CO: Westview Press.

Espinosa, L. M. (2005). Curriculum and assessment considerations for young children from culturally, linguistically, and economically diverse backgrounds. *Psychology in the Schools, 42,* 837–853.

Ferguson, C., Ramos, M., Rudo, Z., & Wood, L. (2008). *The school family connection: Looking at the larger picture.* Austin, TX: National Center for Family and Community Connections with Schools.

Ford, D. Y. (2011). *Reversing underachievement among gifted Black students: Promising practices and programs* (2nd ed.). Waco, TX: Prufrock Press.

Gagné, F. (2000). *A differentiated model of giftedness and talent (DMGT).* Retrieved from http://www.curriculumsupport.education.nsw.gov.au/policies/gats/assets/pdf

Garrett, T., Antrop-Gonzalez, R., & Velez, W. (2010). Examining the success factors of high-achieving Puerto Rican male high-school students. *Roeper Review, 32,* 106–115.

Gay, G. (2010). Acting on beliefs in teacher education for cultural diversity. *Journal of Teacher Education, 6*(1–2), 143–152.

Grantham, T. C., & Henfield, M. S. (2011, March). Gifted ethnic minority student participation in pre-collegiate STEM programs: How to become a STEM parent. *Parenting for High Potential,* 10–15.

Henderson, A. T., & Mapp, K. L. (2002). *A new wave of evidence: The impact of school, family, and community connections on student achievement.* Retrieved from http://www.sedl.org/connections/resources/evidence.pdf

Hertzog, N. B., & Bennett, T. (2004). In whose eyes? Parents' perspectives on the learning needs of their gifted children. *Roeper Review, 26,* 96–104.

Hrabowski, F. A., Maton, K. I., & Greif, G. A. (1998). *Beating the odds: Raising academically successful African American males.* New York, NY: Oxford University Press.

Jeynes, W. (2010). The salience of the subtle aspects of parental involvement and encouraging that involvement: Implications for school-based programs. *Teachers College Record, 112,* 747–774.

Kottak, C. P., & Kozaitis, K. A. (2012). *On being different: Diversity and multiculturalism in the North American mainstream* (4th ed.). New York, NY: McGraw-Hill.

Olszewski-Kubilius, P. (2002). Parenting practices that promote talent development, creativity, and optimal adjustment. In M. Neihart, S. M. Reis, N. M. Robinson, & S. M. Moon (Eds.), *The social and emotional development of gifted children: What do we know?* (pp. 205–212). Waco, TX: Prufrock Press.

Patton, J. M., & Baytops, J. L. (1995). Identifying and transforming the potential of young gifted African Americans: A clarion call for action. In B. Ford,

J. M. Patton, & F. Obiakor (Eds.), *Effective education of African American exceptional learners: New perspectives* (pp. 27–67). Austin, TX: Pro-Ed.

Price-Mitchell, M. (2009). Boundary dynamics: Implications for building parent-school partnerships. *The School Community Journal, 19*(2), 9–26.

Sloane, K. (1985). Home influences on talent development. In B. Bloom (Ed.), *Developing talent in young people* (pp. 439–476). New York, NY: Ballantine.

Villegas, A. M. (1988). School failure and cultural mismatch: Another view. *The Urban Review, 20,* 253–265.

Wegmann, K. M., & Bowen, G. L. (2010). Strengthening connections between schools and diverse families: A cultural capital perspective. *The Prevention Researcher, 17*(3), 7–10.

Yan, W. (1999). Successful Black students: The role of parental involvement. *The Journal of Negro Education, 68,* 5–22.

CHAPTER FOUR

PROBLEM SOLVING: FROM A PROCESS TO A CULTURE

Daphne Pereles and Stuart Omdal

Taking a look at the challenges of education across the country more than a decade into the 21st century provides us with quite a view. The educational landscape, once familiar terrain to many of us, has changed significantly over the years. In today's educational world, students come to us speaking a greater number of languages than ever before; teaching and learning have been significantly changed by advances in technology; the achievement gap across students remains; and requirements for assessing the academic growth of students have increased as schools and districts are held more accountable. Pondering how to best serve the wide variety of student needs has pushed educators across the country to think differently about ways to improve outcomes for students, and changes can be seen in how schools are serving students with academic, behavioral, and language acquisition needs. The increased use of a multi-tiered system of supports (MTSS) like Response to Intervention (RtI) and Positive Behavior Interventions and Supports (PBIS) is reflective of these changes. Indeed, multi-tiered systems of supports are central to many school reform efforts that address today's challenges, and the emerging inclusion of the needs of students with gifts and talents in these reform efforts is a good sign. In this chapter, we will highlight the evolution of RtI and gifted education, discuss the problem-solving process as it applies to improving student outcomes, and explore the need for the development of "problem-solving cultures" at the classroom, school, and district levels, which are essential to the success of multi-tiered approaches to student and school success.

Evolution of RtI and Gifted Education

With the reauthorization of the Elementary and Secondary Education Act (ESEA) on the horizon, the opportunity presents itself to integrate these concepts into legislation that will guide educational systems across the country to put a new model of effective reform into action. The successful experiences of innovative RtI implementers have influenced the movement from the use of the term *Response to Intervention* to a *Multi-Tiered System of Supports*. MTSS is the term that has been integrated into the recommendations for the language to be included in the Elementary and Secondary Education Act.

RtI is often perceived and implemented as a deficit-driven model with a focus on interventions for struggling learners. Because of this, the term *intervention* has been perceived as a description for remediation, and often little thought has been given to the needs of students with gifts and talents. The challenges and successes of RtI implementation have directly informed the evolution of the framework. Innovative educators began to see this implementation as an opportunity to think in broader terms and to create responsive educational systems that would improve outcomes for *all* students. Many school leaders are rethinking this approach to include more emphasis on first/best instruction for all and on providing advanced learning opportunities. Educators and administrators in gifted education also began exploring the possibility of using RtI to address the academic and affective needs of students with gifts and talents.

When applied in a comprehensive manner, the RtI framework provides the opportunity to embed gifted identification and programming within a system of multi-tiered supports. The use of MTSS is not new in gifted education. For decades, many school systems have implemented the Levels of Service approach (Treffinger, Young, Nassab, & Wittig, 2003) and the Purdue Three-Stage Enrichment Model (Feldhusen & Kolloff, 1986). Gifted education is also familiar with multiple types of services that provide support for emerging potential, such as Renzulli's Enrichment Triad Model (Renzulli & Reis, 1985); Betts's Autonomous Learner Model (Betts & Kercher, 1999); and Coleman's U-STARS~PLUS (Coleman & Shah-Coltrane, 2010). A closer look at the

Levels of Service approach (Treffinger et al., 2003) illustrates how the educational needs of students can be met in a tiered system.

Treffinger et al. (2003) identified four levels of service to address the development of gifts and talents for students. These levels describe strategies and programming options that, at the base level, are for *all* students as a matter of course. The programming options increase in depth and intensity across the levels as the needs of advanced learners increase. The resultant levels then become more appropriate for fewer and fewer students, with the next three levels representing the programming needs of *many* students, *some* students, and *few* students across the levels of service, respectively. For example, services at the *few* level usually involve radical adaptation of either content or the environment (Brown, 2012). Options at this level of service might include across-grade, in-school, between schools, and beyond school alternatives.

This idea of all, some, many, and few for the development of gifts and talents can be intentionally incorporated into a comprehensive, cohesive continuum of service options for the needs of all students within a school system. The approaches mentioned above fit well across the tiers of service. Looking at how these approaches fit provides an opportunity for gifted education to be part of a shift to redefining educational need so that it includes the needs of advanced learners. The potential impact on gifted students is that attention can be given to their academic advancement as well as their personal interests and social-emotional and behavioral needs.

The development of a solid problem-solving process and culture supports a model that encompasses all educational needs of students within that system and gives gifted education an opportunity to be an equal partner in the development of this system.

Collaborative Problem Solving as a Process

Educational challenges are problems that must be solved and the problem-solving process often starts with a focus on student outcomes. Gifted educators may have difficulty perceiving how an advanced student's need for acceleration is similar to a struggling student's need for remediation. Both cases, however, can be framed as "problems" whose solutions address student needs in the most effective way. A problem is a question to be considered, solved, or answered. It can also be defined as a situation, matter, or person that presents perplexity or difficulty.

The traditional problem-solving process involves four steps: (1) define the problem, (2) analyze the data to determine the intervention, (3) implement the intervention, and (4) evaluate the effectiveness of the intervention. When gifted education is included, this process can be effective in identifying and addressing the needs of advanced learners. For example, in schools that utilize this approach, it is typical for a team composed of gifted and general education teachers, administrators, and other relevant staff to meet regularly. In Step 1, when considering a student with perceived advanced academic needs, this team reviews data addressing the academic performance level (as informed by achievement data and classroom performance) as well as information regarding social interactions, areas of interest, and any other pertinent information gathered through teacher observations in order to define the problem. In this case, the problem may include an inappropriate instructional level for the student, resulting in lack of challenge and therefore lack of engagement.

In Step 2, an analysis of the data in light of the identified problem leads to the decisions about an appropriate intervention. In this particular case regarding a lack of challenge and engagement, the analysis may lead to the determination that some type of academic acceleration would be the appropriate intervention. Additional data collection could further inform the best type of acceleration for this student. Level of intensity and duration of this intervention will also be determined in this step.

Step 3 involves the implementation of the selected intervention. In this case, it could be subject acceleration with careful progress monitoring of engagement and student response to increased rigor. Evaluating the effectiveness of the intervention occurs in Step 4 through the evaluation of the collective progress monitoring data and other pertinent information over the specified duration. For example, the initial duration could be 6 weeks, at which point the team would review the effectiveness of the intervention and recommend modifying or continuing it.

The four steps of the problem-solving process are effective when used as part of an integrated schoolwide approach. Although problem solving is important as a process used in planning for student success, the greater impact is in the creation of problem-solving cultures that support a comprehensive approach to schoolwide improvement.

Creating Problem-Solving Cultures

Given the challenges of the new educational landscape and the use of multi-tiered solutions, a broader definition of problem solving is important. The creation of a culture of problem solving (rather than only a process) helps us understand how problem solving supports school improvement. Using the problem-solving approach in this way, leads to the development of effective, safe, and trusting cultures within our schools and districts that support the necessary systems and structures that result in successful learning environments for all students.

In fact, we believe that the development of a problem-solving culture is key to the success of effective implementation of MTSS. The problem-solving culture is not a new concept. It has been used successfully in the business world (Goh, 2002; Verble, 2011), as well as in public health/disease prevention (Elstein, Shulman, & Sprafka, 1990). A problem-solving culture is most successful when a shared set of assumptions and values exists that seeks to improve current practices and continually improve progress of all students within that environment. Toyota is frequently used as an example of a successful company that has been built upon a culture of problem solving. The company has created what it calls the "Toyota Way" (Liker & Meier, 2005).

> In the Toyota Way, it's the people who bring the system to life: working, communicating, resolving issues, and growing together. It was clear that the workers were active in making improvement suggestions. But the Toyota Way goes well beyond this; it encourages, supports, and—in fact—demands employee involvement. It is a system designed to provide the tools for people to continually improve their work. The Toyota Way means more dependence on people, not less. It is a culture, even more than a set of efficiency and improvement techniques. (Liker, 2003, p. 36)

Toyota has determined that there are two distinguishing features of its model that make it successful in building a culture that is always in a process of continuous improvement. The first is the requirement that every problem brought forward for discussion or review is based on confirmed facts and not assumptions and interpretation. The second is an understanding that problem solving actually *begins* rather than ends when implementation starts (Verble,

2011). These elements of success can be helpful in their application to an educational setting. This would mean that data are used on an ongoing basis to make decisions—data about the system of the school (e.g., attendance data, suspension/expulsion data), individual grade levels, groups of students, or individual students. Successful systems identify any situation when a student is not reaching his or her potential as a problem to be solved. In addition, there is shared ownership for all students, and teachers and administrators work together on an ongoing basis to improve effectiveness and create a culture that embraces a collaborative problem-solving approach. The development of such a culture in an educational setting can support better educational decisions for all students.

Students must have access to rigorous curricula and high-quality instruction within an effective problem-solving culture that addresses barriers to learning by providing services that address the whole child. As these cultures emerge and are developed, MTSS provides an opportunity for gifted educators to have a genuine place at the table. There are many implications for gifted education within an MTSS/problem-solving culture. As a field, we have to reexamine how gifted students are identified, served, and supported. Beginning to think about these implications is important because there is growing evidence that successful school systems are creating problem-solving cultures to support systemic reform and high levels of expectations for their students and their staff.

A Case in Point: Thompson School District

An example of the benefits of a problem-solving culture can be seen in the Thompson School District in Loveland, CO. A case study was conducted at an elementary, middle, and high school. This district has been implementing RtI and PBIS with some success for 5 years. PBIS is a "decision making framework that guides selection, integration, and implementation of the best evidence-based academic and behavioral practices for improving important academic and behavior outcomes for all students" (Office of Special Education Programs Technical Assistance Center on Positive Behavioral Interventions and Supports, 2012, para. 1).

The Thompson study focused on identifying the root causes that led to success in this district. The five major factors that predicted success in implementing RtI and PBIS at these target schools include:

➢ a shared vision that leadership is everyone's responsibility and the realization that we are better together than we are alone;

➢ a belief that all students can be successful if given appropriate support;

➢ a strong culture of collaboration, partnerships, and relationships built on trust, open communication, and respect;

➢ an honoring of diversity and inclusion; and

➢ a problem-solving, continuous improvement focus that uses data to inform decisions at all levels, from individual students to systemic planning.

These five factors deeply anchor the district and the schools, forming the philosophical foundation for how decisions are made, policies are established, and work gets done (Colorado Department of Education, 2012).

Applying these principles in the development of a problem-solving continuous improvement process addresses a system-wide continuum of evidence-based resources, strategies, structures, and practices to support an agile response to academic and social-emotional needs. MTSS focuses on change across the classroom, school, and district to meet the academic and social-emotional needs of all students. It provides high-quality universal educational experiences in a safe and supporting learning environment for all. Targeted and intensive academic and/or behavioral supports are provided for students who have demonstrated mastery of concepts and advanced skills or who experience academic and/or social-emotional difficulties.

The inclusion of gifted education in the development of such a framework is necessary to ensure that systems are intentionally being created to address the needs of all students within the school environment. In many districts and schools, RtI addresses only the needs of students who are struggling or falling below grade-level expectations, and gifted students' needs are not considered. This perpetuates the deficit way of thinking. Another way that RtI is implemented in relation to gifted learners is the creation of a separate, disconnected RtI system to address the needs of gifted learners. This approach maintains the "silo" mindset and works in conflict to an integrated system of supports. Both of these approaches can dilute the use of existing resources and marginalize the educational needs of advanced learners. The MTSS approach allows for a broader interpretation of systemic reform that can intentionally include the needs of these students.

To better understand what a problem-solving culture would look like, lets look at it through the eyes of Suzy Jones, a student, and Mrs. Green, her teacher.

A Problem-Solving Culture in Action

Suzy: I am Suzy, a fourth grader at Rogers Elementary School in a large city in the Eastern United States. I transferred this fall from a public school in one of the smaller school districts on the other side of town. I am in a hurry to get to school this morning because I think I am a little late. Mrs. Green is my teacher. I like Mrs. Green because she doesn't get mad at me when I don't have my homework done. I do try to work on it, but there is a lot going on at home.

Mrs. Green: I have been teaching for 8 years. The teachers at my school are in the fourth year of implementing an RtI framework. It has improved each year. I was skeptical at first, as it was a tough transition. I realize that now my opinion is really valued in the process and I know I have contributed to schoolwide improvements. We are calling it a Multi-Tiered System of Supports instead of RtI this year. I realized that we are focusing less on interventions because we are continually modifying instruction at the universal tier that more fully addresses the needs of more and more students. I also realize that with this evolving system in place, I have more support than ever!

I have some concerns about Suzy Jones regarding the number of times she has been tardy and the number of times that she has not had her homework done. I have kept track of the days she arrives late and the days she has not completed her homework. I am going to call her parents this evening to see how we can work together to make sure she is at school on time—with her homework.

Suzy: At the beginning of the school year, Mrs. Green had all of us work on some tests in math, reading, and writing. When I came into school the next day, I worked with one group of six kids in math and a different group of kids for reading. Everybody was together for science and social studies on that first day. I noticed that Mrs. Green was always writing things down on her iPad.

Mrs. Green: I was able to do all of the initial content-area assessments with the students in the first couple of days of school in the fall. I laughed when I saw the range of learners in my class. Several students got 100% correct on the math assessment. I decided to give them the initial assessment for fifth grade. I knew from experience what it was like to "teach" kids material that they already knew. I'm planning to talk to the other teachers on my grade-level problem-solving team about possible options. It is not uncommon for students to go to a higher grade level for instruction in a particular subject, or maybe the other fourth-grade teachers will have students whose assessments were at the same or similar level. We might be able to make sure the students are challenged by clustering them together for math.

I will also talk to the members of the problem-solving team about the students whose math assessments indicated that they were working below grade level. I know that there were several curriculum differentiation strategies that Gloria Needham, another fourth-grade teacher, had used successfully last year with kids who assessed at that level. (Now I wish I had gone to that last workshop on differentiation!)

This is the first year that I am using an iPad to record student assessment data and narrative observations. I am always surprised at what I can tell about *my* instruction from student data. I remember "the old days" when I always gave pre- and postassessments to the students and dutifully wrote down their scores, but never did anything with the data. What a waste of time! It was when we had a professional development workshop and follow-up coaching on formative instructional practices that I realized there was more to it than just writing down the numbers—I also needed to change the way I taught! My principal assured us that he was more interested in teachers using that kind of data to influence instruction than keeping perfect records of scores that we never paid attention to.

I called Suzy's home the day before yesterday to see if I could speak to her parents about her being tardy and her incomplete homework. Suzy answered and told me that her parents weren't home and she didn't know how late they would be. I will keep trying.

Suzy: I was a little surprised in science class. It seemed like Mrs. Green didn't know much about the topic that was one of my favorites: rocks and volcanoes. Mrs. Green kept asking the class questions about what they knew and then when a student would ask a question, she usually said, "What do you think?" Funny thing—it seemed like the kids figured out the answer after she asked them a few more questions. A few days later, I thought my teacher made a mistake in something she said. I thought I heard Mrs. Green ask the class what they would like to learn more about. I thought the teachers were supposed to tell us kids that! Mrs. Green told the class that we would be able to choose a topic about rocks or volcanoes and do a special project about it. She told us to think about something we wondered or had questions about. I knew just what I wanted to learn more about.

Whenever we go to visit my grandmother, my parents drive on Highway 44. Part of the roadway goes through a stretch where the construction crews had blasted through a huge rock area many years ago. I always look at these big rock chunks that are on the side of the road. I also look up at the high rock walls of the roadway and see the big holes in the rock. It was just last week that I realized those huge chunks of rock had fallen down on the road. I started to wonder if anyone had gotten hurt—those chunks were pretty big. I wonder why the chunks fell down and whether or not the construction workers can tell when another one is going to fall. I hope that it isn't when we are driving to my grandmother's!

Mrs. Green: The students responded very well in science class. They are always interested in the topic of rocks and volcanoes. In the past, I had focused on having students memorize the names of different rocks and the different kinds of volcanoes. This time I decided to use a concept-based learning approach and focus on the "essential questions" and developing understanding. It was obviously a new approach for them as they just looked at me quizzically when I kept asking them what they thought. I know they were really thinking because when we did an assessment, they demonstrated that they knew the basics of the standards from their previous knowledge and the work we did in class. I decided to do an extension activity with the class by having each student choose a topic of interest to them regarding rocks and volcanoes, focus on a question based on the topic, and communicate that information in a creative and engaging way. I am going to go over rubrics with the class for making posters, doing demonstrations, creating videos, giving a speech, and writing a booklet.

Suzy's eyes lit up when I mentioned the video. I am so glad to see her this excited about school. I have a feeling that this will be an important project for her at this time. I finally got in touch with Suzy's father. He sounded like he wanted to help her and seemed open to the ideas I gave him about making sure she did her homework and got to school on time. He said he would make sure things improved. I am hopeful!

Suzy: I am so excited about the rock project. I checked out a couple of books on rocks and found one on how tunnels are made. I guess that is kind of like the roadway on Highway 44 except it is like a tunnel open to the sky. Mrs. Green said that if we could talk to a person about our topic, that would be considered an interview and we could put that in our project, too. I like talking to people! I'd like to do a video and show the chunks of rock, but I don't have a camera. I guess I'll do a poster.

I'm really liking science, but when I think about math, am I excited? Not so much. I just have a hard time keeping up with it this year. It is so much harder than last year. Mrs. Green tells me to slow down and just think about what I know about multiplication. I'm slowing down and I'm thinking, but I'm not multiplying! I'd rather spend the time I have for homework on the science project. Did you know that people who design roads are called engineers? I thought those were just on trains!

Mrs. Green: I'm so pleased to see that the students are paying attention to the project rubrics; if they follow them, they act as a guide on how to do each project. A couple of students wanted to write a play. I found an article online that had a how-to section on writing plays. I'm noticing that some of the students are able to work pretty independently and manage their time well while others really need help in figuring out what to do. I think I'll see what the others on the grade-level problem-solving team have done to help the students work more independently.

Last week, Suzy got to school on time for 3 days and turned in most of her homework. She has missed 2 days this week and has not turned in any homework. I talked with her mother on the phone, and she said that Suzy just did not like school and that she could not do anything about that. I asked her if there would be a good time for me to meet with her and her husband at school or at their home. She paused and said that she did not think that would work out. I am going to share this information at our problem-solving team meeting tomorrow. I hope they can give me some ideas about how to connect better with Suzy's parents.

Suzy: I am so tired this morning. I know that I haven't done any homework this week, and I hope Mrs. Green won't yell at me. No, she wouldn't do that. She never yells.

I'm going to try and work on my science project, but I have kind of lost interest in it. All of the other kids are making these really neat posters, videos, and other stuff. It is just kind of hard to concentrate on it. I probably wouldn't do very well anyway. It's dumb.

Mrs. Green: Our grade-level problem-solving team met this afternoon. I brought in Suzy's data on attendance. She has missed 6 out of 24 days and been tardy 10 days. As far as homework, she is missing more than half of her assignments. I also have quite a few observations that I jotted down on my iPad. Her mind just seems to be elsewhere. She was so excited about the science project, and her topic and questions were about the best I have ever seen for a fourth grader. I also told my teammates about the contacts I had with her parents. They were supportive of the way I had contacted them. I was encouraged to keep trying, and they recommended that I work with the Individual Problem-Solving Team to see what school-level interventions would be appropriate.

Suzy: Mrs. Green talked to me by myself yesterday. I thought I was in trouble for missing so much school and not turning in assignments. But, I wasn't in trouble. She asked me if I would like to meet another teacher who could help me get caught up with my homework and work with me on my science project about rocks. Mrs. Green came to my house and met with my parents. My mom was embarrassed to tell her that she and dad had lost their jobs and are now working at temporary jobs and sometimes have to leave me alone at home. Mrs. Green told them that if I came early to school, I could get breakfast and could stay after school for help with my homework. I think I'll be finding out about those rocks after all.

Mrs. Green: I took Suzy's attendance and other data, including observations and parent contact information, to the Individual Problem-Solving Team meeting last week. They asked me questions about Suzy's strengths and interests. They agreed that her science project was unique and that we really needed to find a way to provide assistance so she could finish it. The media specialist mentioned that one of the parent volunteers had told her that she had helped several students in Mr. Dowd's class with a video journalism project and was eager to work with other students. We all agreed that I would contact her and set up a meeting with Suzy. The school counselor said she would check to see if Suzy qualified for the before- and afterschool program. The assistant principal wondered if there might be a change in her family's economic situation and, if so, that could account for some of the instability that Suzy was exhibiting. I told them that I was willing to try and set up a home visit after we found out about the instructional assistance and the before- and afterschool program status. I am hopeful that these interventions will work.

Suzy: I finished my science project video yesterday and got to share it with all of the other kids in my class. They all asked how I came up with the idea. Mrs. Green invited Mr. Steve Carboni to my presentation. He is the Highway 44 road supervisor whose job it is to study and predict when falling rocks might come down on the road. He was the guy that I got to interview—we just talked about the rocks and the road.

I am no longer having problems with being tardy and with not doing homework like I had at the beginning of the year. The special teacher is getting me caught up with my homework. I'm even understanding math more now. (Science is still my favorite though!) It is nice to be able to get some breakfast at school and have extra help after school with homework. Things have turned around for me at school. I'm even starting to think about another science project. I think I want to start collecting rocks—small ones!

Conclusion

As shown in the example above, building a problem-solving culture (including collaborative problem solving, formative assessment, and continuous improvement for the student and for the system) is key to meeting the diverse needs of today's student population. When a problem-solving culture is in place, meeting the needs of the student becomes a matter of course. This type of collaborative problem-solving culture is the culminating result of the successful implementation of MTSS approaches. Although problem solving includes the four-step process focused on student needs, this is merely a part of the whole. The four-step process works best if it is embedded within a supportive problem-solving culture that embraces a comprehensive view of continuous school improvement. The intentional inclusion of gifted education within this problem-solving culture is central to a focus on optimizing student success. The early stages of this movement have begun, but there is still much work to be done. The creation of these problem-solving cultures has the potential to make a difference for *all* students.

References

Betts, G. T., & Kercher, J. K. (1999). *Autonomous Learner Model: Optimizing ability.* Greeley, CO: Autonomous Learner Press.

Brown, E. F. (2012). Is Response to Intervention and gifted assessment compatible? *Journal of Psychoeducational Assessment, 30,* 103–116.

Coleman, M. R., & Shah-Coltrane, S. (2010). *U-STARS~PLUS: Professional development kit manual.* Arlington, VA: Council for Exceptional Children.

Colorado Department of Education. (2012). *Creating the conditions for success: A case study of three Thompson schools' RtI and PBIS frameworks.* Denver, CO: Author.

Elstein, A. S., Shulman, L. S., & Sprafka, S. A. (1990). Medical problem solving: A ten-year retrospective. *Evaluation & the Health Professions, 13*(1), 5–36.

Feldhusen, J. F., & Kolloff, P. B. (1986). The Purdue Three-Stage Enrichment Model for gifted education at the elementary level. In J. Renzulli (Ed.), *Systems and models for developing programs for the gifted and talented* (pp. 126–152). Mansfield Center, CT: Creative Learning Press.

Goh, S. C. (2002). Managing effective knowledge transfer: An integrative framework and some practice implications. *Journal of Knowledge Management, 6,* 23–30.

Liker, J. K. (2003). *The Toyota way: 14 management principles from the world's greatest manufacturer.* New York, NY: McGraw-Hill.

Liker, J. K., & Meier, D. (2005). *The Toyota way fieldbook: A practical guide for implementing Toyota's 4Ps.* New York, NY: McGraw-Hill.

Office of Special Education Programs Technical Assistance Center on Positive Behavioral Interventions and Support. (2012). *What is school-wide positive behavioral interventions and supports?* Retrieved from http://www.pbis.org/school/what_is_swpbs.aspx

Renzulli, J. S., & Reis, S. M. (1985). *The Schoolwide Enrichment Model: A comprehensive plan for educational excellence.* Mansfield Center, CT: Creative Learning Press.

Treffinger, D. J., Young, G. C., Nassab, C. A., & Wittig, C. V. (2003). *Programming for talent development: The Levels of Service approach.* Waco, TX: Prufrock Press.

Verble, D. (2011). *Problem solving for lean continuous improvement.* Retrieved from http://www.lean-transform.com/leanculture2.htm

CHAPTER FIVE

USING DATA-DRIVEN DECISION MAKING

Mary Ruth Coleman and Jennifer Job

One of the key components that differentiates Response to Intervention (RtI) from traditional service-delivery approaches is its integrated decision-making approach based on outcomes data—and this is also what often makes it challenging (Cummings, Atkins, Allison, & Cole, 2008; Skalski & Romero, 2011)! Within the RtI approach, data are critical for identifying a student's academic, social, and behavioral needs; data inform instructional planning; data drive the allocation of resources; and data reveal the outcomes of all of our efforts (Ysseldyke, Burns, Scholin, & Parker, 2010). So why is it that the term *data* is often seen as a four-letter word?

Historically, data have often been used for punitive accountability and for the assignment of blame when things go wrong (Skalski & Romero, 2011). Punitive approaches can leave educators feeling vulnerable, frustrated, and gun-shy when the need for data is discussed. As long as data are used to punish students, teachers, principals, and districts, it will be difficult—if not impossible—to build the trust needed for the proactive data-driven decision-making that is central to RtI. Yet, changing to a culture that supports proactive data-driven decision-making is essential for RtI to be successful. In this chapter, using the lens of the educational needs of students who are gifted, we will examine the kinds of data required for proactive data-driven decision-making, look at the changing uses of data within an RtI framework from both a classroom and a systems level, and explore what data-driven decision-making cultures look like.

Data Are More Than Numbers

When we as educators think about data, we sometimes imagine that it is some kind of magical set of numbers that will give us the answers to all of our questions. But data are not magical, and they can only inform our decisions—data cannot provide us the answers. And data are not just numbers. Data can be composed of all kinds of information that help us gain an understanding of current situations and trends over time. With this information, we can review past outcomes, examine current outcomes, and plan to improve future outcomes. In other words, data act as a baseline to see where we are, as checkpoints to guide where we are going, and as endpoints to tell us when we have achieved our goals. Data are used as the navigation system that helps us know what to teach, offers us insights into how to teach, and lets us know whether our teaching has been effective (i.e., Have our students learned?). Without appropriate data, we are operating blindly, and it is difficult to tell if what we are doing is making any meaningful differences. But to be helpful, data must be used correctly.

Within the RtI context, the uses of data are somewhat different than in the past. Ysseldyke et al. (2010) argued that we have entered an era in which our focus on data has "shifted from making predictions about students' lives to making a difference in their lives" (p. 54). They pointed out that we are moving from the use of data primarily for eligibility (entitlement) decisions (e.g., identifying who needs special or gifted education) to the use of data to guide instructional planning. According to Ysseldyke and his colleagues, "The primary purpose of assessment within RtI models is to facilitate decision making that leads to instructional practices that help children with unique needs learn" (p. 55). To accomplish this goal, they described the use of data and assessment as "an interactive, dynamic process, one that is strongly influenced by the student's individual *ecology*" (p. 55, italics in original). This change in focus means that we also must change the kinds of data we collect, how and when we collect these data, who has access to the data, and what we do to analyze the data (Halverson, Grigg, Prichett, & Thomas, 2007). These changes reflect the purposeful use of data to inform specific decisions—otherwise known as data-driven decision making.

What kinds of data are needed for this decision making within an RtI framework? The answer is, "It depends!" It depends, of course, on the specific decision being made for the specific student. The kinds of information that we should have access to if needed, however, can be identified. Table 5.1 shares several kinds of assessments that can provide meaningful data to inform decision making. Some of the information best supports formative decision making and instructional planning whereas other data best support summative or evaluative decisions at periodic endpoints for instruction (e.g., the end of a unit or marking period; Allain & Eberhardt, 2011). The distinction between formative and summative, however, is often blurry, as the appropriate use of all data is to guide us in supporting the continuous learning of the student. The critical aspect of data-driven decision making is to collect the data that are needed for the student and the decision being made. In this way, our use of data becomes more strategic.

Using data to inform instruction is central to the RtI framework; as the student's needs become more intense (i.e., different from his or her normative peer group), the supports and services we provide to address these needs must become more intense (Allain & Eberhardt, 2011). The types and amounts of data needed for decision making also change as the student's needs become more intense. The decision to provide targeted enrichment—a Tier 2 option— to a student based on her interests is rather straightforward, and the only data we really need is the strength of the student's interests. If, however, we are trying to decide whether grade acceleration is appropriate for a student, we need significantly more information (data) that will likely include formal testing of achievement and cognitive abilities, the student's grades, ecological information about the family and school, student interests, and other indications that the student will be better served, across the years, with grade acceleration (Coleman, 2012). Although tests are helpful tools in determining what to teach, other kinds of data are needed to determine how to teach (Ysseldyke et al., 2010). These data will come from direct observations of a student's success during actual teaching and learning, from work samples, and from reviewing the student's learning preferences. As we can see, this use of data within an RtI system goes well beyond determining whether or not a student is gifted.

Data used for instructional planning must be (a) directly related to the instructional purpose, (b) respectful of the student's individual ecology (e.g., his or her strengths, needs, interests, cultural and personal attributes), and (c) able to show growth and mastery across time. The types of data available to teachers must also be broad enough in scope to help them measure general out-

Table 5.1

Types of Data Available for Decision Making

Assessment Type	Definition	Purpose for Decision Making
General outcome measure (formative)	Standardized indicators of basic success (e.g., vocabulary level as an indicator of success for reading) that have multiple equivalent items to allow for progress monitoring over time	To assess growth in the mastery of basic skills needed for a given area of learning (e.g., reading)
Curriculum-based measure (formative)	General outcome measures that are established for specific content areas (e.g., spelling, math, writing) to assess student mastery of the given curriculum and to monitor progress over time	To inform instructional decision making that is tied to the curriculum and that reflects a student's achievements and learning gaps
Formal state or district assessments (summative)	Standardized tests that are given periodically to determine achievement levels within a given curriculum or domain	To evaluate student performance and mastery within a given curriculum or domain
Observational measure (formative)	Systematic tools that allow observers to document student behaviors within the context of their natural environments and activities (e.g., classroom, playground, home)	To inform instructional planning for students given their actual performance and success within the learning context and activities
Benchmark assessment (formative and summative)	Checkpoints of accomplishments on skills within a given domain or curriculum (e.g., adding with multiple digits)	To document proficiency in skills within a given domain or curriculum and determine the need for more targeted supports
Work samples/ portfolios (formative or summative)	Student-generated artifacts that show actual work and accomplishments	To provide evidence of performance and accomplishments
Student interest and learning preferences surveys	Profile a student's interests and learning preferences	To inform instructional planning and differentiation to address a student's strengths and needs
Environmental/ ecological information	Contextual information about a student's family, culture, language, areas of strength, and areas of challenge	To support appropriate planning for family engagement and student success

comes, specific knowledge and skills, and outcomes for more complex learning goals.

Data Use at the Classroom Level

Using data at the classroom level presents different challenges when working with students with gifts and talents as opposed to those with learning disabilities. When examining the data sources listed in Table 5.1, areas of difficulty show up clearly—we can tell when a student has not met a benchmark or is not showing a skill. But if we collect data on our students in a classroom and a student has aced a formal test and excelled in an outcomes measure, is she gifted and does she need special services? Or, has she simply learned that skill set particularly well? How do we tell the difference between outcomes data that show competence and data that show giftedness?

Ms. Reed's third-grade class is studying geometric shapes. Ms. Reed has designed several types of assessments to collect data for this unit: There is a benchmark test designed by her state's Department of Education, two formative assessments, a few group and individual projects, and a formal test that she will give her students at the end of the term.

Sarah, a diligent student who Ms. Reed has recognized for turning in neat, complete assignments, takes particular interest in this unit. When she works through her formative assessments, her work is typical of her—she takes time with the questions and generally gets them right. But when Ms. Reed has her students do projects with manipulatives, including kits to put together shapes and measure size and volume, Sarah really shines. While her fellow students are building cubes and showing a basic understanding of how much matter the shapes can hold, Sarah is building more complex geometric shapes and showing a basic understanding of not only volume, but also how the ratio of the sides of the shapes relates to that volume. To give her more freedom in her work, Ms. Reed borrows a more complex kit that the sixth-grade classes use to learn volume and mass to give to Sarah.

Ms. Reed wonders if perhaps Sarah is gifted in math. She has never noticed anything special about Sarah—she always does well in class, but does not particularly shine over the other students. Sarah is not quick to raise her hand or volunteer to go to the board to demonstrate problems, and her reading skills seem to be just about on grade level. But when Ms. Reed asks for Sarah's test scores from the previous years, she finds that Sarah scored above average in math in first grade, but not in the second grade. Ms. Reed decides to contact the school's RtI coordinator and gifted education specialist to ask for help in not only identifying Sarah's potential, but also developing assignments better suited to her geometry skills.

Ms. Reed's story probably seems familiar to all of us. Luckily, she has the access to data that she can use to make the best choices for Sarah, and she has a team of people within her school who are also invested in Sarah's success. And yet, looking back at the vignette, we can also see ways in which Ms. Reed can make significant changes in the way she approaches her classroom as a whole, as well as how she works with Sarah, in order to truly assure that she is implementing the RtI approach to its fullest potential.

Setting Goals That Produce Meaningful Data

At the beginning of the unit, Ms. Reed's goal was to teach shapes and an introduction to volume. In the state in which she teaches, the standard is very vague, stating that students are to "show understanding of the concepts of measuring and capacity." But how do we as teachers know if a student is showing understanding or not? More important, this standard is a benchmark for the unit—an end goal. Ms. Reed needs to be able to find out whether her students are learning along the way. To accomplish this, she needs to set her own goals that will produce meaningful data she can use to determine whether her students are learning on schedule, experiencing difficulties, or, as in Sarah's case, already understanding the concept and are ready to move on to something more in depth or advanced.

Vanderheyden (2011) emphasized the need for both specificity and variety of data when implementing the RtI framework. Only when we have a multitude of data that all points to a certain direction can we make appropriate decisions for education interventions. To gather such data, Johnston (2010) suggested a model of goal setting she termed ABCD (Audience, Behavior,

Condition, Degree). This model identifies the who, what, when, and extent of the standard and thus makes it much easier to collect data. For example, let us look at one of the formative assessments Ms. Reed designed for her class and see how the ABCD model could be applied.

The formative assessment is a worksheet consisting of 15 shapes. Seven of the shapes are one-dimensional (e.g., rhombus, triangle) and eight of the shapes are three-dimensional (e.g., cube, cone). Students are not only to identify each shape, but also match the three-dimensional shapes to the one-dimensional shapes they are made of. Ms. Reed's original goal for this assessment was that all students would be able to complete the worksheet correctly. However, this goal was vague and not very helpful for collecting data. If Tom answers 10 out of 25 items correctly, what does that mean? If Sarah answers every question correctly after some prompting from Ms. Reed, does that affirm Ms. Reed's instincts about her potential?

If Ms. Reed were to rewrite her goals for this assessment based on the ABCD model, they would look very different. Let us consider that the class has spent the last week studying one-dimensional shapes and has also covered this information in previous years' work. They have spent the past 2 days learning the terms for three-dimensional shapes and how they are formed. If the goal for the assessment were rewritten for the ABCD model, it may look like the following:

> Given 20 minutes for the worksheet and working indepen-
> dently, students will identify 90% of the one-dimensional
> shapes correctly, 60% of the three-dimensional shapes cor-
> rectly, and 50% of the shapes that make up the three-dimen-
> sional shapes correctly.

This goal satisfies the ABCD model: Audience (students), Behavior (answering questions), Conditions (20 minutes and working independently), and Degree (percentage correct). In using this goal, Ms. Reed can identify where students are in relation to the benchmark. Perhaps Tom only answers 50% of the questions relating to one-dimensional shapes correctly, and Ms. Reed can tell that he needs remediation in this area before he moves on to three-dimensional shapes. And if Sarah answers 90% of the three-dimensional shape questions correctly in only 10 minutes rather than taking the entire 20, her teacher then knows that she is ready for more challenging work and per-haps has the potential for more intensive interventions.

Universal Design for Learning: Collecting Multiple Types of Data

Making data-driven decisions requires teachers to have *data literacy*, which is "the ability to accurately observe, analyze, and respond to a variety of different kinds of data for the purpose of continuously improving teaching and learning in the classroom and school" (Love, 2011, p. 1). As shown in Table 5.1, there are multiple sources of data that teachers can pull from, and not all of them can be distilled to numbers. What is essential is gathering a body of evidence for each student that identifies patterns of his or her strengths and needs (Pereles, Omdal, & Baldwin, 2009). This body of evidence can come from standardized test scores and formal assessments, as well as systematic observations of student behavior and abilities in the classroom (Coleman & Shah-Coltrane, 2010). For example, Ms. Reed may decide to design a chart for Sarah and note whenever she sees her taking an interest in more complex math concepts or extending her effort beyond what is asked for (Lee, Vostal, Lylo, & Hua, 2011).

In order to collect such a rich body of evidence that does not rely solely on test scores, teachers can implement Universal Design for Learning (UDL) principles that allow students to express their potential in multiple ways (Kirk, Gallagher, Coleman, & Anastasiow, 2012). The basic principles of UDL hinge on providing multiple ways of representing content or information to be learned, using multiple forms of engagement to immerse students in learning, and offering multiple ways that students can express their learning and show their mastery. By providing a number of different activities to promote learning, such as group work, hands-on modeling and lab interactions, guided reading and practice, and projects, teachers give students the opportunity to shine through learning preferences that may be silenced in strictly direct instruction classrooms. Consider Sarah, whom Ms. Reed observes excelling in modeling geometric shapes, but is typically too shy to volunteer answers in a whole-group setting; assessment based wholly on the whole-group setting would miss her potential. In a classroom where UDL principles are used, assessment and data collection can take place throughout numerous activities to assure that this potential is not missed (Conderman & Hedin, 2012).

Data Mining for Intervention Rather Than Identification

At the end of the geometry unit, Ms. Reed has a wealth of data to pull from. She has her observational charts, the scores from the formative assessments and tests, and the data produced from the state's benchmark assessment. Now, she has to engage in the practice of *data mining*, or "the process of problem iden-tification, data gathering and manipulation, statistical/prediction modeling, and output display leading to deployment or decision making" (Streifer & Schumann, 2005, p. 283). Although data mining can sound overwhelming, the goal is pretty straightforward: to be able to use the collected data purpose-fully in order to decide on the interventions (if needed) for each student. In other words, it is data-driven decision making.

Love (2011) identified the following criteria for interpreting data accurately:

> ➢ Distinguishing between observation and inference
> ➢ Critically examining the assumptions and cultural biases that influence one's data interpretations
> ➢ Applying basic metrics accurately (e.g., percentage, percentile, percent-age change, and percentage point change)
> ➢ Accurately interpreting line graphs, bar graphs, and scatter plots
> ➢ Acting as critical consumers of tests based on an understanding of the importance of reliability, validity, cultural sensitivity, and fairness. (p. 1)

Typically, data mining for giftedness has focused on *identification* (gifted vs. not gifted), but within the RtI model, data mining shifts the focus to *interven-tion* (Coleman, 2012). There are several reasons for this difference. In the past, giftedness was an all or nothing identification—a student was either gifted or not. However, the RtI framework recognizes a much more fluid method of identification and realizes that although a student may show potential in one area, he may not in another (and, in fact, may have needs that require services in other areas; Coleman, 2012). A student such as Sarah may show the need for Tier 2 services in math (e.g., she may work with small groups on more advanced projects or she may be given more difficult assignments) or she may need Tier 3 services (e.g., skipping to a higher level math class or attending pull-out classes designed for gifted students).

In order to make these decisions, teachers actively participate in the prac-tice of data mining. A significant aspect of data mining is noting change in data points—has the student progressed, lost ground, or accelerated? This is why Love (2011) pointed out the need for *data literacy*, the ability to read data and know what they mean. Many teachers find this to be an easier task by making visual models of the data they have collected; Wayman (2005) noted the many computer programs available for data input that teachers can use, and often standardized and common assessment data come to the teacher already plotted on charts and graphs. In order to make the data most useful, it should be broken down by the goals so that the teacher can make the necessary decisions as to how to support her students' needs.

To think about this further, let's examine the differences between using data for formal identification of students (a traditional approach) and using data to determine needed supports and services to help the student meet with optimal success. To explore the difference between using data to *identify* and using data to *intervene*, let's imagine that the entire third grade has taken the benchmark assessment that Ms. Reed gave to her students. The school decides that any student who has scored a 95 (out of 100) or above will be moved to gifted education classes, and any student who has scored below a 45 will be referred for special education. This is a case of using data to identify: The students are now labeled based on their test scores. We see the narrow use of data when we consider three concerns with how data are used in the example above. First, in using the general benchmark, the needs of the students are not determined specifically (consider the case of Tom above, who may only need remediation for a previous year's learning to catch up with his classmates); second, the labels are inflexible and all-encompassing (just because Sarah is gifted in geometry does not mean she will succeed in the rest of the gifted curriculum, which focuses on literature); and third, the data do not provide direction guiding us to the interventions the students may need (how will we help both Tom and Sarah based only on these data?). Although this example is oversimplified, it illustrates the use of data that is primarily focused on eligibility determinations and not on interventions.

Now, consider a situation in which Ms. Reed examines the benchmark scores broken down by goal item and compares them to the scores from the previous unit's tests. She notes that Sarah's identification of shapes and her ability to relate numbers to one another have been consistently higher than the class average on both assessments. She compiles that information with the chart she has created of her observations and decides to increase the complexity and depth of the math assignments she gives to Sarah in the next unit while pairing her with Jorge, who has already been working on accelerated assignments, as a peer helper (Tier 2 services). In this case, Ms. Reed has used data to *intervene*. She may also begin collecting work samples showing Sarah's success and building a body of evidence that may lead to Sarah's formal identification as a student with gifts in math.

Putting Collaboration to Use

The final, and perhaps most important, piece to using data-driven decision making in the classroom is collaborating with other educators. The tasks outlined above can seem very daunting, and teachers are susceptible to "data drown" (which will be discussed in depth in a later section of this chapter). In a best-case scenario, teachers will have coteachers in their classrooms who can assist with both the collection and mining of data. Conderman and Hedin (2012) outlined several best practices for coteachers in practicing co-assessment, including pre-instruction assessments, during-instruction assessments, and post-instruction assessments. Having a coteacher in the classroom allows for freedom and creativity in data collection that is not possible for one teacher alone. Conderman and Hedin described, for example, using "unison responses" to encourage students to participate, with one teacher asking the question and one teacher observing the class to see if any student seems confused or refuses to participate.

The more likely scenario for the classroom teacher, however, is that she will not have a coteacher, but may have part-time access to a paraprofessional, gifted education specialist, resource teacher, and/or guidance counselor. Lingo, Barton-Arwood, and Jolivette (2011) emphasized the need for all educators in a school to participate actively in the collection and mining of data in order to measure progress and make data-driven decisions. Although the classroom teacher may be responsible for collecting classroom observations and analyzing student class work, a resource teacher or testing specialist may take on the analysis of standardized and common assessment. Each person can take on a separate role in what is done with that data; in analysis of student work, for example, the teacher may complete error analysis, the special educator may define behavior and recommend interventions (Lingo et al., 2011), and the gifted education teacher may develop a rubric to review an advanced independent project. What is essential to this process is that it is a team effort focused on providing the right support for the student (Coleman, Gallagher, & Job, 2012).

Recall that Ms. Reed approached the RtI coordinator and gifted education specialist to ask for assistance in providing the right resources for Sarah. Ms. Reed should also include Sarah's parents in the decision-making process. Byrd (2011) explained that educating and involving parents in the RtI process is essential to successful implementation of RtI. Parents who are more aware of the process and who are kept involved with the data that are collected are more likely to be supportive of their child at home and assist with the interventions decided upon. In Sarah's case, her father is her sole caregiver and works many hours during the week to support Sarah and her younger brother. However, he is happy to meet with Sarah's support team during his day off. He has also collected data to contribute to Sarah's body of evidence; he has observed Sarah's reactions at the town's Museum of Life and Science and has taken pictures of the models she has built with her construction sets at home. With these important data, the gifted education specialist and Ms. Reed can work together to design assignments that will pique Sarah's interest and that can be expanded upon at home with her father.

Data at the System Level

Data-driven decision making does not happen by accident, and it cannot happen in a vacuum (Shapiro & Clemens, 2009). Systems support for data collection and use is critical (Wohlstetter, Datnow, & Park, 2008). Creating capacity at the district and school levels for data collection, storage, and analysis is essential (Marsh, Pane, & Hamilton, 2006). This capacity must include expertise as well as the physical and technological storage for data management; building this capacity may be harder than you think (Mandinach, Gummer, & Muller, 2011). Designing data systems begins with identifying meaningful and challenging learning goals, determining appropriate measures to assess progress and mastery of these goals, and linking these measures to interventions (including additional support *and* enhancements or enrichments). These decisions require input at the classroom, school, and district levels and must be aligned with state (and sometimes federal) goals (Burdette, 2011; Wohlstetter et al., 2008). As these data systems are designed, it is critical that they include the ability to incorporate above-grade-level assessments for students with gifts and talents. These systems should also be designed so that they can include data for complex learning outcomes, which may require the use of rubrics, work samples, or portfolio/performance adjudications. These complex learning outcomes are often associated with gifted education; however, if these are built into the data management system, they can be used with all students. There are several additional factors that influence the use of data for decision making and these must be addressed systemically (see Table 5.2).

Each of the areas shared in Table 5.2 need to be addressed in order to support the use of data-driven decision making. Failure to address any one of these areas can mean that although data are collected, they may not be used

Table 5.2

Factors That Can Influence the Use of Data-Driven Decision Making

- *Accessibility of data*: Can those who need the information get it easily?
- *Quality of the data*: Are the data of high quality, accurate, reflective of the population, and valid for the purpose they are being used?
- *Motivation to use the data*: Is there a positive/proactive reason to use the data combined with an intrinsic desire to be informed by data?
- *Timelines of the data*: Are the data available when the decision needs to be made?
- *Staff capacity and support*: Do faculty members have a solid comfort level with use of data and just-in-time support when needed?
- *Curriculum pacing pressures*: Do mandated pacing plans undermine the incentive to use data because there is little or no flexibility to adjust instruction based on data?
- *Lack of time*: Is there limited time to use the data for collecting, analyzing, collaborating, and planning?
- *Organizational culture and leadership*: Is data-driven decision making supported by leadership and is there a culture of professional learning communities and continuous improvement?
- *History of state accountability:* Is there a state context for data collection and use?

Note. Adapted from Marsh et al. (2006).

(Marsh et al., 2006). Perhaps the single most important variable for teachers in their decision to use data is if they can see positive results for their students. This feedback, which shows the beneficial impact of the use of data on student learning, is critical for a teacher (Halverson et al., 2007), and because of this, data systems must also incorporate feedback loops that support intentional and continuous improvement and show the value of data-driven practices. When teachers can see positive student results of data-driven differentiated instruction (remember Sarah), they are more likely to see the value of using data-driven decision making.

Even given a systemic approach to data with support for data usage, data can be overwhelming (Johnston, 2010). The strategic use of data, as discussed in this chapter, means focusing on the decision being made and collecting only the data that are needed for the purpose at hand. If we remember this in our design of data systems, we can help teachers avoid data drowning (Skalski & Romero, 2011). Data drowning happens when we blindly accept the faulty belief that the more data we have, the better our decisions will be. This faulty belief often leads us to collect more data just for the sake of having more data, and it can also delay making appropriate decisions in the belief that if we just had one more piece of data we would make a better decision. A strategic use of data, on the other hand, follows these rules: (a) be clear why you are collecting data (i.e., know your purpose); (b) collect the data you need for the decision at hand; (c) do not collect data that are not relevant to the decision; (d) if the data already exist because they were collected for another purpose (referred to as "indigenous data"), use them rather than collecting more data; (d) if you have more than one option for data collection, select the one that both meets the objective and is most reasonable in terms of cost, effort to administer, and ease of interpretation; and (e) remember that the "best" data collection may be the simplest (i.e., if you want to know what a student is interested in studying for an independent project, ask him). The bottom line in all educational endeavors is learning outcomes for the students: We cannot claim we are teaching if we cannot show learning, and data are how we show learning.

Creating a Positive Data Culture

At the beginning of this chapter we asked the question, "So why is it that the term *data* is often seen as a four-letter word?" We discussed the historic use of data to assign blame to districts, schools, teachers, and even to students. This punitive approach to data and the culture that supports it presents a major challenge to the use of data-driven decision making needed for the successful implementation of RtI (Skalski & Romero, 2011). For the successful implementation of RtI, we must create a culture that supports proactive data-driven decision making.

A culture that supports data-driven decision making is built on a continuous improvement foundation (Halverson et al., 2007). The continuous improvement mindset provides the openness needed to examine results outcomes for students, without assigning blame (Augustine et al., 2009). Key aspects of this culture include trust and collaborative approaches to teaching. Establishing the trust that data will be used proactively and not punitively encourages honesty. Teachers and principals are safe to share areas of concern or challenge with supervisors when they trust that this information will be used to seek ways to strengthen outcomes. Collaborative approaches through teaming help to ensure that individuals have others to help them meet with success. Sarah's teacher, as discussed earlier, had a team of teachers to support her in her work, the gifted teacher being of primary help in planning for differentiated instruction. This collaborative approach to meeting student needs is a cornerstone of RtI, and the team is also critical for data-driven decision making (Allain & Eberhardt, 2011).

The changes we are seeing in cultures that support continuous improvement, build trust, and foster collaborative relationships are all part of a new paradigm of professionalism that supports teaching as a reflective, dynamic process to meet student needs (Coleman et al., 2012). Gifted education specialists must be part of the RtI team to ensure that the needs of students with high potential are included in planning and addressed within the supports and services. As members of the team, gifted educators have an important role in helping to make sure that learning goals are meaningful and challenging, that data thresholds are high enough to reflect off-grade-level learning, and that data collection incorporates information on complex learning outcomes. Skalski and Romero (2011) concluded that "to ultimately change ineffective practices and improve student achievement, data must be used by principals and teachers in practice to promote data-based decision making by all school employees" (p. 16). We could not agree more!

References

Augustine, C. H., Gonzalez, G., Ikemoto, G. S., Russell, J., Zellman, G. L., Constant, L., . . . Dembosky, J. W. (2009). *Improving school leadership: The promise of cohesive leadership systems.* Pittsburgh, PA: Rand.

Allain, J. K., & Eberhardt, N. C. (2011). *RtI: The forgotten tier: A practical guide for building a data-driven Tier I instructional process.* Stockton, KS: Rowe.

Burdette, P. (2011). *Systems for reviewing educational data, including special education information: Four state approaches.* Retrieved from http://projectforum.org/docs/SystemsforReviewingEducationalDataIncludingSpecialEdInfo-FourStateApproaches.pdf

Byrd, E. S. (2011). Educating and involving parents in the Response to Intervention process: The school's important role. *TEACHING Exceptional Children, 43*(3), 32–39.

Coleman, M. R. (2012). RtI approaches to identification practices within gifted education. In C. Callahan & H. L. Hertberg-Davis (Eds.), *Fundamentals of gifted education: Considering multiple perspectives.* New York, NY: Taylor & Francis.

Coleman, M. R., Gallagher, J. J., & Job, J. (2012). Developing and sustaining professionalism within gifted education. *Gifted Child Today, 35*(1), 27–36.

Coleman, M. R., & Shah-Coltrane, S. (2010). *U-STARS~PLUS professional development kit.* Arlington, VA: Council for Exceptional Children.

Conderman, G., & Hedin, L. (2012). Purposeful assessment practices for co-teachers. *TEACHING Exceptional Children, 44*(4), 18–27.

Cummings, K. D., Atkins, T., Allison, R., & Cole, C. (2008). Response to Intervention: Investigating the new role of special educators. *TEACHING Exceptional Children, 40*(4), 24–31.

Halverson, R., Grigg, J., Prichett, R., & Thomas, C. (2007). The new instructional leadership: Creating data-driven instructional systems in schools. *Journal of School Leadership, 17,* 159–194.

Johnston, T. C. (2010). *Data without tears: How to write measurable educational goals and collect meaningful data.* Champaign, IL: Research Press.

Kirk, S., Gallagher, J. J., Coleman, M. R., & Anastasiow, N. (2012). *Educating exceptional children* (13th ed.). Belmont, CA: Cengage.

Lee, D. L., Vostal, B., Lylo, B., & Hua, Y. (2011). Collecting behavioral data in general education settings: A primer for behavioral data collection. *Beyond Behavior, 20*(2), 22–30.

Lingo, A. S., Barton-Arwood, S. M., & Jolivette, K. (2011). Teachers working together: Improving learning outcomes in the inclusive classroom—practical strategies and examples. *TEACHING Exceptional Children, 43*(3), 6–13.

Love, N. (2011). *Data literacy for teachers.* Port Chester, NY: National Professional Resources.

Mandinach, E. B., Gummer, E. S., & Muller, R. D. (2011). *The complexities of integrating data-driven decision making into professional preparation in schools of education: It's harder than you think.* Retrieved from http://educationnorthwest.org/webfm_send/1133

Marsh, J. A., Pane, J. F., & Hamilton, L. S. (2006). *Making sense of data-driven decision making in education: Evidence from recent RAND research.* Retrieved from http://www.rand.org/pubs/occasional_papers/2006/RAND_OP170.pdf

Pereles, D. A., Omdal, S., & Baldwin, L. (2009). Response to Intervention and twice-exceptional learners: A promising fit. *Gifted Child Today, 32*(3), 40–51.

Shapiro, E. S., & Clemens, N. H. (2009). A conceptual model for evaluating system effects of Response to Intervention. *Assessment for Effective Intervention, 35*(1), 3–16.

Skalski, A. K., & Romero, M. (2011, January). Data-based decision making. *Principal Leadership,* 12–16.

Streifer, P. A., & Schumann, J. A. (2005). Using data mining to identify actionable information: Breaking new ground in data-driven decision making. *Journal of Education for Students Placed at Risk, 10,* 281–293.

Vanderheyden, A. M. (2011). Technical adequacy of Response to Intervention decisions. *Exceptional Children, 77,* 335–350.

Wayman, J. C. (2005). Involving teachers in data-driven decision making: Using computer data systems to support teacher inquiry and reflection. *Journal of Education for Students Placed at Risk, 10,* 295–308.

Wohlstetter, P., Datnow, A., & Park, V. (2008). Creating a system for data-driven decision-making: Applying the principal-agent framework. *School Effectiveness and School Improvement, 19,* 239–259.

Ysseldyke, J., Burns, M. K., Scholin, S. E., & Parker, D. C. (2010). Instructionally valid assessment within Response to Intervention. *TEACHING Exceptional Children, 42*(4), 54–61.

CHAPTER SIX

EVIDENCE-BASED PRACTICE MODEL AND RESPONSE TO INTERVENTION FOR STUDENTS WITH GIFTS AND TALENTS

Ann Robinson and Mary Kathryn Stein

The purpose of this chapter is to define the evidence-based practice model, to review how this model and its variants have been applied over time in an analysis of the education of students with gifts and talents, and to align specific practices with research support to selected components of the Response to Intervention (RtI) model for this special population of children and adolescents. In addition, the chapter suggests what is yet to be learned about the application of the RtI model in the context of serving students with gifts and talents.

Education, psychology, and many other helping professions have embraced some form of evidence-based practice (EBP). A model that originated in the medical profession, evidence-based practice is defined as the integration of the best research evidence with patients' values and clinical circumstances in clinical decision making (Shaneyfelt et al., 2006). By substituting students for patients and classrooms for clinical circumstances, evidence-based practice becomes more recognizable to educators. The model prompted a policy statement from the American Psychological Association (APA, 2005), which set out the importance of clinical practice based substantially, although not exclusively, on research evidence. Proctor and Rosen (2004) suggested that evidence-based practice is characterized by decisions based on empirical, research-based support, an assessment of the empirically supported intervention for a goodness of fit to the current situation, and the systematic monitoring of the outcomes to determine if the evidence-based practice currently implemented is in need of revision to serve the best interests of the individual. Described in this way, the medical roots of evidence-based practice are evident. From its medical history, the model was transported to education and has begun to influence practice and policy in schools. The application of an evidence-based practice model in the education of students with gifts and talents can be traced to precursors of the model in the late 1980s and early 1990s.

Early Efforts in Evidence-Based Practice Models in Gifted Education: The Recommended Practice

In the 1970s, Virgil Ward proposed a Knowledge Production and Utilization (KPU) Committee to The Association for the Gifted (TAG), a division of the Council of Exceptional Children (CEC), and served as the first chair of the committee. Ward's vision was to set the field of gifted education on a sound philosophical and theoretical base. Subsequently, Ward asked Bruce Shore of McGill University, a member of the KPU Committee, to succeed him as chair. Shore reconstituted the committee with two new members in addition to Ward (Dewey Cornell and Ann Robinson) and took it in a new direction, beginning with an extensive review of the research underlying practices in the education of students with gifts and talents (B. M. Shore, personal communication, March 25, 2012). The committee began with the practices that educators might encounter in the field, particularly the received wisdom synthesized in textbooks, and then searched for research evidence that might challenge the practice or confirm it. The term *recommended practice* was adopted for this broad examination of the research base supporting the field. It is important to note that recommended does not imply the practice is well supported, only that it repeatedly appears in the literature as exhortatory advice. In *Recommended Practices in Gifted Education: A Critical Analysis*, Shore, Cornell, Robinson, and Ward (1991) identified a list of 120 practices that were combined and reduced to 101 practices found in the textbook literature on giftedness. Then, the journal literature and other research publications were searched to discern the level of support or disconfirmation of each specific practice. Among the conclusions drawn by the authors was that not all recommended practices were well supported by empirical research or by other scholarly evidence. Neither were the practices refuted. Thus, the authors concluded that many, but not all, educational practices related to students with gifts and talents lacked strong support, but the field was not engaged in malpractice either. Two decades ago, they noted, "the major problem facing the field is not malpractice but insufficiently developed and validated curricular and pedagogical alternatives" (Shore et al., 1991, p. 290). Of the 101 practices in the 1991 review, those based on assessment, those that emanated from differential psychology and the studies of individual differences, those that focused on accelerative practices, and those that addressed the differential career exploration and guidance needs stood out as practices with the most extensive and longest research records in the field of gifted education. Of particular relevance to the roots of the RtI model, one of the original strongly supported practices was that students with disabilities and with gifts and talents were best served by interventions that focused on academic strengths as well as weaknesses.

Best Practice and Evidence-Based Practice Models in General Education

More recently, educators from all areas of education have sought to identify *best practices,* in contrast to recommended practices (Zemelman, Daniels, & Hyde, 2005). Presumably, best practices are supported by empirical and other kinds of evidence. In education, best practices are likely to rely on the experiences and insights of skilled practitioners as well as on empirical research studies. Like the EBP model, best practices emerged from other professions, specifically medicine, law, and architecture, to describe reputable work. The term best practices is now ubiquitous. Zemelman et al. (2005) bemoaned the terminological drift, but pointed out most professional associations have generated best practices that have the confidence of the majority of the fields they represent.

Best Practice and Evidence-Based Practice Models in Gifted Education

In gifted education, Robinson and Shore (2009) suggested that the universe of practices that might be termed best was large and generated through multiple approaches. For example, a single recognized authority in a textbook, an edited compendium featuring the work of multiple experts, formal meta-analyses of specific practices, and more recently the broader concept of systematic reviews are all sources of best practices accepted with varying degrees of consensus. They note that the most defensible strategy for the field of gifted education at this time is to give priority to practices with converging and replicable evidence. These might be specific practices such as models of questioning strategies used in the classroom to elicit higher level thinking, or they might be broader programmatic practices such as acceleration (Shore & Delcourt, 1996).

A project to identify best practices in gifted education was funded through the Jacob K. Javits Gifted and Talented Students program in the U.S. Department of Education to examine which of the practices had the most research support. Using an expert advisory group of scholars and practitioners from the field and a modified Delphi technique, a list of practices believed to be supported empirically was generated by the group and subsequently investigated by the research team. The advisory group was asked to respond to three questions:

> ➤ What questions do we need to be able to answer about educational and home practices effective with high-ability youth?
> ➤ How do we frame these questions to be maximally useful to practitioners?
> ➤ What existing research informs these practical questions?

In response to their charge, the advisory group generated 150 questions. Subsequently the research team and Javits program staff met to reduce the 150 questions to 61 electronically searchable terms. These 61 searches produced 31 terms with sufficient empirical research to remain viable as possible best practices. Ultimately, the list of best practices was reduced to 29 when overlapping research literatures emerged. Although there is some alignment between the 101 recommended practices from the initial review of practices, the 29 practices are more focused on the pedagogical and curricular practices. In light of the concerns stated by Shore et al. (1991) that the field suffered from insufficiently validated curricular and pedagogical practices, the shift from the 1991 review to the 2007 review is a positive development. During the 1990s and until recently, the federal funding of a National Research Center on the Gifted and Talented and of several demonstration projects with curricular and pedagogical foci fueled the development, implementation, and evaluation of practices and placed them on a firmer empirical footing. For example, curriculum projects in the major content areas of language arts (Feng, VanTassel-Baska, Quek, Bai, & O'Neill, 2005; Robinson & Stanley, 1989; VanTassel-Baska, Johnson, Hughes, & Boyce, 1996; VanTassel-Baska, Zuo, Avery, & Little, 2002), mathematics (Gavin, Casa, Adelson, Carroll, & Sheffield, 2009; Pierce et al., 2011), reading (Reis, Eckert, McCoach, Jacobs, & Coyne, 2008; Reis et al., 2007), and science (Cotabish, Dailey, Hughes, & Robinson, in press; Cotabish, Robinson, Dailey, & Hughes, 2012; Kim et al., 2011; VanTassel-Baska, Bass, Ries, Poland, & Avery, 1998) informed the field of what works with talented youth and resulted in curriculum products, models, and tools available to schools for adoption and replication. The work from these projects with their substantial research and evaluation designs moved the field forward in terms of curricular and pedagogical best practices. In addition, the focus of the Javits legislation on the development of talents in learners from low-income homes and with culturally diverse backgrounds added to the stock of defensible best practices in the field. Thus, educators will find a richer store of best practices with stronger research support in the first decade of the 21st century than would have been available even 10 years ago.

Finally, in addition to recommended practices and best practices, the most stringent level of scrutiny applied to practice is the evidence-based model, Evidence-Based Practice (EBP). In EBP, education has adopted the full medical model with respect to evidence-based practice, although with far less research funding and with less agreement that the model can capture the complexity of the classroom than the individual patient-physician interaction in the doctor's office or hospital. A proponent of EBP in education, Slavin (2008) reviewed various models and entities for evaluating evidence and proposed reliance on large-scale studies with defensible quantitative research designs as the basis for decisions about which practices are evidence-based. Other researchers are less sanguine about the specific design criteria imposed by Slavin, admit other kinds of evidence in addition to state achievement tests, and acknowledge the usefulness of a more general model of systematic review in addition to meta-analytic approaches (Sloane, 2008).

For clarity, it is useful to distinguish between EBP as defined by the medical and social science community and articulated through the Cochrane (see http://www.cochrane.org/about-us/history) and Campbell (see http://www.campbellcollaboration.org/about_us/index.php) collaborations, respectively, and the model of evidence adopted by the Council for Exceptional Children (CEC) in developing its professional standards for educators. The CEC standards were informed by three general sources of evidence: (a) literature and theory, (b) research, and (c) practice. In the model underlying the CEC standards and subsequently the joint standards of CEC and the National Association for Gifted Children (NAGC) professional standards (Johnsen, VanTassel-Baska, & Robinson, 2008), theory-based knowledge included theoretical and philosophical reasoning represented in position papers, policy analyses, and descriptive reviews. Research-based knowledge was derived from peer-reviewed studies that reported positive effects and were independently replicated. Finally, CEC practice-based knowledge included a range of sources from model programs to professional wisdom (CEC, 2003). In mapping the CEC standards model onto the more general models of practice reviewed in this chapter, the CEC model shares the most features with the best practice conceptualization.

In summary, practices in gifted education could be characterized as falling along a continuum from recommended, to best, to evidence-based in terms of how replicable their research might be. For the purposes of this chapter, we adopted the most restrictive definition of EBP. Few practices in general, gifted, or special education attain the level of replicability associated with EBP, although a number of classroom and school practices in gifted education that can be incorporated into the RtI model could be characterized as strongly research-supported best practices. Table 6.1 summarizes the key features of recommended, best, and evidence-based practices.

Research-supported practice models have moved the credibility of what works in education and other social programs to a new level of acceptance. Each of the models summarized above contributes to an increased research base for our practices. The individual practices identified as recommended, best, or evidence-based form the building blocks of a service delivery framework when applied to RtI.

Applying Best and Evidence-Based Practice Models to Response to Intervention for Students With Gifts and Talents

In 2004, RtI was set out in federal statute as a means of serving students with learning disabilities before their achievement difficulties were sufficiently severe to require intensive intervention. In other words, the developers and advocates of RtI viewed the model as a way to provide appropriate services to learners who had yet to reach the failing criterion that would activate screening and placement through a traditional special education model (Bradley,

Table 6.1
Types and Key Features of Practice-Based Models

Recommended Practices	Best Practices	Evidence-Based Practices
• Recommended by authorities or experts • Take the form of advice • Accepted as received wisdom • Generally found in textbooks • Not all recommended practices are supported by research	• Represent consensus in the field • Supported by empirical research • Informed by clinical practice • Practitioner experience is accepted as part of the evidence	• Empirical research • Emphasize randomized control trials • Characterized by systematic reviews • Include transparent search protocols for the research studies included in the review

Danielson, & Doolittle, 2007). Subsequently, the model is being explored for its applicability as a service delivery framework for students with gifts and talents. Bianco (2010) characterized this application as a strength-based approach to RtI. Coleman and Johnsen (2011) developed a resource guide for educators and included several examples of state and district applications of RtI to gifted programs and services. How might program services appear when an RtI model is applied to a young, precocious child with reliance on the practices for students with gifts and talents that have sufficient support to be considered best practice or EBP options?

Stephen's Story

Stephen is a 5-year-old kindergarten student whose educational needs are being addressed by the RtI team at his elementary school. When he arrived at her door, Stephen's kindergarten teacher, Ms. Monroe, and the gifted educational services teacher for the building, Mr. Lopez, observed Stephen's precocity and ability to read far beyond grade-level expectations. In the early weeks of school, a meeting to determine Stephen's educational needs has been called by Stephen's teacher. Although the school does not yet have a universal screening plan in place, the staff members are alert to children for whom the grade-level curriculum appears to need differentiation. The participants in the meeting include Ms. Monroe, the school counselor, the principal, the ESL coordinator, the special education teacher, and Mr. Lopez. Before the meeting, Mr. Lopez contacted Stephen's parents and gathered information about Stephen's home and his early educational experiences, as well as their ideas about Stephen's educational needs. Mr. Lopez reports that Stephen has been reading since he turned 5 in the spring before beginning kindergarten. According to his parents, his preschool teachers noted that he was reading and that his vocabulary was advanced for his age both in the number of words used and the sophistication of the words. Stephen's parents are aware that he is generally ahead of his peers academically. They report that Stephen is very imaginative in his play and sensitive to intrusions into his fantasy worlds while he is highly engaged in play at home. Both Ms. Monroe and Mr. Lopez have observed Stephen as he becomes immersed in fantasy play at school. Now, Stephen's reading is opening new imaginative worlds for him.

The educational team decides that Mr. Lopez will give Stephen the Dynamic Indicators of Basic Early Literacy Skills (DIBELS; Good et al., 2004) assessment and other assessments beyond kindergarten grade level to determine where he is academically in reading and math. The educational team decides that these tests may be relevant as above-grade-level assessments required by the Iowa Acceleration Scale in the event that Stephen is a candidate for grade acceleration. The school psychologist will observe Stephen and visit with him to discuss his feelings in a general way to determine whether his social and emotional needs are being well served in the kindergarten class. The team decides to accelerate Stephen into a reading group in a third-grade classroom determined by the observations and tests administered by the professionals in the group. Then, Mr. Lopez will work with Stephen in a Tier 3 setting by pulling him into a cross-grade group of gifted students who are working on a project to write fairy, folk, and pourquoi tales for the 21st century.

Mr. Lopez will give Stephen an interest survey to guide in the selection of additional curriculum projects to meet his advanced literary requirements. Mr. Lopez and Ms. Monroe will also consult regularly to share how Stephen's literacy skills are progressing. Stephen will spend part of his day in the kindergarten classroom, but he will continue to go to the third-grade classroom for his literacy instruction and to Mr. Lopez for Tier 3 small-group project work. Stephen will also meet on a monthly basis with Mr. Lopez to continue formal testing for gifted services. Mr. Lopez will share the results with the RtI team when it reviews Stephen's case. Mr. Lopez, Ms. Monroe, and the third-grade teacher will share Stephen's progress with the RtI team annually or as needed. Table 6.2 summarizes the services in the strength-based RtI approach for Stephen.

The RtI model seems especially promising for young gifted children entering preschool or kindergarten. Early childhood educators are comfortable with close observation, and schools have screening protocols that can be tweaked to

Table 6.2
RtI Research Supported Tiered Services for Stephen

Student: Stephen	Tier 1 General Education Classroom	Tier 2 General Education Classroom	Tier 3 Gifted Programs and Services
• Current grade level: kindergarten • Current strength areas: reading and writing • Current interests: fantasy worlds and fantasy play	• Universal screening with DIBELS and additional assessments • Encouraging creativity • Encouraging higher order thinking • Compacting curriculum	• Differentiated language arts instruction • Appropriate reading materials for enrichment	• Accelerating to appropriate reading group • Participating in a multigrade project to write fairy, folk, and pourquoi tales for the 21st century

locate advanced as well as struggling students. Flexible schedules in primary and elementary schools are more likely to accommodate Tier 3 adaptations, which move children around to meet their instructional needs.

How would RtI be deployed at the secondary level? What best or evidence-based practices might provide the spine for services that meet the needs of the talented adolescent?

Rosalinda's Story

Rosalinda is a ninth grader who seems to be a 40-year-old living in a 14-year-old's body. She has surprising wisdom and often is perturbed by what she views as the immaturity of her classmates. Nevertheless, Rosalinda tries to model a more adult approach to life rather than pointing out the follies of her peers to them. Rosalinda seems to be worried about her future. She is not sure of her pathway to college, nor whether her interests in history will lead to a career opportunity. The RtI team at her high school meets to determine the educational needs of freshmen students who either need interventions for services because they are academically behind their peers or because they are academically ahead of the grade-level expectation. Both groups of students require services to address their academic and their social and emotional needs to help them adjust comfortably to high school. The team of professionals includes the school psychologist, the special education teacher, the gifted education teacher, an administrator, and lead teachers from the core academic areas and technology classes. Based on the observations of her gifted education teacher, her past grades, an early score on the ACT (26 as a seventh grader), and additional testing data, the team determines that Rosalinda's needs would best be met by having her begin taking Advanced Placement (AP) classes as a sophomore and continuing throughout her junior and senior years so that she can begin doing college-level work early.

The gifted education teacher, Ms. Cho, has observed that Rosalinda's greatest area of interest lies in the social sciences. She shared with Ms. Cho that she loves her history classes and might want to major in history, but she is not sure about a career in that field. What can she do with a history major in college? Visiting with Rosalinda's parents, Ms. Cho found that they are worried Rosalinda will lower her expectations and not reach her full potential because of social pressures. The gifted education teacher will meet with Rosalinda as part of a group of gifted students to discuss social and emotional issues and to provide special guidance as she determines her further studies. Ms. Cho will share the range of career paths that Rosalinda's interest in the social sciences could lead to, including careers in historical research in higher education, in museum curatorship, as an archivist, or in the law. Rosalinda's interest in world cultures could be enhanced by taking AP World History as a sophomore and choosing from among other AP courses in the social sciences such as AP Human Geography, AP U.S. History, AP European History, AP Art History, or AP Comparative Government and Politics in her junior and senior years. She would have the opportunity to begin college with a semester or two of credit in her area of interest already in hand. Ms. Cho will guide her career exploration formally with suggested internship placements in the rare books and manuscripts collection at a local university and, with the assistance of her parents for transportation, a summer placement in a law office that specializes in patent law. Table 6.3 summarizes the services in the strength-based RtI approach for Rosalinda.

The RtI Model: Key Features

The previous cases are applications of the RtI model at the early childhood and secondary levels. They look different, but each case applies one or more of the key features of the RtI model. For emphasis, we review those key features needed for the strength-based application of RtI to advanced learners.

Table 6.3
RtI Research Supported Tiered Services for Rosalinda

Student: Rosalinda	Tier 1 General Education Classroom	Tier 2 General Education Classroom	Tier 3 Gifted Programs and Services
• Current grade level: ninth grade in a high school building (grades 9–12) • Current strength areas: history and historiography • Current interest: world cultures	• Progress monitoring of student academic records • Encouraging creativity • Encouraging higher order thinking	• Using primary sources in history • Differentiated language arts instruction • Reading	• Social and emotional support • Advanced Placement classes in the social sciences • Specific career explorations

The Team Approach

RtI's key component is a team approach to determining how to best develop the potential in a child. Much like a medical diagnosis group, the team consists of all of the trained adults possible, including the general education teacher, the special education teacher, an administrator, a social worker, the school psychologist, various therapists, and the gifted education teacher. This group would also receive input from parents about interests and abilities. The information from screenings and observations of all students would result in plans to best develop potential in each child. This approach has been called "creative planning for success" for students (Coleman, Coleman, Johnsen, & Southern, 2011). In the strength-based application of RtI to advanced learners, teachers will need to use screening measures that allow for above-grade-level performance so the advanced students' skill levels will not be obscured by ceiling effects (Coleman & Johnsen, 2011).

The Tiered Approach

RtI has a tiered approach that many gifted education program models already use to deliver services to gifted students (Coleman & Hughes, 2009). Tier 1 includes general education screenings for potential and mastery of curriculum. Tier 2 includes small groups in the regular classroom working to enhance individual student strengths. Tier 3 is more like the traditional delivery of services to formally identified gifted and talented students. Because RtI does not require formal identification, but does assume universal screening, services can begin as soon as students enter school. In the state of Arkansas, all students in kindergarten through second or third grade currently receive whole-class enrichment weekly, supervised or delivered by a licensed gifted education teacher, as a means of screening students over time to identify those who need additional services. This practice is compatible as a Tier 1 activity in RtI. Full implementation of RtI could include offering some whole-group enrichment activities for additional grades to identify student strengths. Offering services to more students in the general classroom would make gifted services more "inclusive rather than exclusive" (Hughes et al., 2009, pp. 58–59) as gifted education is often accused of being. The image of gifted education as a "silo" program could be erased. The gifted education teacher could assist the general education teacher with implementing flexible grouping, pacing, and scheduling; offering appropriate activities for higher order thinking; setting up learning stations; finding mentors; and helping students conduct independent studies.

Assessment

Universal screenings of students are essential to determine the educational needs of both very young students and older students. Likewise, educators are becoming more used to the concept of educational decisions being data-driven (Bender & Shores, 2007). Hughes, Rollins, and Coleman (2011) recommended universal screening to determine which students are "performing significantly above or significantly below their peers" (p. 13) so educational decisions can be made. These preassessments may be in the form of teacher recommendations based on observations and behavioral checklists as well as more formal testing data. The following tests and assessment approaches have been suggested for identifying students who are performing below their peers: Curriculum-Based Measurement (CBM; Deno, 1985), which assesses reading, writing, and math; DIBELS (Good et al., 2004); and subtests of the Woodcock Reading Mastery Test-Revised. If these screenings indicate which students are performing below 25% of their peers, then those students who are performing better than 75% of their peers should be referred to the gifted education teacher who could administer several of the assessment measures designed to identify giftedness and share that information with the RtI team to help determine Tier 2 and Tier 3 placements. Some teams may have access to information from pre-K teachers if the school district provides those services. Teams should also consider information on students based on parent input on background forms or in interviews, along with information about a student's social or cultural background and physical condition, particularly in the case of twice-exceptional students. Assessment and progress monitoring for students beyond the early grades can take the form of state exams, other standardized tests, classroom achievement, and teacher recommendations based on observations. The gifted education teacher would have to determine if these measures provide advanced students with the opportunity to show the extent of their progress without hitting a ceiling. For example, a middle-level student may need to take an early ACT exam to show what she is capable of doing. Assessment should also take place periodically to continue to compile data as decisions are reviewed by the RtI team for progress monitoring to see if the data indicate the educational decisions being made are effective or not.

Specialized Teacher Training

As in any model, the preparation of the teacher is crucial to meeting the needs of students. Meeting the needs of gifted and talented learners is no exception, particularly in grade-level classroom settings. Robinson, Shore, and Enersen (2007) reviewed the research on teacher professional preparation with respect to talented learners and found that trained teachers are more sensitive to the needs and interests of talented learners and have more strategies to use to meet those needs. Tomlinson et al. (1994) conducted a qualitative study of preservice teachers and found that they were aware of the special needs of gifted children, but were unsure about how to assess their needs or to act on them. Without training and experience, they lacked a repertoire of strategies that would allow them to serve gifted students effectively in the general classroom. Because the classroom is the location of Tier 1 and Tier 2 activities in the RtI model, effective teacher preparation and professional development is a key feature for success.

Teacher preparation is no less important for in-service teachers than it is for preservice teachers. A more extensively researched practice, in-service preparation of teachers to meet the needs of gifted students demonstrates that when provided with training on the nature and needs of talented students and given preparation and coaching in appropriate strategies for advanced learners, in-service teachers are better able to identify advanced learners and modify instruction (Cashion & Sullenger, 2000; Gentry & Keilty, 2004; Hansen & Feldhusen, 1994; Robinson, 1985).

Selecting Tier 1, 2, and 3
Best Practices for Advanced Learners

Using research-based strategies for gifted education within the RtI model will ensure that students are receiving appropriate services. Currently, identified gifted students may not be receiving services that are appropriate for them. Carol Tomlinson (2008) reported that high-achieving students receive little regular, planned differentiation. Robinson et al. (2007) identified a group of "evidence-based strategies that work with talented youth" (p. 2). Some of the strategies are more likely to be used in the early grades when children enter school and with the universal screening that is a foundational component of RtI. These research-based strategies include encouraging creativity, higher level thinking, and inquiry-based learning and teaching; compacting the curriculum; and utilizing flexible grouping. Other research-based strategies are recognizable in high schools, such as using primary sources in history; implementing various forms of acceleration, including Advanced Placement; and offering career exploration and guidance for students who may very well be on career trajectories that involve more than a decade of postsecondary study.

It is essential to include services to students of high potential in the RtI strategy because high-achieving students need interventions just as much as students who have traditionally recognized disabilities. If these students are not exposed to evidenced-based strategies for gifted learners, their potential will go wanting, and it is vital to develop the potential in every student. RtI can become an integral part of achieving Common Core State Standards because it will provide students who already have met standards an opportunity to go in depth in an area of interest. Using RtI to provide gifted services to more students will require a paradigm shift in many school districts and gifted programs, but with supportive leadership, RtI has the potential to be a strategy to develop an appropriate instructional intervention for every child—and to develop each child's individual potential. Figure 6.1 summarizes the best practices for advanced learners with sufficient research support to include as examples within the strength-based RtI model.

Through the examples of Stephen and Rosalinda that were presented earlier, a strength-based approach to RtI has been explored for advanced learners. Several of the individual practices embedded in Stephen's and Rosalinda's plans include practices that the consensus of the field identifies as best practice. Thus, several strategies that could form the application of RtI for advanced learners are supported by research. At present, however, the implementation of RtI

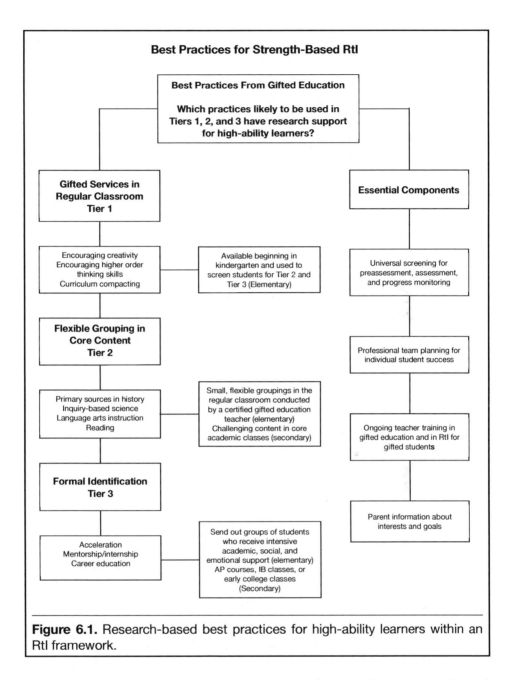

Figure 6.1. Research-based best practices for high-ability learners within an RtI framework.

as an overall service model for students with gifts and talents cannot be said to be evidence-based. Recall that to be truly evidence-based, a practice must have been subjected to a systematic review (either meta-analytic or narrative in nature) in which the protocols for searching the literature and for including or excluding studies on a practice are available for other researchers to examine and presumably replicate. The difficulties associated with moving educational interventions into the category of evidence-based practices present us with challenges (Cook, Smith, & Tankersley, 2012).

Too little research has been done on RtI as a means of serving an individual gifted student, although students with gifts and talents *and* a disability will most likely provide the first systematic empirical examinations of the practice. In terms of implementing RtI at the school level, the field of gifted education is just beginning to explore this approach to service delivery. At the state level, where policy will drive practice, at least four states have explored RtI either as a framework (Wisconsin and Colorado) or as one option a district might select for service delivery (Ohio and Utah).

No systematic, large-scale studies applying RtI to students with gifts and talents have been undertaken. Thus, at present RtI is best characterized as a recent recommended practice as defined in the first section of this chapter. Systematic inquiry is needed for the RtI framework, as applied to students with gifts and talents, to move from the status of recommended to either best practice or to the level of validation through systematic review and replication—Evidence-Based Practice (EBP).

References

American Psychological Association. (2005). *Policy statement on evidence-based practice in psychology.* Washington, DC: Author.

Bender, W. N., & Shores, C. (2007). *Response to Intervention: A practical guide for every teacher.* Thousand Oaks, CA: Corwin Press.

Bianco, M. (2010). Strength-based RtI: Conceptualizing a multi-tiered system for developing gifted potential. *Theory Into Practice, 49,* 323–330.

Bradley, R., Danielson, L., & Doolittle, J. (2007). Responsiveness to Intervention: 1997–2007. *TEACHING Exceptional Children 39*(5), 8–12.

Cashion, M., & Sullenger, K. (2000). "Contact us next year": Tracing teachers' use of gifted practices. *Roeper Review, 23,* 18–21.

Coleman, L., Coleman, M. R., Johnsen, S. K., & Southern, T. (2011, November 4). *Are Response to Intervention and gifted education compatible? A dialogue in 4 parts.* Paper presented at the 58th annual National Association for Gifted Children Conference, New Orleans, LA.

Coleman, M. R., & Hughes, C. E. (2009). Meeting the needs of gifted students within an RtI framework. *Gifted Child Today, 32*(3), 14–17.

Coleman, M. R., & Johnsen, S. K. (Eds.). (2011). *RtI for gifted students.* Waco, TX: Prufrock Press.

Cook, B. G., Smith, G. J., & Tankersley, M. (2012). Evidence-based practices in education. In K. R. Harris, S. Graham, T. Urdan, C. B. McCormick, G. M. Sinatra, & J. Sweller (Eds.), *APA educational psychology handbook, Vol. 1: Theories, constructs and critical issues* (pp. 495–527). Washington, DC: American Psychological Association. doi:10.1037/13273-017

Cotabish, A., Dailey, D., Hughes, G., & Robinson, A. (in press). The effects of a STEM intervention on elementary students' science knowledge and skills. *School Science and Mathematics.*

Cotabish, A., Robinson, A., Dailey, D., & Hughes, G. (2012). *The effects of a gifted education STEM project on elementary teachers' science process skills and knowledge of science content.* Manuscript submitted for publication.

Council for Exceptional Children. (2003). *What every special educator must know: Ethics, standards, and guidelines for special educators* (5th ed.). Arlington, VA: Author.

Deno, S. L. (1985). Curriculum-based measurement: The emerging alternative. *Exceptional Children, 52,* 219–232.

Feng, A. X., VanTassel-Baska, J., Quek, C., Bai, W., & O'Neill, B. (2005). A longitudinal assessment of gifted students' learning using the Integrated Curriculum Model (ICM): Impacts and perceptions of the William and Mary language arts and science curriculum. *Roeper Review, 27,* 78–83.

Gavin, M. K., Casa, T. M., Adelson, J. L., Carroll, S. R., & Sheffield, L. J. (2009). The impact of advanced curriculum on the achievement of mathematically promising elementary students. *Gifted Child Quarterly, 53,* 188–202.

Gentry, M., & Keilty, B. (2004). Rural and suburban cluster grouping: Reflections on staff development as a component of program success. *Roeper Review, 26,* 147–155.

Good, R. H., Kaminski, R. A., Shinn, M., Bratten, J., Shinn, M., Laimon, L., . . . Flindt, N. (2004). *Technical adequacy and decision making utility of DIBELS* (Technical Report No. 7). Eugene: University of Oregon.

Hansen, J. B., & Feldhusen, J. F. (1994). Comparison of trained and untrained teachers of gifted students. *Gifted Child Quarterly, 38,* 115–121.

Hughes, C. E., Rollins, K., & Coleman, M. R. (2011). Response to Intervention for gifted learners. In M. R. Coleman & S. K. Johnsen (Eds.), *RtI for gifted students* (pp. 1–20). Waco, TX: Prufrock Press.

Hughes, C. E., Rollins, K., Johnsen, S. K., Pereles, D. A., Omdal, S., Baldwin, L., . . . Coleman, M. R. (2009). Remaining challenges for the use of RtI with gifted education. *Gifted Child Today, 32*(3), 58–61.

Johnsen, S. K., VanTassel-Baska, J., & Robinson, A. (2008). *Using the national gifted education standards for university teacher preparation programs.* Thousand Oaks, CA: Corwin Press.

Kim, K. H., VanTassel-Baska, J., Bracken, B. A., Feng, A., Stambaugh, T., & Bland, L. (2011). Project Clarion: Three years of science instruction in Title I schools among K–third grade students. *Research in Science Education.* Advance online publication. doi:10.1007/s11165-011-9218-5

Pierce, R. L., Cassady, J. C., Adams, C. M., Speirs Neumeister, K. L., Dixon, F. A., & Cross, T. L. (2011). The effects of clustering and curriculum on the development of gifted learners' math achievement. *Journal for the Education of the Gifted, 34,* 569–594.

Proctor, E. K., & Rosen, A. (2004). Concise standards for developing evidence-based practice guidelines. In A. R. Roberts & K. R. Yeager (Eds.), *Evidence-based practice manual: Research and outcome measures in health and human services* (pp. 193–199). New York, NY: Oxford University Press.

Reis, S. M., Eckert, R. D., McCoach, D. B., Jacobs, J. K., & Coyne, M. (2008). Using enrichment reading practices to increase reading fluency, comprehension, and attitudes. *Journal of Educational Research, 101,* 299–315.

Reis, S. M., McCoach, D. B., Coyne, M., Schrieber, F. J., Eckert, R. D., & Gubbins, E. J. (2007). Using planned enrichment strategies with direct instruction to improve reading fluency, comprehension, and attitude toward reading: An evidence-based study. *The Elementary School Journal, 108,* 3–23.

Robinson, A. (1985). Summer Institute on the Gifted: Meeting the needs of the regular classroom teacher. *Gifted Child Quarterly, 29,* 20–23.

Robinson, A., & Shore, B. M. (2009). Best practices. In B. Kerr (Ed.), *Encyclopedia of giftedness, creativity, and talent* (Vol. 1, pp. 89–92). Thousand Oaks, CA: Sage.

Robinson, A., Shore, B. M., & Enersen, D. L. (2007). *Best practices in gifted education: An evidence-based guide.* Waco, TX: Prufrock Press.

Robinson, A., & Stanley, T. D. (1989). Teaching to talent: Evaluating an enriched, accelerated mathematics program. *Journal for the Education of the Gifted, 12,* 253–267.

Shaneyfelt, T., Baum, K. D., Bell, D., Feldstein, D., Houston, T. K., Kaatz, S., . . . Green, M. (2006). Instruments for evaluating education in evidence-based practice. *Journal of the American Medical Association, 296,* 1117–1127.

Shore, B. M., Cornell, D. G., Robinson, A., & Ward, V. S. (1991). *Recommended practices in gifted education: A critical analysis.* New York, NY: Teachers College Press.

Shore, B. M., & Delcourt, M. A. B. (1996). Effective curricular and program practices in gifted education and the interface with general education. *Journal for the Education of the Gifted, 20,* 138–154.

Slavin, R. (2008). What works? Issues in synthesizing educational program evaluations. *Educational Researcher, 37,* 5–14.

Sloane, F. (2008). Through the looking glass: Experiments, quasi-experiments, and the medical model. *Educational Researcher, 37,* 41–46.

Tomlinson, C. A. (2008). Differentiated instruction. In J. A. Plucker & C. M. Callahan (Eds.), *Critical issues and practices in gifted education: What the research says* (pp. 167–179). Waco, TX: Prufrock Press.

Tomlinson, C. A., Tomchin, E. M., Callahan, C. M., Adams, C. M., Pizzat-Tinnin, P., Cunningham, C. M., . . . Imbeau, M. (1994). Practices of preservice teachers related to gifted and other academically diverse learners. *Gifted Child Quarterly, 38,* 106–114.

VanTassel-Baska, J., Bass, G., Ries, R., Poland, D., & Avery, L. (1998). A national study of science curriculum effectiveness with high ability students. *Gifted Child Quarterly, 42,* 200–211.

VanTassel-Baska, J., Johnson, D. T., Hughes, C., & Boyce, L. N. (1996). A study of language arts curriculum effectiveness with gifted learners. *Journal for the Education of the Gifted, 19,* 461–480.

VanTassel-Baska, J., Zuo, L., Avery, L. D., & Little, C. A. (2002). A curriculum study of gifted-student learning in the language arts. *Gifted Child Quarterly, 41,* 42–51.

Zemelman, S., Daniels, H., & Hyde, A. (2005). *Best practice: Today's standards for teaching and learning in America's schools* (3rd ed.). Portsmouth, NH: Heinemann.

GIFTED EDUCATION MODELS THAT FIT WITHIN TIERED FRAMEWORKS

CHAPTER SEVEN

THE SCHOOLWIDE ENRICHMENT MODEL

Responding to Talent Within an RtI Framework

Sally M. Reis, Nicholas W. Gelbar, and Joseph S. Renzulli

In many schools across the country, various types of enrichment opportunities are offered to students that both enhance and extend the regular curriculum. Some of these enrichment opportunities are designed to enable students to be exposed to and develop specific talent areas. For example, enrichment programs in music involve multiple opportunities for talent development. Most schools provide some music instruction for all students and typically offer a general chorus for interested students with some musical talent. However, if students demonstrate advanced musical talents, they may also audition to participate in a more advanced school or regional chorus. This process enables every child to have an opportunity to demonstrate his or her musical potential. As students grow older and their musical talents begin to emerge, some learn to expend extended effort and practice. These students generally qualify for even more challenging levels of music while others stop taking music instruction altogether. In essence, music serves as a way to enable students to demonstrate their abilities and to further develop their skills and performances through authentic musical experiences. This process is important because, for example, advanced orchestra performances are not appropriate for beginning players or for players who do not have a passion for playing more complicated musical pieces. Accordingly, scaffolded musical enrichment programs serve as an example of a talent development approach that can also be applied to other curricular and extracurricular opportunities, such as advanced science fair projects for scientifically talented students or advanced history projects for students with historical interests and talents.

Can an enrichment-based approach and opportunities for academically advanced and talented students fit into a Response to Intervention (RtI) approach? Could the implementation of RtI within some districts actually enable more services to be given to academically talented students? This chapter suggests that the use of the Schoolwide Enrichment Model (SEM) could be integrated into a district RtI approach to increase and enhance services to academically talented students.

Response to Intervention

The RtI model employs the same logic as the music enrichment example described above. The original purpose of RtI was to replace the ability-achievement discrepancy model that has been used in the past to identify students with learning problems, which had resulted in a disproportionately higher identification of culturally diverse students and students with learning disabilities (Shifrer, Muller, & Callahan, 2011). Further, the discrepancy between a student's ability (as measured by a cognitive assessment or IQ test) and performance on a standardized achievement assessment documented the evidence of a learning disability, but did not indicate the types of interventions that could be utilized to remediate the problem (McCoach, Kehle, Bray, & Siegle, 2001). More importantly, because the gap between ability and achievement had to become wide enough to be significant, the discrepancy model could best be conceptualized as a wait-to-fail approach, as it often involved waiting for this gap to widen in order to warrant entry into special education services (Bradley, Danielson, & Doolittle, 2007; Fuchs & Fuchs, 2006; Glover & DiPerna, 2007).

In contrast, the RtI model involves the process of screening students who are at-risk for learning difficulties and offering these students instructional supports that are matched to the level of their difficulties. Similar to the music example, these supports are often tiered (Bradley et al., 2007; Fletcher & Vaughn, 2009; Fuchs & Fuchs, 2006; Hoover & Patton, 2008). Tier 1, the general education curriculum, is delivered to all students, hopefully with high-quality instruction utilizing evidence-based practices. Thus, Tier 1 has been conceptualized as effective teaching in general instructional situations (Brown

& Abernethy, 2009). Tier 2 involves targeted small-group instruction to remediate specific skills deficits (Bradley et al., 2007; Fletcher & Vaughn, 2009; Fuchs & Fuchs, 2006; Hoover & Patton, 2008). With our musical enrichment example or for students with scientific talent, this would be additional lessons or opportunities to enhance their talents. Tier 3 consists of more intense one-on-one interventions and serves the needs of approximately 5% of students (Bradley et al., 2007; Fletcher & Vaughn, 2009; Fuchs & Fuchs, 2006; Hoover & Patton, 2008). Giving students opportunities to learn challenging content, monitoring their errors in that process, and utilizing these data to provide higher level and appropriately challenging tasks to students are ways in which this tier could be conceptualized in our music or science examples. In more academic settings, the student's progress is monitored in these groups using dynamic assessment to continually adjust learning experiences to match student strengths and needs (Fuchs & Fuchs, 2006). The interventions delivered in this RtI model can be individualized to the student (the problem-solving model) or can be scripted (the standard treatment protocol; Fuchs & Fuchs, 2006; Glover & DiPerna, 2007).

The appeal of the RtI model is that it matches the intensity of instructional support to the needs of the students and also utilizes a preventive (as opposed to a reactive) approach (Fletcher & Vaughn, 2009; Grigorenko, 2009). The preventive approach focuses on early instruction in basic academic skills that will generalize to other academic contexts (Daly, Martens, Barnett, Witt, & Olson, 2007). This approach could be particularly effective for identifying twice-exceptional students, because their high ability often delays the diagnosis of a learning disability (Crepeau-Hobson & Bianco, 2011; Pereles, Omdal, & Baldwin, 2009). Although the RtI model as defined above does not specifically address the needs of gifted students, The Association for the Gifted (TAG), a division of the Council of Exceptional Children (CEC), has offered a framework for how gifted students can be served using this approach by "advanc[ing] learning needs of children in terms of a faster paced, more complex, greater depth and/or breadth with respect to their curriculum and instruction" (CEC-TAG, n.d., pp. 1–2). An individualized process of developing talent in students serves as the basis of an enrichment framework and is particularly appropriate because it focuses on matching services to the individual's needs, not on labels (Hughes et al., 2009; Pereles et al., 2009).

The Role of Gifted Pedagogy in the RtI Framework

The RtI model was originally designed to serve as a preventive, early intervention approach to remediate learning difficulties. Indeed, it appears as if its primary strength lies within this domain. As is often the case, the strength of this model also serves as its major limitation. The continued evolution of RtI/multi-tiered service delivery models has raised a series of implementation dilemmas. In essence, these models can be oversimplified as a reconceptualization of the discrepancy model (Fletcher & Vaughn, 2009; Reynolds & Shaywitz, 2009). Klingner and Edwards (2006) noted a major limitation of the RtI model: "we are concerned that if we do not engage in dialogue about the critical issues raised . . . RtI models will simply be like old wine in a new bottle, in other words, just another deficit-based approach to sorting children" (p. 115). Clearly, RtI models are not one-size-fits-all solutions to educational service delivery. This model of service delivery is evolving, and one of the dilemmas of this evolution is to ensure that sound pedagogical frameworks, including gifted pedagogy, are utilized to drive instructional practices within multi-tiered service delivery models.

Adding gifted pedagogy to RtI does not improve some inherent weaknesses of the RtI model, but could it increase some services to academically advanced students? We believe that gifted pedagogy and the RtI model both have a place in the current educational context but as separate ingredients in a child's educational program. The RtI model monitors and remediates students' progress in attaining basic academic skills; gifted pedagogy focuses on strengths, challenging students with depth and complexity and engaging them in creative productive experiences as they develop critical thinking and other 21st-century skills. Clearly, both of these approaches are necessary to address the needs of all students.

Gifted pedagogy can be seen as a response to a talent framework in which multiple tiers of services can be incorporated to not only remediate weaknesses in the attainment of basic literacies, but also to challenge students to develop 21st-century skills. Central to this response to talent framework is the assessment of students' strengths and interests and matching enrichment opportunities that engage and challenge students. The SEM is one response to talent approach that can be utilized in schools to appropriately expose and challenge all students. This promotes a focus on the student's continuous progress and the provision of extending enrichment and gifted education pedagogy beyond that offered by the regular curriculum. Can this approach be integrated within the context of a district RtI model to increase services to talented students? In this chapter, we discuss the integration of the SEM into an RtI district framework and offer suggestions for how this might work in practice.

Schoolwide Enrichment Model

The key question concerning the applications of gifted pedagogy in an RtI context is: How can we develop the potential of our academically able children? Further, what services should be provided to students who are identified for gifted and talented programs, as opposed to those for all students? Can creative productivity be enhanced when students participate in enrichment or gifted programs? The answers to these questions represent the core of the Schoolwide Enrichment Model, which was developed to encourage and develop creative productivity in young people.

In this chapter, a description of the SEM is presented as is a summary of pertinent research highlights (Renzulli & Reis, 1994) and a description of Renzulli Learning, a new SEM service delivery resource that uses a computer-generated profile of each student's academic strengths, interests, learning styles, and preferred modes of expression. The ways in which the SEM could enhance Tier 1 in an RtI service delivery model is also explored. For example, Tier 1 can include enrichment experiences for all students, known in the SEM as Type I and II Enrichment, or simply *general* enrichment. Students who have met the learning objectives of Tier 1 instruction qualify for Type II Enrichment, which consists of specific enrichment and curriculum differentiation using curriculum compacting targeted for a talent pool of approximately 10–15% of the student population. Students who are significantly advanced in relation to the regular curriculum could engage in Type III Enrichment, which includes more intense one-on-one project- and problem-based independent and small-group learning opportunities that serve the needs of approximately 5–10% of the general population of students, the vast majority of those identified as gifted, who complete Type III in-depth self-selected studies.

The SEM promotes engagement using these three types of enjoyable, challenging, and interest-based enrichment experiences. Separate studies on the SEM have demonstrated its effectiveness in schools with widely differing socioeconomic levels and program organizational patterns (Reis & Renzulli, 2003; Renzulli & Reis, 1997). The SEM was developed using Renzulli's Enrichment Triad Model (Renzulli, 1977; Renzulli & Reis, 1985, 1997) as a core and has been implemented in thousands of schools across the country and internationally. The effectiveness of the SEM has been studied in more than 30 years of research and field tests, suggesting that the model is effective at serving high-ability students and providing enrichment in a variety of educational settings, including schools serving culturally diverse and low socioeconomic populations (Reis & Renzulli, 2003; Renzulli & Reis, 1997).

The Theoretical Underpinnings of the SEM: Developing Academic Giftedness and Creative Productivity

The SEM focuses on the development of both academic and creative-productive giftedness. Creative-productive giftedness describes those aspects of human activity and involvement where a premium is placed on the development of original material and products that are purposefully designed to have an impact on one or more target audiences. Learning situations designed to promote creative-productive giftedness emphasize the use and application of information (content) and thinking skills in an integrated, inductive, and real-problem-oriented manner. Our focus on creative productivity complements our efforts to increase academic challenge when we attempt to transform the role of the student from that of a learner of lessons to one of a firsthand inquirer who can experience the joys and frustrations of creative productivity (Renzulli, 1977).

Three-Ring Conception of Giftedness. The SEM is based on Renzulli's (1978) "three-ring" conception of giftedness (see http://www.gifted.uconn.edu/sem/semart13.html for a diagram and more detail), which defines gifted behaviors rather than gifted individuals. This conception encompasses three interrelated components and is described as follows:

> Gifted behavior consists of behaviors that reflect an interaction among three basic clusters of human traits—above average ability, high levels of task commitment, and high levels of creativity. Individuals capable of developing gifted behavior are those possessing or capable of developing this composite set of traits and applying them to any potentially valuable area of human performance. Persons who manifest or are capable of developing an interaction among the three clusters require a wide variety of educational opportunities and services that are not ordinarily provided through regular instructional programs. (Renzulli & Reis, 1997, p. 8)

Longitudinal research supports this distinction between academic giftedness and creative-productive giftedness. For example, Perleth, Sierwald, and Heller (1993) found differences between students who demonstrated creative-productive giftedness as opposed to traditional academic giftedness. Renzulli's (1988a) research has suggested that gifted behaviors can be developed "in certain people, at certain times, and under certain circumstances" (p. 21).

These questions have led us to advocate that we *label the services students receive rather than labeling the students,* for we believe that a shift should occur from an emphasis on the traditional concept of "being gifted" (or not being gifted) to a concern about the development of gifted and creative behaviors in students who have high potential for benefiting from more advanced educational opportunities, as well as the provision of some types of enrichment for all students. This change in terminology may also provide the flexibility in both identification and programming endeavors that encourages the inclusion of at-risk and underachieving students in enrichment programs. Our ultimate goal is the development of a total school enrichment program that benefits all students and focuses on making schools places for talent development for all young people. In the context of RtI, it would, for example, be appropriate to incorporate elements of gifted pedagogy into the general educational curriculum and to use data to appropriately monitor and challenge students to make continuous progress toward becoming critical thinkers and problem solvers and to engage in higher levels of enrichment and talent development opportunities.

The Enrichment Triad Model. The Enrichment Triad Model (Renzulli, 1977), the curricular basis of the SEM, was originally designed as a gifted program model to encourage creative productivity in young people by exposing them to various topics, areas of interest, and fields of study and to further train them to *apply* advanced content, process-training skills, and methodology training to self-selected areas of interest using three types of enrichment. The original Triad Model with three types of enrichment was implemented in programs designed for academically talented and gifted students. In the Enrichment Triad Model, Type I enrichment is designed to expose students to a wide variety of disciplines, topics, occupations, hobbies, persons, places, and events that would not ordinarily be covered in the regular curriculum. In schools using this approach, an enrichment team of parents, teachers, and students often organizes and plans Type I experiences by contacting speakers; arranging mini-courses; conducting overviews of enrichment clusters, demonstrations, and performances; using Internet resources; or by ordering and distributing films, slides, CDs and DVDs, videotapes, or other print or non-print media. Type I Enrichment is mainly designed to stimulate new interests leading to Type II or III follow up for students who become motivated by Type I experiences. Type I Enrichment can be provided for general groups or for students who have already expressed an interest in the topic area. It is our belief that educators could, as stated earlier, augment Tier 1 of RtI (the regular curriculum) with Type I Enrichment for all students.

Type II Enrichment includes materials and methods designed to promote the development of thinking and feeling processes. Some Type II Enrichment is general, and it is usually provided to groups of students in their classrooms or in enrichment programs. This general Type II training includes the development of (a) creative thinking and problem solving, critical thinking, and affective processes; (b) a wide variety of specific learning how-to-learn skills; (c) skills in the appropriate use of advanced-level reference materials; and (d) written, oral, and visual communication skills. The more general Type II Enrichment could, we believe, also be associated with implementing Tier I in the RtI approach.

Other Type II Enrichment is specific, as it cannot be planned in advance and usually involves advanced instruction in an interest area selected by the student. For example, students who become interested in botany after Type I Enrichment on this topic would pursue advanced training in this area by reading advanced content in botany; compiling, planning, and carrying out plant experiments; and undertaking more advanced methods training for those who want to go further and pursue Type III Enrichment in that area. It is this specific Type II training that could be used with curriculum compacting as a differentiation strategy to meet the needs of students who have already mastered the learning objectives for specific units of the regular curriculum. This would be considered a Tier 2 service within an RtI framework.

Type III Enrichment enables students who become interested in pursuing a self-selected area and are willing to commit the time necessary for advanced content acquisition and process training to assume the role of a first-hand inquirer. Type III products can be completed by individual or small groups of students and are always based on students' interests. Type III Enrichment enables students to:

> ➢ apply interests, knowledge, creative ideas, and task commitment to a self-selected problem or area of study;

➢ acquire advanced-level understanding of the knowledge (content) and methodology (process) used within particular disciplines, artistic areas of expression, and interdisciplinary studies;

➢ develop authentic products that are primarily directed toward bringing about a desired impact upon a specified audience;

➢ develop self-directed learning skills in the areas of planning, organization, resource utilization, time management, decision making, and self-evaluation; and,

➢ develop task commitment, self-confidence, and feelings of creative accomplishment.

It is this most advanced component of the SEM that we regard as most beneficial to students who have demonstrated mastery of the course curriculum. Type III activities are a way to implement differentiation for students who will require different types of support and guidance as they pursue advanced mastery of an interest area. Students pursuing advanced Type III activities would be served within a Tier 3 RtI framework.

The Schoolwide Enrichment Model: Enrichment for all. With the Enrichment Triad Model as its theoretical and curricular basis, the SEM identifies a talent pool of approximately 10–15% of above-average ability/high-potential students through a variety of measures, including achievement tests, teacher nominations, and assessments of potential for creativity and task commitment, as well as through alternative pathways of entrance (e.g., self-nomination, parent nomination). High achievement tests and/or IQ test scores automatically place a student in the talent pool, enabling those students who are underachieving in their academic schoolwork to be included.

Once students are identified for the talent pool, they are eligible for several kinds of services to challenge them to move beyond the learning objectives covered in the regular curriculum. First, interest and learning style assessments are used with talent pool students in the development of a Total Talent Portfolio for each student. Informal and formal methods are used to identify and assess students' interests and to encourage students to further develop and pursue these interests in various ways. Learning style preferences include projects, independent studies, teaching games, simulations, peer teaching, computer-assisted instruction, lecture, drill and recitation, and discussion. Second, curriculum compacting and other forms of differentiation and curricular modification are provided to all eligible students to adjust the regular curriculum to meet their needs. This elimination or streamlining of curricula enables above-average students to avoid repetition of previously mastered work and guarantees mastery while simultaneously finding time for more appropriately challenging activities (Reis, Burns, & Renzulli, 1992; Renzulli, Smith, & Reis, 1982). Third, a series of enrichment opportunities organized around the Enrichment Triad Model offers three types of enrichment experiences through various forms of delivery, including enrichment clusters. Type I, II, and III Enrichment are offered to all students; however, Type III Enrichment is usually more appropriate for students of higher levels of ability, interest, and task commitment.

The SEM has three major goals that are designed to challenge and meet the needs of high-potential, high-ability, and gifted students and at the same time provide challenging learning experiences for all students. These goals are: (a) to maintain and expand a continuum of special services that will challenge students with demonstrated superior performance or the potential for superior performance in any and all aspects of the school and extracurricular program; (b) to infuse into the general education program a broad range of activities for high-end learning that will challenge all students to perform at advanced levels and allow teachers to determine which students should be given extended opportunities, resources, and encouragement in particular areas where superior interest and performance are demonstrated; and (c) to preserve and protect the positions of gifted education specialists and any other specialized personnel necessary for carrying out these goals.

Implementing the SEM

The SEM has three service delivery components that provide services to students, namely the Total Talent Portfolio, curriculum modification techniques, and enrichment learning and teaching (see Figure 7.1). These three services are delivered through the regular curriculum, a continuum of special services (see http://www.gifted.uconn.edu/sem/semhand.html under "Continuum of Special Services"), and a series of enrichment clusters.

Total Talent Portfolio. In the SEM, teachers help students better understand dimensions of their learning, abilities, interests, and learning styles. This information, focusing on their strengths rather than deficits, is compiled in a management form called the Total Talent Portfolio that can be subsequently used to make decisions about talent development opportunities in general education classes, enrichment clusters, and/or in the continuum of special services (see http://www.gifted.uconn.edu/sem/semhand.html under "Dimensions of the Total Talent Portfolio"). The major purposes of the Total Talent Portfolio are: (a) to *collect information* about students' strengths on a regular basis; (b)

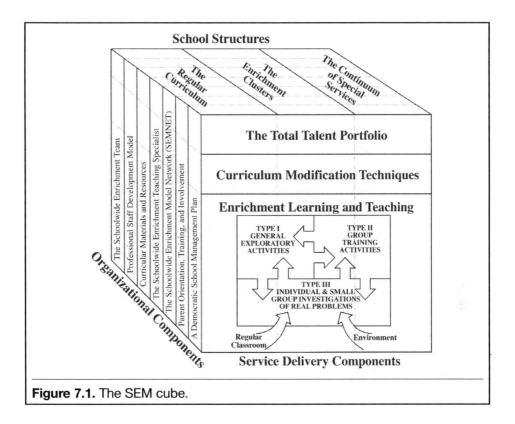

Figure 7.1. The SEM cube.

to *classify* this information into the general categories of abilities, interests, and learning styles; (c) to periodically *review and analyze* the information in order to make decisions about providing opportunities for enrichment experiences in the general education classroom, the enrichment clusters, and the continuum of special services; and (d) to use this information to *make decisions* about acceleration and enrichment in school and in later educational, personal, and career decisions. This expanded approach to identifying talent potential is essential if we are to make genuine efforts to include a broader, more diverse group of students in enrichment programs. This approach is also consistent with the more flexible conception of *developing* gifts and talents that has been a cornerstone of the SEM, addressing concerns for promoting more equity in special programs. This could be regarded as the process by which we collect data for movement between the different types of enrichment opportunities. The use of data-driven decision making is a cornerstone of the RtI approach and fits well with the Total Talent Portfolio.

Curriculum modification techniques. The second service delivery component of the SEM is a series of curriculum modification techniques that can: (a) adjust levels of required learning so that all students are challenged, (b) increase the number of in-depth learning experiences, and (c) introduce various types of enrichment into general education curricular experiences. The procedures that are used to carry out curriculum modification include implementing curriculum differentiation strategies, such as curriculum compacting, and infusing greater depth into regular curricular material (Reis et al., 1993; Renzulli, 1994). Tier 1 instruction will not adequately challenge high-ability students, so enhancing it with enrichment and other differentiation strategies is essential.

Curriculum compacting is one such approach. It is a differentiation technique designed to make appropriate curricular adjustments for students in any curricular area and at any grade level, by (a) defining the goals and outcomes of a particular unit or segment of instruction, (b) determining and documenting which students already have mastered most or all of a specified set of learning outcomes, and (c) providing replacement strategies for material already mastered through the use of instructional options that enable a more challenging and productive use of the student's time. Teachers should fill out one Compactor form per student or one form for a group of students with similar curricular strengths (see http://www.gifted.uconn.edu/siegle/CurriculumCompacting/ccaf.html for the form). Completed Compactors should be kept in students' academic files and updated on a regular basis. The form can also be used for small groups of students who are working at approximately the same level (e.g., a reading or math group). The Compactor is divided into three sections:

> The first column should include information on learning objectives (being covered in Tier 1 instruction) and student strengths in those areas. Teachers should list the objectives for a particular unit of study, followed by data on students' proficiency in those objectives, including test scores, behavioral profiles, and past academic records.

> In the second column, teachers should detail the assessment tools or procedures they select, along with test results. The pretest instruments can be formal measures, such as pencil-and-paper tests, or informal measures, such as performance assessments based on observations of class participation and written assignments.

> The third column is used to record information about acceleration or enrichment options; in determining these options, teachers must be aware of students' individual interests and learning styles. If, for example, a student loves working on science fair projects, that option may be used to replace material that has been compacted from the regular curriculum. We should also be careful to help monitor the challenge

level of the material that is being substituted, as we want students to understand the nature of effort and challenge, and we must ensure that we are not simply replacing the compacted material with basic reading or work that is too easy. Replacement learning activities may require Tier 2 or even Tier 3 supports, as they will often extend well beyond the general curriculum.

Enrichment learning and teaching. The third service delivery component of the SEM, based on the Enrichment Triad Model, is enrichment learning and teaching, which has roots in the ideas of a small but influential number of philosophers, theorists, and researchers such as Jean Piaget (1975), Jerome Bruner (1960, 1966), and John Dewey (1913, 1916). The work of these theorists, coupled with our own research and program development activities, has given rise to the concept we call enrichment learning and teaching. The best way to define this concept is in terms of the following four principles:

➢ Each learner is unique, and therefore, learning experiences must be examined in ways that take into account the abilities, interests, and learning styles of the individual.

➢ Learning is more effective when students enjoy what they are doing, and therefore, learning experiences should be constructed and assessed with as much concern for enjoyment as for other goals.

➢ Learning is more meaningful and enjoyable when content (i.e., knowledge) and process (i.e., thinking skills, methods of inquiry) are learned within the context of real and present problems, and therefore, attention should be given to opportunities to personalize student choice in problem selection, the relevance of the problem for individual students at the time the problem is being addressed, and authentic strategies for addressing the problem.

➢ Some formal instruction may be used in enrichment learning and teaching, but a major goal of this approach to learning is to enhance knowledge and thinking skill acquisition that is gained through formal instruction with applications of knowledge and skills that result from students' own constructions of meaning. (Renzulli, 1994)

The ultimate goal of learning guided by these principles is to replace dependent and passive learning with independence and engaged learning. Although all but the most conservative educators will agree with these principles, much controversy exists about how these (or similar) principles might be applied in everyday school situations. A danger also exists that these principles might be viewed as yet another idealized list of glittering generalities that cannot be manifested easily in schools that are entrenched in the deductive model of learning. Developing a school program based on these principles is not an easy task. Over the years, however, we have achieved success by gaining faculty, administrative, and parental consensus on a small number of easy-to-understand concepts and related services and by providing resources and training related to each concept and service delivery procedure.

The importance of not losing sight of these principles in an RtI framework cannot be understated. Although direct instruction in basic literacies is an important function of school, schools can also provide opportunities to challenge students to become creative and productive members of our society. Using these principles to guide instruction would benefit all students by providing opportunities for them to demonstrate their strengths as opposed to merely receiving instruction in areas of weakness. Both approaches are necessary in the current educational climate.

School Structures in SEM Schools

The general education curriculum. The general education curriculum consists of everything that is a part of the predetermined goals, schedules, learning outcomes, and delivery systems of the school. The general education curriculum might be traditional, innovative, or in the process of transition, but its predominant feature is that authoritative forces (e.g., policy makers, school councils, textbook adoption committees, state regulators) have determined that the general education curriculum should be the centerpiece of student learning. Hence, Tier 1 in RtI is the general education curriculum. Application of the SEM influences the general education curriculum in the differentiation of the challenge level of required material using curriculum compacting and the enrichment recommended in the Enrichment Triad Model (Renzulli, 1977) integrated into general education curriculum activities. Although our goal in the SEM is to influence rather than replace the general education curriculum, the application of certain SEM components and related staff development activities has resulted in substantial changes in both the content and instructional processes of the entire general education curriculum.

Enrichment clusters. The enrichment clusters, the second component of the SEM, are nongraded groups of students who share common interests and who come together during specially designated blocks of time during school to work with an adult who shares their interests and who has some degree of advanced knowledge and expertise in the area. The enrichment clusters usually meet for a block of time weekly during a semester. All students complete an interest inventory developed to assess their interests, and an enrichment team of parents and teachers tally all of the major families of interests. Faculty, staff, parents, and community members are recruited to facilitate enrichment clusters based on these interests, such as creative writing, drawing, sculpting, archeology, and other areas. Training is provided to the facilitators who agree to offer the clusters, and a brochure can be developed and sent to all parents and students that emphasizes the importance of student interests and their own choices of enrichment clusters. Students select their top three choices for the clusters, and scheduling is completed to place all children into their first or, in some cases, second choice. Like extracurricular activities and programs such as 4-H and Junior Achievement, the main rationale for participation in one or more clusters is that students and teachers want to be there. All teachers (including music, art, physical education, and so forth) are involved in teaching the clusters, and their involvement in any particular cluster is based on the same type of interest assessment that is used for students in selecting clusters of choice.

The model for learning used with enrichment clusters is based on an inductive approach to solving real-world problems through the development of authentic products and services using the Enrichment Triad Model to create a learning situation with the use of specific methods authentically applied to creative and productive situations. Enrichment clusters promote real-world problem solving, focusing on the belief that "every child is special if we create conditions in which that child can be a specialist within a specialty group" (Renzulli, 1994, p. 70).

Enrichment clusters are organized around various characteristics of differentiated programming for gifted students on which the Enrichment Triad Model (Renzulli, 1977) was originally based, including the use of major disciplines, interdisciplinary themes, or cross-disciplinary topics (e.g., a theatrical/television production group that includes actors, writers, technical specialists, and costume designers). The clusters are modeled after the ways in which knowledge utilization, thinking skills, and interpersonal relations take place in the real world. Thus, all work is directed toward the production of a product or service.

Enrichment clusters incorporate the use of advanced content, providing students with information about particular fields of knowledge. The methods used within a field are also considered advanced content by Renzulli (1988b), involving the use of knowledge of the structures and tools of fields, as well as knowledge about the methodology of particular fields. Enrichment clusters are not intended to be the total program for talent development in a school or to replace existing programs for talented youth. Rather, they are one component of the SEM that can stimulate interests and develop talent in the entire school population. They can also serve as staff development opportunities, as they provide teachers with an opportunity to participate in enrichment teaching and subsequently to analyze and compare this type of teaching with traditional methods of instruction. In this regard, the model promotes a spillover effect by encouraging teachers to become better talent scouts and talent developers and to apply enrichment techniques to general education classroom situations. Research on enrichment clusters also has found that their use results in both higher use of advanced thinking and research skills in gifted and nongifted students in both clusters and regular classrooms settings as well (Reis, Gentry, & Maxfield, 1998).

The continuum of special services. A broad range of special services is the third school structure targeted by the model, as represented at http://www.gifted.uconn.edu/sem/semhand.html under "Continuum of Special Services." Although the enrichment clusters and the SEM-based modifications of the regular curriculum provide a broad range of services to meet individual needs, a program for total talent development still requires supplementary services that challenge our most academically talented young people who are capable of working at the highest levels. These services, which cannot ordinarily be provided in enrichment clusters or the regular curriculum, typically include individual or small-group counseling, acceleration, direct assistance in facilitating advanced-level work, mentorships with faculty members or community persons, and connections between students, their families, and out-of-school persons, resources, and agencies.

Direct assistance also involves setting up and promoting student, faculty, and parental involvement in special programs such as Future Problem Solving; Odyssey of the Mind; Model United Nations; state and national essay competitions; and mathematics, art, and history contests. Another type of direct assistance consists of arranging out-of-school involvement for individual students in summer programs, on-campus courses, special schools, theatrical groups, scientific expeditions, and apprenticeships at places where advanced-level learning opportunities are available. Provision of these services is one of the responsibilities of the SEM teaching specialist or an enrichment team of teachers and parents who work together to provide options for advanced learning. Most SEM teaching specialists spend 2 days a week in a resource capacity to the faculty and 3 days providing direct services to students. Again, this continuum of services fits well within the RtI multi-tiered supports and services approach.

SEM as Evidence-Based Practice

A collective body of research on the SEM (Gubbins, 1995; Reis & Renzulli, 2003; Renzulli & Reis, 1994) suggests that the model is effective at serving high-ability students in a variety of educational settings and in schools serving diverse ethnic and socioeconomic populations. Separate studies on the SEM have demonstrated its effectiveness in schools with widely differing socioeconomic levels and program organization patterns (Olenchak, 1990; Olenchak & Renzulli, 1989). The effectiveness of the model has been studied in more than 30 years of research and field-testing on (a) the effectiveness of the model as perceived by key groups, such as principals; (b) student creative productivity; (c) personal and social development; (d) the use of SEM with culturally diverse or special needs populations; (e) student self-efficacy; (f) the use of SEM as a curricular framework; and (g) learning styles and curriculum compacting, along with other longitudinal research on the SEM.

This research suggests:

> ➢ the model is effective at serving high-ability students in a variety of educational settings and in schools serving diverse ethnic and socioeconomic populations.
> ➢ the pedagogy of the SEM can be applied to various content areas, resulting in higher achievement when implemented in a wide variety of settings.
> ➢ the pedagogy of the SEM can be used with diverse populations of students, including high-ability students with learning disabilities and those who underachieve.
> ➢ the use of the SEM results in more use of advanced reasoning skills and thinking skills.
> ➢ students who are involved in SEM activities achieve at higher levels on traditional achievement tests than students who continue to use regular curricular or remedial activities.

A table of relevant research and pertinent references is available at http://www. gifted.uconn.edu/sem/rrsem.html. Clearly, the breadth and depth of research supporting the implementation of this model illustrate its utility as an evidence-based practice in schools.

SEM in the 21st Century: Renzulli Learning

Renzulli Learning is the newest component of the SEM. It is an interactive online program that aids in the implementation of SEM by matching student interests, expression styles, and learning styles with a vast array of educational enrichment activities and resources, designed to enrich high-potential students' learning processes. Using Renzulli Learning, students independently explore, discover, learn, and create using the SEM on the most current technology resources in a safe environment. It consists of a series of services that represent the various components of SEM. Renzulli Learning automatically differentiates learning experiences to challenge and engage students. Thus, it can be a potentially useful tool to augment Tier 1 instruction.

In order to differentiate for students, this system utilizes the Renzulli Profiler, which is an interactive assessment tool that identifies students' talents, strengths, interests, and preferred learning and expression styles, providing a comprehensive student learning profile. It consists of carefully selected, user-friendly, research-based questions related to a student's particular interests in 13 major categories. Students' expression styles are also assessed. Whether through writing, oral debates, stage performance, sculpture, dance, or a host of other expressive techniques, the student shares how he or she most enjoys interacting with the world. The Renzulli Profiler also assesses learning styles, or the ways students like to learn new information, ranging from individualized study or large-group learning, to paper-based review or digital technology, focusing on nine learning styles: Lecture, Computer-Assisted Instruction, Discussion, Peer Tutoring, Group Work, Learning Games, Technology, Simulations, and Independent Studies. Students answer questions about their interests and learning and product styles in 30–50 minutes, and the Profiler produces an accurate, printable assessment of each student's interests and abilities and how that individual best learns. The Renzulli Profiler reflects the world of learning from the *student's* perspective, not necessarily that of his or her parents or teachers. This makes it possible to provide enrichment based on the Enrichment Triad Model with optimum effectiveness and efficiency.

The Renzulli Enrichment Database includes thousands of carefully screened, grade-level appropriate, child-safe enrichment opportunities that are regularly monitored, updated, enhanced, and expanded at a rate of more than 500 per month. To truly individualize and differentiate for students of various needs, teachers using Renzulli Learning have easy access to an unlimited supply of enrichment activities and resources that make such differentiation possible. All enrichment database entries are carefully researched by Renzulli Learning educational specialists, screened for grade-level applicability, and coded as one of the 14 enrichment categories. Elements of each category are then matched to students' top three choices of interests, learning, and expression styles, providing each student with a unique personalized selection of enrichment opportunities. The search automatically links each student's profile (interests, learning styles, and expression styles) with the Enrichment Database to generate a customized list of activities designed to appeal to that student's grade level, interests, and abilities, as well as his or her learning and expression styles.

A secondary self-directed search enables students and teachers to enter a set of one or more self-selected keywords to locate specific database entries from their own individual activity list or from the entire database. This feature is particularly useful for selecting a particular topic for project work or for in-depth study. A global search capability enables students and teachers to access the entire Enrichment Database, across all interests, expression styles, learning styles, or even grade levels. This permits students with above-grade capabilities to locate and pursue new activities and threads of interest, all within the safety of a prescreened information environment. It also helps teachers identify possible projects and other curriculum enhancements so their students can receive more in-depth, personalized instruction to augment the regular curriculum. Renzulli Learning's combined search facilities offer children an extensive, expanding menu of learning opportunities and offer teachers a new and valuable resource for their classroom preparation.

The Total Talent Portfolio provides a complete record of the student's online learning activities and academic progress and an online portfolio to save students' best work. The Total Talent Portfolio enables students to create and post writings, Internet links, images, and other work on projects or areas of interest. This portfolio can help to solve some of the assessment dilemmas in a multi-tiered service delivery system, including progress monitoring. By keeping a record of student progress in an environment that fosters critical thinking and problem solving, this portfolio provides valuable data formatively to ensure students are being engaged and challenged by the work they are completing in Renzulli Learning. Further, this portfolio can demonstrate the knowledge and skills they are acquiring beyond the competencies covered in the general education curriculum. The Wizard Project Maker is an online project-management tool that helps students to create their own high-interest projects and store them in their own Total Talent Portfolios. More than 200 Super Starter Projects have been added to the Wizard Project Maker to enable students to begin the process of doing projects on a small-scale, short-term basis that may later enable them to initiate and complete projects more independently. The students' ability to create their own projects is a unique feature of Renzulli Learning that can be viewed as a student-driven problem-solving model in a multi-tiered response to talent system.

In an era of accountability, Renzulli Learning also offers a series of management tools for teachers, administrators, and parents, designed to help follow individual students' learning progressions, analyze group usage patterns, and formulate lesson plans and classroom organization. Renzulli Learning features a collection of administrative reports designed to help make the process of enriching each student's learning process more efficient. Reports include printable listings of individual and group interests and individual and group summaries of student expression styles and learning styles. Also available are teacher learning maps for enrichment differentiation activities, downloadable enrichment projects, downloadable creativity training activities, background articles by leading educational practitioners, lesson plans for using Renzulli Learning effectively, and outstanding websites for teachers.

Perhaps the most significant aspect of Renzulli Learning is its emphasis on students' strengths, celebrating and building upon students' academic abilities and interests in the tradition of SEM. It gives teachers a virtual equivalent of multiple "teaching assistants" in their classrooms—each and every day—to implement the SEM. This approach can also be viewed as a standard protocol treatment, because Renzulli Learning includes activities that are matched to the student but are not teacher-created. Teachers can access exciting websites to help their own teaching and download creative activities to use in their classroom. They can monitor students' progress by accessing their profiles and viewing all of the activities and assessments that they have completed. Teachers using this system can even submit their own ideas for activities and interact with other teachers, enrichment specialists, curriculum coordinators, and administrators from around the country. The creation of specific activities tailored to their students' needs and interests also represents how Renzulli Learning can be used in a problem-solving model of a multi-tiered service delivery system.

Finally, parents can view their child's progress, his or her profile, and the choice of enrichment activities and projects.

Field (2009) studied the use of Renzulli Learning by students in both an urban and suburban school. In this 16-week experimental study, both gifted and nongifted students who participated in this enrichment program and used Renzulli Learning for 2–3 hours each week demonstrated significantly higher growth in reading comprehension than control group students who did not participate in the program. Students also demonstrated significantly higher growth in oral reading fluency and in social studies achievement than those students who did not participate. Experimental group gains over the control group were also shown in science, although these gains were not statistically significant (Field, 2009).

Meeting the Needs of Gifted Students With RtI

Although some high-potential and gifted students could be served by using the emerging SEM/RtI model described in this chapter, caution should be utilized when integrating frameworks that have different theoretical underpinnings and purposes. The focus of gifted education is on the development of students' talents and strengths in individuals and not on remediating student weaknesses. Further, the RtI model is evolving and will continue to do so. Several researchers have discussed the issues presented by the wide-scale adoption of this approach to service delivery (Fletcher & Vaughn, 2009; Reynolds & Shaywitz, 2009). Undoubtedly, individual variations of this model will be developed as educational institutions mold this framework to their unique contexts, but several issues exist with the current conceptualization of this service delivery model. Challenges emerge, for example, with regard to serving the needs of students who are English language learners (Klingner & Edwards, 2006) and the appropriateness of the RtI model for service delivery at the secondary level needs further examination (Mastropieri & Scruggs, 2005). These challenges have not been fully addressed or articulated in the current RtI model, and, as Reynolds and Shaywitz (2009) have also argued: "Whereas seemingly intuitively appealing, RtI has, in fact, a very weak experimental base, particularly longitudinal studies of the effects of RtI on a student's progress toward high school graduation and beyond" (p. 133).

Further, the RtI model places an emphasis on the regular curriculum (Tier 1) as a vehicle for meeting the needs of all students. When the RtI model is applied to gifted education, Tier 1 would represent the general education classroom where gifted students would receive the majority of their instruction. Given that a significant portion of the general education curriculum can be eliminated for gifted students (Archambault et al., 1993; Reis et al., 1993), it appears that Tier 1 would not serve the needs of these students, as it does not focus on ensuring that they will be challenged and make continued academic progress. The RtI model does not address whether students are interested or engaged in the general education curriculum. Although Tier 1 could involve curriculum compacting or other differentiation strategies (Coleman & Hughes, 2009), differentiation is not actively practiced in most schools (Reis et al., 2004).

In discussing a report released by the National Association of State Directors of Special Education (NASDSE) about the RtI initiative, Pereles et al. (2009) noted that the report on RtI fails to address the needs of gifted children, "nor does it define high-quality instruction as opportunities for acceleration or enrichment" (p. 40). Further, the screening measures utilized by this approach often focus on the grade-level curriculum and do not identify those students who have the ability to grapple with more complex or difficult material (Brown & Abernethy, 2009). These screening measures will not appropriately identify potential areas for talent development because of their focus on basic academic skills and their failure to consider the development of creative and critical thinking skills (Daly et al., 2007). In essence, "to recognize whether talent exists there must be opportunities for talent to emerge" (Gentry, 2009, p. 265). The RtI model is not designed to identify the potential talents in students. The lack of focus on developing talent could have serious repercussions, as too few students develop their talents in school. As we have argued for the last three decades, schools should be places for talent development. Although some educators may believe that adding tiers to the RtI model would solve this problem, substantial challenges continue to be posed by the implementation of the current RtI conceptualization on a large scale.

The Schoolwide Enrichment Model can serve as an addendum to the RtI approach to service delivery. The SEM mitigates several of the major weaknesses of the RtI approach. Utilizing both approaches would enable educators to address the learning needs of all students by developing both basic and 21st-century skills. Schools that implement the SEM give students the opportunity to demonstrate their potential as opposed to demonstrating weakness or mastery of basic academic skills. Thus, the SEM can be conceptualized as a "Response to Talent" framework. If schools are to prepare our students to meet the demands placed on them by the revolution in access to knowledge through technology and complexities created by a modern global economy, it is essential that educators consider how to assess the ways in which students respond to interventions, as well as the ways that educators develop talent and talent potential in all students.

References

Archambault, F. X., Jr., Westberg, K. L., Brown, S., Hallmark, B. W., Zhang, W., & Emmons, C. (1993). Regular classroom practices with gifted students: Findings from the classroom practices survey. *Journal for the Education of the Gifted, 16,* 103–119.

Bradley, R., Danielson, L., & Doolittle, J. (2007). Responsiveness to Intervention: 1997 to 2007. *TEACHING Exceptional Children, 39*(5), 8–12.

Brown, E. F., & Abernethy, S. H. (2009). Policy implication at the state and district level with RtI for gifted students. *Gifted Child Today, 32*(3), 52–57.

Bruner, J. S. (1960). *The process of education.* Cambridge, MA: Harvard University Press.

Bruner, J. S. (1966). *Toward a theory of instruction.* Cambridge, MA: Harvard University Press.

Coleman, M. R., & Hughes, C. E. (2009). Meeting the needs of gifted students within an RtI framework. *Gifted Child Today, 32*(3), 14–19.

Council for Exceptional Children, The Association for the Gifted (n.d.). *Response to Intervention for gifted children.* Retrieved from http://cectag.com/wp-content/uploads/2012/04/RTI.pdf

Crepeau-Hobson, F., & Bianco, M. (2011). Identification of gifted students with learning disabilities in a Response-to-Intervention era. *Psychology in the Schools, 48,* 102–109.

Daly, E. J., Martens, B. K., Barnett, D., Witt, J. C., & Olson, S. C. (2007). Varying intervention delivery in Response to Intervention: Confronting and resolving challenges with measurement, instruction, and intensity. *School Psychology Review, 36,* 562–581.

Dewey, J. (1913). *Interest and effort in education.* New York, NY: Houghton Mifflin.

Dewey, J. (1916). *Democracy and education.* New York, NY: Macmillan.

Field, G. B. (2009). The effects of using Renzulli Learning on student achievement: An investigation of Internet technology on reading fluency, comprehension, and social studies. *International Journal of Emerging Technology, 4,* 29–39.

Fletcher, J. M., & Vaughn, S. (2009). Response to Intervention: Preventing and remediating academic difficulties. *Child Development Perspectives, 3*(1), 30–37.

Fuchs, D., & Fuchs, L. S. (2006). Introduction to Response to Intervention: What, why, and how valid is it? *Reading Research Quarterly, 41,* 93–99.

Gentry, M. (2009). Myth 11: A comprehensive continuum of gifted education and talent development services. *Gifted Child Quarterly, 53,* 262–265.

Glover, T. A., & DiPerna, J. C. (2007). Service delivery for Response to Intervention: Core components and directions for future research. *School Psychology Review, 36,* 526–540.

Grigorenko, E. L. (2009). Dynamic assessment and Response to Intervention: Two sides of one coin. *Journal of Learning Disabilities, 42,* 111–132.

Gubbins, E. J. (Ed.). (1995). *Research related to the Enrichment Triad Model* (Research Monograph 95212). Storrs: University of Connecticut, The National Research Center on the Gifted and Talented.

Hoover, J. J., & Patton, J. R. (2008). The role of special educators in a multi-tiered instructional system. *Intervention in School and Clinic, 43,* 195–202.

Hughes, C. E., Rollins, K., Johnsen, S. K., Pereles, D. A., Omdal, S., Baldwin, L., . . . Coleman, M. R. (2009). Remaining challenges of the use of RtI with gifted education. *Gifted Child Today, 32*(3), 58–61.

Klingner, J. K., & Edwards, P. A. (2006). Cultural considerations with Response to Intervention models. *Reading Research Quarterly, 41,* 108–117.

Mastropieri, M. A., & Scruggs, T. E. (2005). Feasibility and consequences of Response to Intervention: Examination of the issues and scientific evidence as a model for the identification of individuals with learning disabilities. *Journal of Learning Disabilities, 38,* 525–531.

McCoach, D. B., Kehle, T. J., Bray, M. A., & Siegle, D. (2001). Best practices in the identification of gifted students with learning disabilities. *Psychology in the Schools, 38,* 403–411.

Olenchak, F. R. (1990). School change through gifted education: Effects on elementary students' attitudes toward learning. *Journal for the Education of the Gifted, 14,* 66–78.

Olenchak, F. R., & Renzulli, J. S. (1989). The effectiveness of the Schoolwide Enrichment Model on selected aspects of elementary school change. *Gifted Child Quarterly, 32,* 44–57.

Pereles, D. A., Omdal, S., & Baldwin, L. (2009). Response to Intervention and twice-exceptional learners: A promising fit. *Gifted Child Today, 32*(3), 40–51.

Perleth, C. H., Sierwald, W., & Heller, K. A. (1993). Selected results of the Munich longitudinal study of giftedness: The multidimensional/typological giftedness model. *Roeper Review, 15,* 149–155.

Piaget, J. (1975). *The development of thought: Equilibration of cognitive structures.* New York, NY: Viking.

Reis, S. M., Burns, D. E., & Renzulli, J. S. (1992). *Curriculum compacting: The complete guide to modifying the regular curriculum for high ability students.* Mansfield Center, CT: Creative Learning Press.

Reis, S. M., Gentry, M., & Maxfield, L. R. (1998). The application of enrichment clusters to teachers' classroom practices. *Journal for the Education of the Gifted, 21,* 310–324.

Reis, S. M., Gubbins, E. J., Briggs, C. J., Schreiber, F. J., Richards, S., Jacobs, J. K., . . . Renzulli, J. S. (2004). Reading instruction for talented readers: Case studies documenting few opportunities for continuous progress. *Gifted Child Quarterly, 48,* 315–338.

Reis, S. M., & Renzulli, J. S. (2003). Research related to the Schoolwide Enrichment Triad Model. *Gifted Education International, 18*(1), 15–40.

Reis, S. M., Westberg, K. L., Kulikowich, J., Caillard, F., Hébert, T. P., Plucker, J. A., . . . Smist, J. M. (1993). *Why not let high ability students start school in January? The curriculum compacting study* (Research Monograph 93106). Storrs: University of Connecticut, The National Research Center on the Gifted and Talented. Retrieved from http://www.gifted.uconn.edu/nrcgt/reports/rm93106/rm93106.pdf

Renzulli, J. S. (1977). *The Enrichment Triad Model: A guide for developing defensible programs for the gifted and talented.* Mansfield Center, CT: Creative Learning Press.

Renzulli, J. S. (1978). What makes giftedness? Re-examining a definition. *Phi Delta Kappan, 60,* 180–184, 261.

Renzulli, J. S. (1988a). A decade of dialogue on the three-ring conception of giftedness. *Roeper Review, 11,* 18-25.

Renzulli, J. S. (1988b). The multiple menu model for developing differentiated curriculum for the gifted and talented. *Gifted Child Quarterly, 32,* 298–309.

Renzulli, J. S. (1994). *Schools for talent development: A practical plan for total school improvement.* Mansfield Center, CT: Creative Learning Press.

Renzulli, J. S., & Reis, S. M. (1985). *The Schoolwide Enrichment Model: A comprehensive plan for educational excellence.* Mansfield Center, CT: Creative Learning Press.

Renzulli, J. S., & Reis, S. M. (1994). Research related to the Schoolwide Enrichment Model. *Gifted Child Quarterly, 38,* 2–14.

Renzulli, J. S., & Reis, S. M. (1997). *The Schoolwide Enrichment Model: A how-to guide for educational excellence* (2nd ed.). Mansfield Center, CT: Creative Learning Press.

Renzulli, J. S., Smith, L. H., & Reis, S. M. (1982). Curriculum compacting: An essential strategy for working with gifted students. *The Elementary School Journal, 82,* 185–194.

Reynolds, C. R., & Shaywitz, S. E. (2009). Response to Intervention: Ready or not? Or, from wait-to-fail to watch-them-fail? *School Psychology Quarterly, 24,* 130–145.

Shifrer, D., Muller, C., & Callahan, R. (2011). Disproportionality and learning disabilities: Parsing apart race, socioeconomic status, and language. *Journal of Learning Disabilities, 44,* 246–257.

CHAPTER EIGHT

RESPONSE TO INTERVENTION AND THE AUTONOMOUS LEARNER MODEL

Optimizing Potential

George T. Betts and Robin Carey

Potential
Is a moment, a thought, a flicker,
a chance, a change, an idea of what
may become . . .
Potential
Is the feeling that I can do that,
I want to do that,
I will learn to do that . . .
Potential
is usually felt within,
but it can be seen by others
even before you know it . . .
Potential is courage,
a risk, an opportunity,
the possibility of a passion,
the opportunity for the beginning
of a life-changing moment . . .
Potential is
what you may become . . .

—George T. Betts

Rarely do we have total freedom to develop programming with students in a public school. In the case of the Autonomous Learner Model for the Gifted and Talented (ALM), we did not develop a program *for* them, but *with* them, and the results are still relevant today in schools throughout the world. Although the model was originally developed for gifted learners, it has proven to be effective in developing lifelong learning for all students (Betts & Kercher, 1999). The ALM and a multi-tiered instructional framework are strongly aligned to serve the diversified cognitive, emotional, social, and physical needs of all learners. Implementing the Response to Intervention (RtI) framework in concert with the ALM allows us to focus on the learners and not the labels acquired as they pass through the school system. Together, RtI and the ALM provide a complete approach to meeting the needs of the learner.

We have both been involved in gifted education and special education, and we have seen many changes in both fields. However, there is one foundation that does not change: meeting the cognitive, emotional, social, and physical needs of the individual. This is true whether the diversified needs are shown through potential or performance. Combining the ALM and RtI provides a potential-based approach, responding to and nurturing learners' potential and performance.

Potential and Performance

Merriam-Webster defines potential as, "existing in possibility: capable of development into actuality." American Heritage Dictionary definitions highlight the growth nature inherent in potential: "capable of being but not yet in existence; having possibility, capability, or power; something possessing the capacity for growth." With both the ALM and RtI approaches, the focus is on those possibilities, with support for the learner's development in reaching his or her full potential. The teacher/facilitator recognizes and nurtures that potential through the activities in the five dimensions of the ALM, with the intensity of support determined by the needs and potential of the individual learner.

Many gifted learners already demonstrate a high level of performance. By this, we mean they respond to challenging opportunities, demonstrate depth and complexity of thought in process and product, and thrive in a learning environment that encourages continual growth and new learning experiences. The ALM and RtI approaches respond to the needs of performing gifted learners by providing a venue for the highest levels of learning.

Three Levels of Curriculum

The three levels of curriculum (Betts, 2004) provide curriculum for differentiated instruction by the teacher and for the learner. The three levels are Standard-Based-Curriculum, Standards-Based Differentiated Curriculum, and Learner-Based Differentiated Curriculum.

Level One: Standards-Based Curriculum

Within the ALM approach, Level One, Standards-Based Curriculum, is providing basic skills and content for all learners in the regular classroom. The goal for this potential-based approach is to discover and develop the potential of all children, not just achieving children. Specific activities, based on standards, are included here. This curriculum provides the foundation for skills and content, but does not include depth and complexity for learners that need greater challenges. The Standards-Based Curriculum includes components such as:

➢ prescribed content and basic standards;

➢ teacher-developed and teacher-implemented content;

➢ textbooks and worksheets;

➢ teacher instruction;

➢ cooperative learning;

➢ knowledge, comprehension, and application levels of thinking;

➢ daily assignments (retention); and

➢ similar curriculum for all students.

Level Two: Standards-Based Differentiated Curriculum

The Standards-Based Curriculum may not contain the depth and complexity necessary to meet the diversified affective and cognitive needs of the high-ability learners in our classrooms. The curriculum must be differentiated to encourage critical and creative thinking, problem solving, communication, and collaboration. Level Two supports the development of a Standards-Based Differentiated Curriculum by teachers, making it more meaningful and engaging for learners. The Standards-Based Differentiated Curriculum includes components such as:

➢ the learning experience, which consists of the content, process, and product;

➢ teacher-developed and learner-implemented content;

> ➢ the teacher becoming facilitator;
> ➢ higher level thinking skills;
> ➢ depth and complexity;
> ➢ integrated in-depth knowledge;
> ➢ pretesting and curriculum compacting;
> ➢ high-level differentiated curriculum; and
> ➢ development of independent learning skills.

Level Three: Learner-Based Differentiated Curriculum

Within Learner-Based Differentiated Curriculum, there are three subareas. Students are introduced to Explorations to discover how to learn independently and what is available to learn, and Investigations allow them to go deeper into the topics they have found meaningful in their Explorations. In-Depth Study is the highest level of learning, and it provides passion-developed experiences for the learner. (Please note: The students begin as *students* and progress through learning processes to the role of *learners*). The Learner-Based Differentiated Curriculum includes components such as:

> ➢ learner-developed and learner-implemented content,
> ➢ the teacher becomes the facilitator and the student becomes the learner,
> ➢ applications and extensions of the standards,
> ➢ passion-based learning,
> ➢ application of independent learning skills,
> ➢ mentorships with producing adults in fields of passions,
> ➢ opportunities for becoming producers of knowledge, and
> ➢ beginning of the "quest."

The following are the basic components of the three subareas of Learner-Based Differentiated Curriculum. Students begin with Explorations, which are teacher developed/student based; include diverse possibilities, information gathering, and knowledge/comprehension; are short term; and have an emphasis on content. These lead to Investigations, in which the student is becoming a learner and the teacher is becoming a facilitator. Investigations include diverse possibilities, the discovery of a passion area, and an emphasis on content and process. These are long-term studies with multiple means of reporting. Investigations lead to In-Depth Study. The teacher is now a facilitator and the student is now the learner. The In-Depth Study is implemented and assessed by the learner who learns that social and emotional growth is the foundation for lifelong learning. The focus is on high-level content that features depth and complexity. The learner will work with a mentor who is involved in all aspects of the learner's experience. This subarea features long-term involvement to provide gifted learners with the experience to develop their potential of becoming producers of knowledge rather than consumers of knowledge

Modification of Roles in the Three Levels of Curriculum

In Level One, the students are working as students and responding to the goals and strategies of the teachers. In Level Two, the students are now involved in some decision making, goal development, and the completion of strategies and are seen as students/learners. The teachers are also in transition and are considered teachers/facilitators. In Level Three, the students are now learners and are responsible for their own learning while the teachers are facilitators of the learning process and work directly with the learners but do not define or limit the content, process, or product of the learner.

Summary of the Three Levels of Curriculum

In summary, it is essential to provide differentiated curriculum, instruction, and experiences for all learners who demonstrate potential and for those identified for gifted programming (Betts, 2004). As Betts (2004) explained:

> ➤ Level One, Standards-Based Curriculum (Prescribed Curriculum and Instruction), may not be challenging for gifted learners.
> ➤ Teachers move on the continuum of teaching from dispenser of knowledge to facilitator of the learning process. Teachers of gifted learners are able to fulfill both roles.
> ➤ Students move on the continuum of learning from the role of student to the role of learner.
> ➤ All three levels are necessary for total growth of the learner. This includes implementation of specific standards in the affective domain of learning.
> ➤ Level Two, Standards-Based Differentiated Curriculum (Teacher-Differentiated Curriculum and Instruction), provides learners with challenging and exciting curriculum. Most of the learners' time should be devoted to Level Two.
> ➤ Level Three, Learner-Based Differentiated Curriculum, permits the discovery and development of passion areas that may be unique to each learner.

> Level Three encourages development of self-discovery, self-esteem, creativity, and autonomy. Ten percent of classroom time should be devoted to Level Three.

> The Level Three In-Depth Study is the highest level of learning and provides learners experiences that are selected, developed, completed, and assessed by the learners. (p. 191)

The Autonomous Learner Model: Optimizing Potential

Unless we open the door to possibilities and nurture the development of the learner, the potential may go unrealized. The Autonomous Learner Model, designed by and for gifted learners, does not rely on test scores or labels to provide a powerful potential-laden environment. The model's five dimensions tap into unique areas not found in many traditional classroom settings, allowing the individual potential of all learners to blossom to the fullest.

The ALM was developed specifically to meet the diversified cognitive, emotional, and social needs of learners (see Figure 8.1). The model is currently implemented at all grade levels with the gifted and talented, as well as all learners in the regular classroom. Emphasis is placed on meeting the individualized cognitive and affective needs of learners through the use of activities in the five major dimensions of the model. The standards and activities are such that all incorporate specific elements intended to address the affective needs of the learner. Without attending to the heart, we cannot hope to develop the mind.

Dimension One: Orientation

What do students need to know, understand, and be able to do? What can they become? What is talent? What is potential? What are group-building skills? What school opportunities are available? Dimension One, Orientation, is the foundation of the Autonomous Learner Model: optimizing potential. In this dimension, the students (and teachers and parents) will not know the essential components of the approach, why it is being used, and what the outcomes will be. There are four separate areas in this dimension:

> *Understanding giftedness, talent, intelligence, and creativity.* All learners come to us with potential; some have giftedness, talent, higher levels of intelligence, and different forms of creativity. While moving toward performance, potential is the foundation.

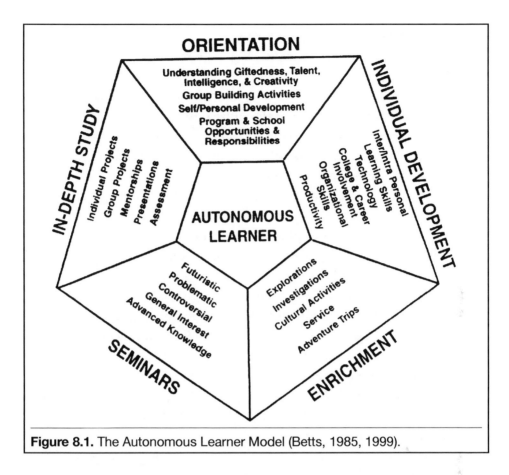

Figure 8.1. The Autonomous Learner Model (Betts, 1985, 1999).

> *Group-building activities.* The need for belonging is addressed through group-building activities that break boundaries, provide opportunities for working together, and plant the seeds of friendship.

> *Self-/personal development.* Emphasis on cognitive and affective development includes formal and informal involvement with the students in terms of who they are, how they can accept themselves, and what they are capable of becoming.

> *Program and school opportunities and responsibilities.* A 3-year plan of what is available in the classroom, the school, and the community is presented to the students so they can look at their areas of potential and performance and begin to make decisions based on what is available in the future. It is important to note that the students are in the role of students and the teachers are still in the role of teachers. The transition to learners and facilitators has not yet begun in this dimension.

Dimension Two: Individual Development

Individual Development provides for growth through the development of cognitive, emotional, social, and physical skills, as well as attitudes necessary for lifelong learning. Teachers discover potential and performance and decide what is necessary for each child and the entire class.

> ➤ *Inter-/intrapersonal.* The continuation of self-/personal development, which is initiated in the Orientation Dimension, is integrated and extended throughout the entire model.

> ➤ *Learning skills.* Learning skills (creativity, problem finding and problem solving, thinking skills, writing skills, and research skills) are presented and are implemented throughout the model.

> ➤ *Technology (next generation).* To be a 21st-century learner, the understanding and implementation of new technology is an ongoing process and necessary for lifelong, autonomous learners.

> ➤ *College and career involvement.* Students become aware of the preparation necessary, and the pathways available, to be successful in their chosen careers, tapping into the expertise of guidance counselors and professionals in the field.

> ➤ *Organizational skills.* This area explores the students' learning style in terms of organization (e.g., sequential or random approaches, lists or graphic organizers).

> ➤ *Productivity.* This area provides students with the opportunity to develop the skills necessary in planning, developing, and completing products.

Dimension Three: Enrichment

What does the learner want to explore and to investigate? How do these areas fit into lifelong learning? The Enrichment dimension of the model provides learning in the students' areas of interest, not in the content provided by the teachers. This is the opportunity for students to learn to develop content, to process, and to enhance their own potential and performance through Explorations, Investigations, Cultural Activities, Service Projects, and Adventure Trips.

> ➤ *Explorations.* Many times students are limited because they do not know what is available or how to learn more about their interests. This area provides students with the basic skills and knowledge of how to learn independently. The teacher provides opportunities for the stu-

dents to explore for themselves, in and outside of the classroom and school.

➢ *Investigations.* After the successful completion of several Explorations, students become aware that they are ready to begin Investigations. It is not the teacher who decides this, but the student. The students approach the teacher and explain why these areas are important and indicate possible topics they want to learn at a deeper level over an extended period of time. A contract is essential at this time, with the idea that flexibility is always needed. Changes are essential when we truly learn on a deeper level.

➢ *Cultural Activities.* The students are not always aware of their culture or the cultures of other people. Through involvement in a wider community, the students learn about government, art galleries, places of business, museums, and individuals who are making a difference in their communities from a cultural point of view. These must be hands-on, chaperoned experiences that take place in the community. For example, sitting in the first row at a dress rehearsal of the symphony orchestra can open new areas of interest, especially if a student meets the conductor and members of the symphony informally. The best experiences are realized when students decide where to go, make the preparations themselves, process the experience afterward, and write the thank-you notes on personalized cards.

➢ *Service Projects.* Service projects have become an essential ingredient in education. They allow the learner to serve, give, help, care for, and have empathy for others. Students find this area to be one of the most fulfilling in their entire learning experience.

➢ *Adventure Trips.* Have the students draw a circle of 1,000 miles around their community, and then have them study the map and decide where they want to go. All of the knowledge, the planning, the fundraising, the contacting of people, and the final adventure trip must be developed by the students. Then, it is time to go! Many groups are successful in this area, while others learn because they are not able to succeed.

Dimension Four: Seminars

In Dimension Four, Seminars, the students are moving toward the roles of learners and are more autonomous in their participation than they have been in the previous dimensions. They now have the appropriate skills and the developed passions to work on short-term group or individual projects that demonstrate their autonomy. One to three Seminars need to be completed before they select Dimension Five, In-Depth Study, for their long-term participation.

Basic components. Facilitators provide the following guidance and parameters to the learners. As a student develops his or her Seminar, there are three basic components to include (Betts & Kercher, 2009):

> *Presentation of factual information.* This means basic knowledge of a concept or skill will be demonstrated through a handout or PowerPoint, Prezi, or other type of presentation so the audience has the requisite information to gauge the learner's depth of knowledge and understanding.

> *Group activity.* Develop an activity in which the audience members can participate. It can be a small- or large-group activity involving them in making a decision or solving a problem related to the Seminar and the student's passion area of learning.

> *Closure.* After the activity, the student should bring the Seminar to closure by asking the audience members the following questions:
>   ◈ What did you learn?
>   ◈ What did you experience?
>   ◈ And now what?
>   ◈ How will you use this new information?

Different types of Seminars. Facilitators provide the learners with the following areas to explore:

> *Futuristic.* Present one component of your passion area to a group of people from a futurist's point of view. Include techniques used today by futurists.

> *Problematic.* Define a major problem within your passion area and design a presentation that includes major problems and at least three solution scenarios.

> *Controversial.* Within your passion area, select information that is controversial to different groups of people at this time. Present a Seminar that describes many different points of view.

> *General interest.* Select an aspect of your passion area that would be relevant to many students and adults and make a presentation to the appropriate audience.

> *Advanced knowledge.* Present your Seminar to selected audience members that already have in-depth knowledge of your area of pursuit.

Dimension Five: In-Depth Study

The In-Depth Study is the highest level of learning within the ALM. Involvement in this dimension is based on the development of the appropriate skills necessary for passion learning. The learners are responsible for the entire project and have a support team that includes the facilitator, the mentor, and other learners as they process through this complex method of thinking and learning. Facilitators provide guidance and parameters for the learners, who will demonstrate their ability to complete an In-Depth Study. A contract is completed before the learner begins the In-Depth Study. This guarantees that the basics for the study have been developed by the learner and have been demonstrated throughout the completion of projects in the Enrichment Activities (Dimension Three) and the Seminars (Dimension Four). The contract addresses the following information:

- the topic,
- a description,
- the content standards,
- materials,
- human resources (including the mentor),
- final product details,
- presentations, and
- assessment.

Standards of the Autonomous Learner Model

Basic standards of the Autonomous Learner Model (Betts, 1985; Betts & Kercher 1999, 2009) provide a fundamental background for the model. The standards presented here have been modified as the ALM continues to be assessed and evaluated by teachers, learners, and administrators. Learners will:

- Develop more positive self-concept and self-esteem.
- Comprehend their own abilities in relationship to self and society.
- Develop skills to interact effectively with peers, siblings, parents, and other adults.
- Develop critical thinking, creative thinking, decision-making, and problem-solving skills.
- Increase knowledge in a variety of areas.
- Discover and develop individual passion area(s) of learning.

> ➢ Integrate activities that facilitate responsibility for learning in and out of the school setting.
> ➢ Ultimately become responsible, creative, independent, and lifelong learners.

Develop More Positive Self-Concept and Self-Esteem

In order to meet this standard, the learners will:
> ➢ Continue to develop a deeper understanding of self, abilities, interests, aptitudes, and areas of strengths.
> ➢ Develop appropriate social skills, including communication, problem-solving, decision-making, and conflict resolution skills.
> ➢ Critique their social skills and what is needed for ongoing development.
> ➢ Comprehend inter-/intrapersonal development of self.

Comprehend Their Own Abilities in Relationship to Self and Society

In order to meet this standard, the learners will:
> ➢ Develop an understanding of the terms "potential," "giftedness," "talent," "intelligence," and "creativity."
> ➢ Relate these concepts to their own lives.
> ➢ Understand eminent people who are seen as gifted and talented.
> ➢ Comprehend the current approaches to the education of gifted and talented learners in today's society.
> ➢ Develop their own definitions of ability and how it relates to their potential.

Develop Skills to Interact Effectively With Peers, Siblings, Parents, and Other Adults

In order to meet this standard, the learners will:
> ➢ Comprehend the dynamics of the group process.
> ➢ Apply the dynamics of the group process to their environment.
> ➢ Comprehend different group roles that facilitate or deter group development.
> ➢ Assess the dynamics of the interaction of the small and large groups within the class.
> ➢ Understand the importance of developing skills, concepts, and attitudes for lifelong learning.

➢ Participate in activities developed to provide skills, concepts, and attitudes for lifelong learning.

➢ Demonstrate the skills, concepts, and attitudes that have been presented in this area.

➢ Comprehend the importance of organizational skills in their lives.

➢ Explore the organizational skills that they believe they already possess.

➢ Develop organizational skills they believe they will need for future development.

Develop Critical Thinking, Creative Thinking, Decision-Making, and Problem-Solving Skills

In order to meet this standard, the learners will:

➢ Comprehend critical thinking, creative thinking, decision-making, and problem-solving skills.

➢ Apply critical thinking, creative thinking, decision-making, and problem-solving skills to learning.

➢ Create Seminars and In-Depth Studies that involve the use of critical and creative thinking.

➢ Continue to analyze the use of critical and creative thinking in everyday life.

➢ Identify the technology available in the world today.

➢ Decide what technology is needed in the next few months and the next year.

Increase Knowledge in a Variety of Areas

In order to meet this standard, the learners will:

➢ Demonstrate the ability to select a topic that is meaningful.

➢ Successfully complete group and/or individual enrichment activities.

➢ Verbally report what was learned and how it was learned.

➢ Comprehend the process of an investigation.

➢ Successfully complete an investigation.

➢ Comprehend and share the process of completing an investigation.

Discover and Develop Individual Passion Area(s) of Learning

In order to meet this standard, the learners will:

➢ Comprehend the process of an In-Depth Study.

➢ Select a passion area for an In-Depth Study.
➢ Design a learning contract for an In-Depth Study.
➢ Participate in an In-Depth Study.
➢ Create ongoing and final presentations demonstrating what has been experienced and what has been learned in the In-Depth Study.
➢ Evaluate their personal participation and their In-Depth Study.
➢ Become a practicing "professional" within the passion area.
➢ Receive appropriate feedback from involved audiences concerning the In-Depth Study.
➢ Develop appropriate products that are visual, oral, kinesthetic, written, and technological.
➢ Incorporate appropriate products in passion areas of learning.

Integrate Activities That Facilitate Responsibility for Learning in and Out of the School Setting

In order to meet this standard, the learners will:
➢ Comprehend the importance of college and career involvement.
➢ Explore colleges and careers of their choice.
➢ Complete college and career projects.
➢ Comprehend the definition of involvement in ongoing cultural activity.
➢ Comprehend the basic format of a Seminar.
➢ Select interest topics in the areas of futuristic, problematic, controversial, general interest, and advanced knowledge.
➢ Develop, present, and assess a complete Seminar.
➢ Receive feedback from appropriate audiences concerning the Seminar.
➢ Demonstrate lifelong learning skills through informal projects outside of school.

Ultimately Become Responsible, Creative, Independent, and Lifelong Learners

In order to meet this standard, the learners will:
➢ Seek feedback from facilitators, peers, and other appropriate audiences concerning lifelong learning activities.
➢ Participate in ongoing service activities in the community.
➢ Focus on passion learning as the highest level of learning.

➢ Develop, participate in, complete, present, and assess ongoing Seminar and In-Depth Studies throughout life. Include appropriate products that become a capstone of their content, process, and product.

➢ Comprehend the concept of lifelong learner and complete several Seminar and In-Depth Studies that provide them with the opportunities for creative production.

➢ Ultimately commit to the goal of being one that can impact the world in a positive direction through their abilities, their skills, and the ability to work in collaboration with other learners on passion projects.

➢ Facilitate others in their quests of becoming . . .

➢ Begin their own journey of lifelong learning.

Blending the ALM and RtI

Response to Intervention and the Autonomous Learner Model share common ground, as they both address the cognitive, academic, social, emotional, and physical needs of all learners and are potential-based, allowing us to discover, feed, and nurture the potential of *all* learners. These needs are determined by the learners, the parents, the educators, and community members.

The Three-Tiered Approach

When ALM activities are introduced, the learner may require scaffolding in order to be successful, may engage in the activity at a basic level, or may excel by adding depth, complexity, and additional understanding because he or she has the opportunity to "go beyond." The activity is appropriate for all three levels of learners if it is open-ended and requires creativity and deeper thought. The ALM has proven to be successful with all learners, as it is responsive to the needs of all learners. Some gifted learners will take an activity like "Night of the Notables" and become completely immersed in the life and times of the person they chose. Others will learn basic research techniques from the activity but may not engage at a higher level with the same passion. The activity may tap into a learner's potential in a way other assignments have not, allowing the learner to engage more deeply than ever before. Again, you will notice the elements that specifically attend to the affective needs of the learner, providing growth and development in that area, as well as in the cognitive domain.

Table 8.1 shows how the dimensions of the Autonomous Learner Model are appropriate across the three-tiered Response to Intervention framework, with Tier 3 taking the dimension to the highest level of learning.

Universal level (Tier 1). In the universal classroom setting, progress monitoring and pre-/postassessments are utilized to inform instructional decisions. All adults work collaboratively to determine the expectations to be taught, reinforced, and monitored. Differentiated instruction is critical at the universal level; teachers and support staff adjust instruction based on the needs of the learner. Through schoolwide screening and ongoing progress monitoring, students are identified for more intense support at Tiers 2 and 3.

In Tier 1, all students engage in learning opportunities via the Orientation and Individual Development dimensions of the ALM as a foundation to become autonomous. All students benefit from identifying:

➢ How do I learn?
➢ How can I work effectively in group situations and develop collaboration skills?
➢ What does it mean to be an autonomous, lifelong learner?

Targeted level (Tier 2). Targeted interventions are provided to students identified as at risk for academic and/or social challenges and/or students identified as underachieving who require specific supports to make sufficient progress in general education. This holds true for struggling learners and highly able learners. Interventions at the targeted level are typically delivered in a small-group setting for a portion of the school day. It is expected that the instruction will be more intense and explicitly targeted to the needs of the learner. Depending on the resources at hand and student need, interventions may be delivered via a push-in model, wherein additional adult support is provided in the classroom setting for small-group work, or in a pull-out model, where small groups of students work outside the classroom environment. The students' response to intervention is carefully monitored and instruction is adjusted as appropriate. In Tier 2, the classroom teacher and the gifted specialist collaborate to determine possible constructs for the Enrichment dimension of the ALM. The Enrichment dimension components are an excellent way to provide learners who are ready to engage in targeted opportunities that include a greater level of depth and complexity. Students who demonstrate the potential for needing more depth, complexity, and interest- and passion-based curricula than their age peers self-differentiate the standard curriculum to develop

Table 8.1

Autonomous Learner Model Dimensions and the Three-Tiered Approach

	Tier 1	Tier 2	Tier 3
Dimension One: Orientation (and the four areas)	• Understanding giftedness, talent, intelligence and creativity • Group building • Self-/personal development • Program and school opportunities and responsibilities	• Understanding giftedness, talent, intelligence and creativity • Group building • Self-/personal development • Program and school opportunities and responsibilities	• Revisit basic areas of Orientation that would provide a deeper foundation for the learner
Dimension Two: Individual Development (and the six areas)	• Inter-/intrapersonal • Learning skills • Technology • College and career involvement • Organization skills • Productivity	• Inter-/intrapersonal • Learning skills • Technology • College and career involvement • Organization skills • Productivity	• Continue with additional skills (e.g., creativity, research, communication) to enhance the learner
Dimension Three: Enrichment (and the five areas)	• Explorations • Investigations • Cultural Activities • Service Projects • Adventure Trips	• Explorations • Investigations • Cultural Activities • Service Projects • Adventure Trips	• Continue Explorations and Investigations; most of the learner's time is dedicated to the In-Depth Study
Dimension Four: Seminars	• Futuristic • Problematic • Controversial • General interest • Advanced knowledge	• Futuristic • Problematic • Controversial • General interest • Advanced knowledge	• Continue to discover new content to be presented in the Seminar format after the completion of the In-Depth Study
Dimension Five: In-Depth Studies	• Introduction to In-Depth Studies • Completion of Explorations, Investigations	• Completion and continuation of Explorations, Investigations, and Seminars • Review of the individual learning process for becoming an autonomous learner	• Individual projects • Group projects • Mentorships • Presentations • Assessment (All of the above are fully developed for the highest level of learning.)

a course of study that goes beyond the traditional curriculum in a way that best fits their learning, their strengths, and their interests.

Intensive level (Tier 3). Intensive interventions are provided to students with the highest level of academic and/or behavior needs based on ongoing progress monitoring and/or diagnostic assessment. For the high-ability or gifted learner whose needs are intensive, a self-contained classroom setting for a particular subject or full day may be required. For the learner who continues to struggle after small-group instruction, interventions at the intensive level are typically longer in duration and may be delivered one-on-one. In Tier 3, as learner potential continues to develop, more intensive opportunities are required to ensure optimal growth. The Seminar and In-Depth Study dimensions of the ALM provide a powerful venue for those learners who need the most intensive programming. These are learners for whom the foundation has been established to allow the highest level of self-directed learning to emerge. The gifted specialist and support staff utilize the ALM's Seminar and In-Depth Study dimensions with learners who are ready for intense group and individual learning opportunities. The criteria for learning and the criteria for assessment of that learning are developed by the learner.

Autonomous Learner Model and the Three-Tiered Approach

Table 8.2 describes how different activities for gifted students fit across the three RtI Tiers using the Autonomous Learner Model.

Summary

The ALM and RtI provide a problem-solving approach embracing collaboration. The collaborative conversations occur among teachers, with parents, and with students to glean a full picture of each learner's potential, strengths, interests, passions, and talents. Classroom teachers collaborate with other teachers, gifted education specialists, parents, and the learner to discuss strengths, interests, and areas for growth. The ALM provides the vehicle for the learners to personalize learning and make it their own.

Bringing the learner's voice into the process is an essential component of ALM and RtI.

Table 8.2

Sample Activities Within the Three-Tiered Approach

ALM Dimensions	Tier 1	Tier 2	Tier 3
Dimension One: Orientation	• Temperature Readings • I Am Poem • Teacher Questionnaire • Student Questionnaire • Discussion of the Teacher and Student Questionnaire	• Temperature Readings • I Am Poem	
Dimension Two: Individual Development	• Guess Who's Coming to Dinner?	• Personalized Learning Portfolio	
Dimension Three: Enrichment	• 5-minute Exploration • 9-step process of an Exploration	• 8 levels of Explorations • Beginning Investigations	• Advanced Investigations • In-Depth Studies (one for a long period of time or several that relate to the learner's passion development)
Dimension Four: Seminars		• Development and completion of the Learner Seminar • 10 steps of the Learner Seminar	
Dimension Five: In-Depth Studies			• Development and completion of first In-Depth Study • 12 steps of the In-Depth Study • Questions to ponder for In-Depth Study Closure

Giftedness is not an activity but the response to the appropriate activity.

—George T. Betts

References

Betts, G. T. (1985). *Autonomous Learner Model for the Gifted and Talented.* Greeley, CO: Autonomous Learning Publications and Specialists.

Betts, G. T. (2004). Three levels of curriculum and instruction. *Roeper Review, 26,* 190–191.

Betts, G. T., & Kercher, J. K. (1999). *Autonomous Learner Model: Optimizing ability.* Greeley, CO: Autonomous Learning Publications and Specialists.

Betts, G. T., & Kercher, J. K. (2009). The Autonomous Learner Model for the Gifted and Talented. In J. Renzulli (Ed.), *Systems and models for developing programs for the gifted and talented* (2nd ed.). Wethersfield, CT: Creative Learning Press.

Potential. (n.d.). In *Merriam-Webster's online dictionary.* Retrieved December 11, 2011 from http://www.merriam-webster.com/dictionary/potential

Potential. (n.d.). In *The American Heritage® Dictionary of the English Language, Fourth Edition.* Retrieved December 11, 2011 from http://www.thefreedictionary.com/potential

CHAPTER NINE

THE INTEGRATED CURRICULUM MODEL

A Basis for RtI Curriculum Development

Joyce VanTassel-Baska

This chapter will address the features of the Integrated Curriculum Model (ICM), the research base for its use, and the applications of the model to curricula for gifted learners in each subject area. The application of the model to the RtI initiative is also explored, showing its efficacy for working with myriad students with special needs.

Overview of the ICM Model

The Integrated Curriculum Model was first proposed in 1986, based on a review of the research literature on what worked with gifted learners, and further expounded upon in subsequent publications (VanTassel-Baska, 1986; VanTassel-Baska & Little, 2011; VanTassel-Baska & Stambaugh, 2006). The model is comprised of three interrelated dimensions that are responsive to different aspects of the gifted learner:

> ➤ *Emphasizing advanced content knowledge that frames disciplines of study.* Honoring the talent search concept, this facet of the model ensures that careful diagnostic-prescriptive approaches are employed to enhance the challenge level of the curriculum base. Curricula based on the model would represent advanced learning in any given discipline.

> ➤ *Providing higher order thinking and processing.* This facet of the model promotes student opportunities for manipulating information at complex levels by employing generic thinking models like Paul's Elements of Reasoning (Paul & Elder, 2001) and more discipline-specific models like Sher's (2003) Nature of the Scientific Process. This facet of the ICM also promotes the utilization of information in generative ways, through project work and/or fruitful discussions.

> ➤ *Organizing learning experiences around major issues, themes, and ideas that define understanding of a discipline and provide connections across disciplines.* This facet of the ICM scaffolds curricula for gifted learners around the important aspects of a discipline and emphasizes these aspects in a systemic way (Ward, 1981). Thus, themes and ideas are selected based on careful research of the primary area of study to determine the most worthy and important ideas for curriculum development, a theme consistent with reform curriculum specifications in key areas (American Association for the Advancement of Science, 1990; Perkins, 1992). The goal of such an approach is to ensure deep understanding of disciplines, rather than misconceptions.

These three relatively distinct curriculum dimensions have proven successful with gifted populations at various stages of development and in various domain-specific areas. Taken together, these research-based approaches formed the basis of the Integrated Curriculum Model (VanTassel-Baska, 1986, 1998; VanTassel-Baska & Little, 2011; VanTassel-Baska & Stambaugh, 2006). Figure 9.1 portrays the interrelated dimensions of the ICM.

The ICM approaches the design and implementation process of working with gifted learners in schools as comprehensive. Too often gifted learners end up with a curriculum diet that is composed of a little acceleration, a little project work, and a few higher level thinking opportunities. The ICM organizes these features into one package, thus allowing gifted learners and others to experience a more integrated pattern of learning. This integrated approach also reflects recent research on learning. Studies have documented that better transfer of learning occurs when higher order thinking skills are embedded in subject matter (Minstrell & Kraus, 2005; National Research Council, 2000; Perkins & Salomon, 1989), and teaching concepts in a discipline is a better way to produce long-term learning than teaching facts and rules (Marzano, 1992). Our understanding of creativity also has shifted toward the need for strong subject matter knowledge as a prerequisite (Amabile, 1996). Because the

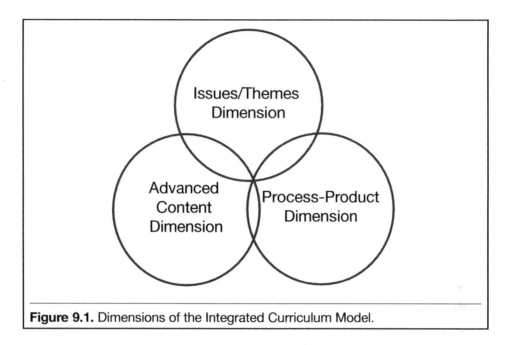

Figure 9.1. Dimensions of the Integrated Curriculum Model.

ICM is organized around the subject matter standards, it uses the content core as a basis for modification and integration.

Recent reviews of curricular interventions for the gifted have found that the content modification features exemplified in the ICM have the greatest prevailing effect on an accelerative approach (Johnsen, 2000; Van Tassel-Baska & Brown, 2007). The fusion of these approaches is central to the development of a coherent curriculum that is responsive to diverse needs of talented students while also providing rich challenges to all for optimal learning.

Theoretical Underpinnings

The theoretical support for the Integrated Curriculum Model comes primarily from learning theory and development. One source is the work of Vygotsky (1978). One aspect critical to the model is the zone of proximal development, where learners must be exposed to material slightly above their tested level in order to feel challenged by the learning experience. This idea was expanded on by Csikszentmihalyi (1991) in his concept of flow where gifted learners demonstrated a broader and deeper capacity to engage learning than did typical students (Csikszentmihalyi, Rathunde, & Whalen, 1993).

A second aspect of this theory of learning is the view of interactionism, whereby the learner increases learning depth by interacting with others in the environment to enhance understanding of concepts and ideas. Ideas are validated and understood through the articulation of tentative connections made based on a stimulus such as a literary artifact, a film, a piece of music, or a problem. Learning increases as interactions provide the scaffolding necessary to structure thinking about the stimulus (Vygotsky, 1978).

A theory of constructivism whereby learners construct knowledge for themselves is also central to the instructional emphases within the application of the ICM. This theory is central to the tenets of the teaching and learning models found in the ICM curriculum and a central thesis to the model itself as students must be in charge of their own learning in respect to each dimension of the model, whether it be content acceleration, project-based learning opportunities, or discussion-laden experiences in which concepts, issues, and themes are explored.

Another theoretical influence on the model was the work of Mortimer Adler and his Paideia Proposal (1984) that posited the importance of rich content representing the best products of world civilization coupled with the relevant cognitive skills to study them, appropriately linked to the intellectual ideas that spawned the work of the disciplines and philosophy. His worldview of curriculum was highly influential in thinking about the role of academic rationalism in a curriculum for the gifted, even as cognitive science was the predominant force in the larger environment.

Finally, the theory of multiculturalism espoused by James Banks (1994a, 1994b, 2001) and more recently by Donna Ford (2005; Ford & Harris, 1999) speaks to the aspect of the ICM concerned with students making a better world through deliberate social action, whether through the resolutions brought to policy makers as a result of Problem-Based Learning (PBL) work or the studies of technology use in researching issues or the concerns for censorship in the history of great literature. Moreover, this theoretical orientation also provides a major emphasis on the works of minority authors both in this country and abroad, as well as an attempt to acknowledge multiple perspectives in student understanding of any content area, especially history.

Application

The application of the ICM was the basis for all of the William and Mary units of study. Whether the unit was in science, language arts, social studies, or math, it employed a curriculum framework that was based on the model—using advanced content, higher level thinking, and problem solving and developing a macro concept. This framework was then structured into a set of goals and outcomes for each domain of study, assessments were designed to address important outcomes in the domain, and instructional strategies like PBL were designed into the units to promote student engagement. Other teaching-learning models also were deliberately designed to promote constructivism and student-created meaning. Metacognitive tools such as reflection emphasized student self-efficacy. Affective components were addressed through the choice of readings and viewings that required an affective response.

Current work on the ICM for the gifted has continued to focus on a merger with the curriculum reform principles advocating world-class standards in all traditional curricular areas (VanTassel-Baska & Little, 2011). The major shift in thinking regarding this orientation is from one that looks only at the optimal match between characteristics of the learner and the curriculum to a model based on performance in various domains, thereby letting the level of functioning determine who is ready for more advanced work in an area rather than a predictive measure. Thus, differentiation for any population is grounded in differential standards of performance at a given period of time. Standards are constant; time is the variable. Such an approach holds promise for gifted students in that the level and pace of curriculum *can* be adapted to their needs, and the existing and new Common Core State Standards call for the kind of focus that curriculum makers for gifted students have long advocated—higher level thinking, interdisciplinary approaches, and an emphasis on student-centered learning. All of these features were designed into the William and Mary units of study, using the ICM as the template.

Gifted students need high but realizable expectations for learning at each stage of development. Other students can benefit also from working to attain such standards. By the same token, gifted students can also benefit from a developmental and personal perspective on fostering their abilities at a close-up level, an emphasis requiring organizational models such as tutorials, mentorships, and small clusters to support it.

What types of students are best served using the ICM? The ICM was designed for students who have strong intellectual abilities and/or strong academic aptitudes in the areas in which curriculum units have been designed. In the last several years, however, the research on effectiveness that has been conducted suggests that more students benefit from the curriculum beyond the population for whom it was intended (e.g., Swanson, 2006). The collection of research on the units of study that used the ICM as the organizing framework has increasingly shown that the benefits of the units for all students is significant and important educationally in respect to achievement and motivation.

Because the units are content-based, students who are strong in only one area can benefit greatly from their use. For example, strong readers can grow from exposure to the language arts units even if they are not identified as gifted, as the readings in the unit can be used with strong readers, and the other differentiation features of the units serve to enrich their understandings in key ways. Because the units employ open-ended opportunities to learn, higher level opportunities to learn, and the use of multicultural literature, they work very well with promising learners from low-income backgrounds and children of color. Moreover, the consistent use of instructional scaffolds becomes a critical aspect in elevating the level of learning for these groups.

In the final analysis, the model has been useful in designing curriculum that can be used with all learners, although the gains have suggested the greatest growth has occurred for promising learners, high-level readers, and students who are gifted in relevant subject areas of the curriculum.

Research on the Effectiveness of the Integrated Curriculum Model

Studies have been conducted over the past decade to discern the learning gains of gifted learners, promising learners from low-income and minority backgrounds, and typical learners exposed to the units of study based on the model. Both quasi-experimental and experimental designs have been employed to demonstrate differences among similar ability groups of learners using curricula based on the model compared to those who have not been exposed to such curricula. An overview of these studies and their results in language arts, science, and social studies follow.

The ICM has been tested substantially in the areas of science and language arts in particular, using quasi-experimental research designs that compared pretest-posttest performance of students participating in the William and Mary units in these areas with the performance of similar students who were not taught using the units. The presentation of claims for student learning in each area follows, demonstrating the results related to the specific curriculum, as well as supporting the notion of ongoing data-collection efforts to maintain high-quality curriculum development and implementation. In each content area, details and results of earlier studies are presented first, followed by discussion of more recent studies.

Science curriculum effectiveness data. The William and Mary problem-based science curricular units for high-ability learners in grades 2–8 have been rigorously evaluated to ensure both effectiveness in promoting student learning gains and acceptance by teachers. Not only have the units and accompanying training materials undergone four major revisions in the course of their development but also the next-to-last edition of the units was field tested across multiple school districts. The goals of the program across all of the units have consistently been threefold: (a) to develop student understanding of the concepts of systems and change, (b) to develop specific content learning that is unit dependent, and (c) to develop scientific research processes. More specific learning outcomes have been delineated under each of these broad overarching goals, in keeping with the intent of the National Science Education Standards and the Benchmarks for Science Literacy that call for substantive content linked to high-level scientific processes and the understanding of meaningful scientific concepts (American Association for the Advancement of Science, 1990; National Research Council, 1996).

Evidence of effectiveness for Project Clarion. Although the problem-based units discussed above address all three major goals in the science curriculum framework (i.e., the concepts of systems and change, specific content learning, and scientific reasoning), the PBL curriculum studies focused explicitly on student application of scientific research and integrating students' understanding of science content and inquiry, reasoning, and problem-based reasoning skills. In the more recent units developed under Project Clarion, we addressed the development of curiosity in science and critical and creative thinking and emphasized concept development in systems and change and the scientific research process. The PBL was part of the ICM units, not the lead feature. Goals and student outcomes are aligned to the National Science Education Standards. Each lesson includes instructions that detail the purpose, time needed, suggestions on how to implement the lesson, and ways to conclude and extend the lessons.

Language arts curriculum effectiveness data. The William and Mary curricular units have also been evaluated for effectiveness in terms of teaching literary analysis and interpretation and persuasive writing as language arts manifestations of higher level thinking (VanTassel-Baska, Zuo, Avery, & Little, 2002). As such, the research findings contribute to our understanding of the importance of embedding higher order skills into content and build on prior understanding of effective research-based strategies for teaching writing (e.g., Burkhalter, 1995). Specifically, they suggest that gifted learners who deliberately receive instruction in literary analysis and interpretation and persuasive writing demonstrate significant and important growth when compared to equally able students not receiving such instruction. Each unit of study has 4–5 lessons that focus on the development of these skills, using short literary selections to buttress discussion and interpretation. Writing prompts are derived from the readings. After 6 weeks of classroom instruction, differential gains have consistently been recorded across units, teachers, and school types.

Evidence of effectiveness for Project Athena. Based on the growing research evidence on the use of the William and Mary language arts units with gifted learners, the team at William and Mary began a 3-year longitudinal study of using the curriculum in Title 1 schools and inclusive classrooms with all learners (VanTassel-Baska, Bracken, Feng, & Brown, 2009). This new effort used the William and Mary language arts units in high-poverty settings with all learners.

The results of this 3-year study demonstrated the power of using more high-level materials with all learners, not just the gifted. In addition, they illustrated the importance of using multiple approaches to assess learning and multiple pathways for learning, as the project team also developed a reading comprehension program, entitled *Jacob's Ladder*, to enable students to move to higher level thinking once comprehension has been attained.

Social studies curriculum effectiveness data. One comprehensive study has been conducted to date to examine the efficacy of the social studies units of study developed by the Center for Gifted Education at William and Mary under the Javits-supported Project Phoenix (Little, Feng, VanTassel-Baska, Rogers, & Avery, 2007). In a quasi-experimental study in which social studies units modeled on the ICM were used with Title I students in grades 3–8, results suggested that significant and important learning gains were accrued by students in selected classrooms in the dimensions of content mastery, concept development, and higher level thinking. Teacher results confirmed the unevenness of student learning as connected to implementation fidelity, although group analyses suggested that teachers enhanced their ability to use selected differentiation strategies as a result of the training and curriculum differentiation use designed into the units. Subanalyses showed growth for both gifted and nongifted students in the study and for low socioeconomic learners as well as minority students.

Research evidence for use of the ICM with special populations. The Center for Gifted Education's studies of science and language arts curriculum effectiveness in heterogeneous Title I classrooms have shown that a curriculum written for gifted learners is also effective with nongifted learners, given the use of proper differentiation, scaffolding, and flexible grouping techniques (VanTassel-Baska et al., 2008). Scaffolding may be in the form of a supplemental curriculum or specific differentiated strategies and pacing. In language arts, *Jacob's Ladder* was developed to provide additional scaffolding in reading to expose less-experienced students to models that bridge lower level to higher level thinking. *Navigator* novel studies were written so that students could have more choice in novel selections and differentiated activities at a given reading level. In science, specific models were developed to scaffold students' thinking in planning scientific investigations. Pacing of units was also modified within the regular classroom, and instructional grouping encouraged effective discussions.

The research evidence we have collected over multiple projects, as well as evidence collected by our colleagues (e.g., Swanson, 2006), suggests that the William and Mary units are effective with these special populations of promising learners. In fact, the data suggest that, given enough time, these students perform at comparable levels to more advantaged learners in selected areas like persuasive writing (VanTassel-Baska et al., 2002). In Title I schools, all groups showed significant and important growth in key areas of language arts, social studies, and science learning after using the units, including groups of diverse learners. The use of such curricula, however, must be accompanied by faithful use of the teaching-learning models provided that scaffold instruction at higher levels of discourse and thought, particularly for less-experienced learners in a subject area.

Examples of Curricula and Instructional Modifications Using the ICM

The examples provided in Table 9.1 illustrate the major dimensions of the ICM and the translation of those dimensions into differentiated approaches in each major content domain. Each of these translations have been developed into full-blown units of study with both pre- and postassessments to assess the extent of student learning. Most units of study have also been judged exemplary by the National Association for Gifted Children (NAGC) annually since 1999, when the standards for curricula were established.

The examples demonstrate the ways in which accelerated learning is promoted; the ways in which the higher level processes of thinking, problem solving, and research are exploited; the types of generative products that students create; and the conceptual foundation for given units of study. These dimensions then frame the units of study for each area of learning, with varying units by grade level that typically cut across two grades. The shorthand table descriptions also suggest the nature of instructional approaches employed.

Each unit of study also has student outcomes that focus on content, process, product, and concept learning matched to unit-based assessments. For

Table 9.1
The Integrated Curriculum Model by Subject Area and Dimensions of Sample Unit Study

Content Area and Topic	Accelerative Approaches	Higher Level Thinking/ Problem Solving	Product Tasks	Concept and Theme
Science: botany, plants	Pretesting and compacting, study of botany at primary level	Reasoning model, scientific investigation skills, questions	Logs, experimental designs, PBL resolution project and presentation	Systems: understanding the elements, boundaries, interactions, inputs, and outputs of cells, plants, and terrariums
Language arts: autobiographies of writers	Reading selections calibrated two grade levels above	Reasoning model, literature web, persuasive writing, research project	Autobiographical project with talent development markers	Change: understanding that change is everywhere, related to time, caused by people or nature, and so forth
Mathematics: study of animal populations	Advanced math skills in graphing, statistics, and estimation	PBL	Problem resolution in oral and written forms for a real-world audience	Models that are conceptual and physical are applied to understand phenomena
Social studies: ancient Egypt	Emphasis on the systems of ancient civilizations that made them great	Emphasis on historical analysis, document study, and trends	Research paper on an historical issue	Change: patterns of change over time as chronicled by historical events within and across cultures

example, teachers may assess students on critical thinking, concept development, content acquisition, and product sophistication using the tools of instrumentation and rubrics provided. Exemplars also provide guidance for judgment regarding student performance.

Funded for 20 years by the United States Department of Education, these units of study were intended not only as models of exemplary curriculum but also as the basis for differentiation in classrooms. They have been successfully used in all states and 18 countries to provide the modifications needed for gifted learners.

Use of the ICM for Tiered Instruction in RtI

The ICM adapts well to the demands of the RtI model in that it can be used with all populations in respect to the teaching and learning models and then be applied in more targeted ways as advanced content and higher level processes are employed (see Table 9.2). The aspects of the model that have universal application for use at Tier 1 of the RtI model are the use of critical and creative thinking skills and problem-solving processes, resulting in high-level products. The incorporation of these skills into deliberate scaffolds allows the universal application to be successful for all learners. Thus, the use of a literature web to explore literary elements such as theme, symbolism, and structure may be used with all students even as the level of the reading material may be adjusted. In a similar way, Problem-Based Learning scaffolds may be used with all learners, even as the sophistication of the products will vary, based partially on ability.

At Tier 2, the use of advanced readings in the language arts curriculum renders the activities and questions relevant to the literature selected accessible only to advanced readers, typically those two grade levels above the norm and those identified as gifted. Literature for the units has been deliberately and carefully selected to respond to the needs of intellectually gifted students. This same reading issue extends to the social studies curriculum. In math and science, the targeted aspects of the units based on the ICM lay in the manipulation of advanced concepts and the higher level problem-solving processes employed.

At Tier 3, ICM units may be used to promote individual learning through their many opportunities for choice in assignments, readings, and special projects. Each unit also has a research project with options for issue exploration,

Table 9.2
Application of the ICM to the Demands of RtI

Advanced Content	Higher Level Skills/Product Generation	Concepts, Themes, and Issues
Tier 1: not applicable	Tiers 1–3 with product expectations aligned with capacity	Tier 1: some applicability, based on content knowledge attained and transferred
Tier 2: accessibility of readings based on level	See above	Tier 2: accessible, based on advanced content attainment
Tier 3: accessibility for advanced independent work, resulting in relevant products for the discipline under study	See above	Tier 3: accessible, based on independent exploration at more advanced and in-depth levels of work, resulting in high-quality interdisciplinary products

Note. The model also supports the other features of the RtI framework in more indirect ways.

again allowing for independent use by gifted students. Additional resources accompany each unit and provide deeper exploration of issues, themes, and topics of interest related to the focus of the unit. Interdisciplinary explorations are also encouraged and may be most fruitful for students in need of greater challenge.

Screening, Assessment, and Progress Monitoring in the ICM

The ICM model employs pre- and post-performance-based assessments in each of its dimensions within each unit of study. Thus, teachers can easily determine the baseline level of students in respect to content learning, capacity to engage in higher level thinking tasks, and conceptual levels across subject areas via the use of a macro-concept assessment tool. The preassessment data may be used as an instructional tool to adjust the teaching needed in key areas of the units of study. These data may also be used to determine student outcome data after a unit has been taught, thus providing ongoing information for planning the next instructional module needed in a given subject area in respect to content skills, higher level thinking, and concept development.

In addition to the use of pre- and postassessments to document positive growth in learning overall, the units use formative assessments for purposes of progress monitoring during the teaching of a given unit of study. This progress monitoring may involve a collection of activities designed to assess how well students are applying their understanding to new material in the areas of content, process, and concept dimensions of the curriculum. For example, as students study the concept of systems in science, they are asked to apply their understanding of systems to the social science system of state transportation. The activity, which they also illustrate and articulate to their peers, suggests their understanding of the concept at a level necessary for transfer to new applications. Such evidence of student performance provides the teacher the information necessary to modify instruction for individuals or groups of learners, based on the result. In several of our studies, we have found that students have difficulty transferring their understanding of boundaries as a part of a system. Consequently, teachers target that component of a system for further teaching.

The units also provide evidence from longer term individual products of the progress in learning that has accrued for students in all three dimensions of the model. Assessment forms are provided for teacher use to chart the extent to which the product meets the standards of higher level thinking, problem solving, and cross-disciplinary content expected.

Self, peer, and teacher assessment approaches are used for writing in both social studies and language arts in order to provide a way for all three groups to chart the baseline and progress on important dimensions of the writing process and key models of writing. Journal writing may be examined by the teacher and the student to determine appropriateness to the prompt, fluency, and use of language devices.

How Is Differentiation Addressed in the Model?

At the most basic level, differentiation for the gifted is addressed through the construction of the ICM to begin with. It was designed based on the research evidence of 50 years in working with the gifted in multiple settings as to what has worked with them. Thus, the dimensions of advanced content, the use of higher level processes with a high-quality product expectation, and higher level concept development that allows for interdisciplinary connections distill that research base.

At the level of translation of the model into practical use, the units of study designed around the ICM also employ deliberate features of differentiation that include the use of acceleration, including pretesting and streamlining, complexity, depth, challenge, abstractness, and creativity. Each unit has designed activities and questions that incorporate these features in a systematic way. Question asking is a major feature of the units, with questions designed around higher level thinking models that frame the use of critical and creative thinking at levels of analysis, synthesis, and evaluation. The creation level of prompts is often included in the scaffolding. Other models of thinking are also used to provide open-endedness in questions and depth of understanding.

Family Engagement Through the ICM

The ICM has proven to be an effective support for parents who want to work with their children on the improvement of skills or deeper understanding of concepts. Parent training sessions have been held where selected activities in the units have been modeled and practiced with an eye to home application. In one project, we made refrigerator magnets for parents to have at home on the scaffolds their children were learning to think at higher levels, encouraging parents to hold conversations, using the language of the thinking processes, and applying it to current events and issues. In other instances, the use of reading lists for parents, accompanied by sample questions, has provided a home-based application for them to use with their children. Moreover, many of the units of study are regularly used by homeschooling parents who find the units easy to follow for purposes of such individualized instruction.

The Use of Collaborative Problem Solving in the ICM

The ICM routinely includes opportunities for collaborative problem solving in all dimensions of the model. Students work together in dyads, triads, and quads to solve problems, design projects, and discuss text. Although some independent work is encouraged, the units portray a collaborative model of learning as the ideal, especially for project-based learning. In the problem-based science units, for example, students work in small investigative teams throughout the unit to address the real-world problem they have been given as stakeholders.

The expectations for collaborative learning clearly delineate individual accountability and specific product outcomes according to a predetermined deadline. Although the student teams are encouraged to do their own assessments of tasks, responsibility, and timeline, teachers engage in helpful monitoring of these metacognitive tasks to ensure efficient and effective use of time and appropriate allocation of workload and resources.

Outcomes anticipated from such collaborative work include growth in oral and written communication skills, interdisciplinary application capacity, and facility with the use of resources for research. In addition, it is anticipated that students will gain significant skills in metacognition as assessed by reflection papers and planning, monitoring, and assessment tools that they construct.

Beyond the units of study themselves, the implementation of such differentiated learning opportunities requires the strong problem-solving abilities of teachers, parents, and others in the environment. Such collaborative conversations can have a positive impact on the optimal match of curriculum and instruction to student needs.

Concerns About the Use of the ICM: What Supports Must Be in Place?

As in the use of any curriculum that is going to be successful, it is critical to consider certain variables related to effective implementation. These variables include the nature and extent of professional development, the leadership for innovation in a school and district, and the commitment of teachers to positive change in their classrooms. Obviously, the ICM will not work well in contexts that do not evidence these three variables.

In respect to professional development, the ICM requires that teachers have systematic training in the scaffolds and models that are built into the curriculum for 2–4 days per year with follow-up support in their buildings in the form of observation and coaching. Professional development is best accomplished by using the unit materials as the basis for it, as teacher inferencing is reduced with ease of implementation being the result. The nature of the professional development should include the performance-based assessments that are central to understanding authentic growth in the students using the units, key activities that highlight how the models are employed, and the features of differentiation that are built into the units of study.

In respect to leadership for innovation, no curriculum will be successful if the principal and superintendent are not willing to support experimentation and positive change for gifted learners in the school and district. Principals must see their central role as that of instructional leader, and superintendents must see that everyone learning something new every day is a central tenet necessary for a school system to work properly. The ICM requires flexibility in terms of implementation, with teachers, principals, and central office staff supporting the efforts of teachers to elevate instruction in a consistent way for the gifted learner and others who can benefit from the model.

With respect to teacher commitment, the ICM is not a formulaic curriculum approach but rather one that requires thoughtful interpretation for use in the classroom. Teachers will need to stay with it over a number of years in order to improve their skills at using such an integrated and differentiated curriculum base. For teachers who lack such commitment over time, the model as translated into the units of study may be too complex for them to handle effectively. Although it has shown success in being used by trained regular classroom teachers, it is ideally implemented by teachers trained in gifted education.

Conclusion

The Integrated Curriculum Model represents one of only a few curriculum models designed for gifted learners in specific subject matter domains that have been fully developed into usable units of study at all stages of development K–12, have been piloted and field tested consistently across districts and states, and have demonstrated impressive growth gains for students in content, higher level process skills, and concepts. The model has consistently demonstrated coherence in its design and development and fidelity of implementation in selected contexts. It has been enthusiastically received by teachers of the gifted as a powerful way to ensure challenge and sufficient differentiation for the gifted. It has proven to be a basis for motivating both students and their teachers to learn more at higher levels. In sum, it represents an important baseline for future work in curricula for the gifted: work that provides both a model and its practical applications and demonstrates how our best learners can show significant and important intellectual growth through the process of systematic differentiation practices, especially within an RtI framework.

References

Adler, M. (1984). *The Paideia Program*. New York, NY: Macmillan.

Amabile, T. (1996). *Creativity in context*. Boulder, CO: Westview Press.

American Association for the Advancement of Science. (1990). *Science for all Americans: Project 2061*. New York, NY: Oxford University Press.

Banks, J. (1994a). *Multiethnic education: Theory and practice* (3rd ed.). Boston, MA: Allyn and Bacon.

Banks, J. (1994b). *An introduction to multicultural education*. Boston, MA: Allyn and Bacon.

Banks, J. (2001). *Cultural diversity and education: Foundations, curriculum, and teaching*. Boston, MA: Allyn and Bacon.

Burkhalter, N. (1995). A Vygotsky-based curriculum for teaching persuasive writing in the elementary grades. *Language Arts, 72,* 192–196.

Csikszentmihalyi, M. (1991). *Flow: The psychology of optimal experience.* New York, NY: Harper Perennial.

Csikszentmihalyi, M., Rathunde, K. R., & Whalen, S. (1993). *Talented teenagers: The roots of success and failure.* New York, NY: Cambridge University Press.

Ford, D. (2005). Integrating multicultural and gifted education: A curricular framework. *Theory Into Practice, 44,* 125–138.

Ford, D., & Harris, J. J. (1999). *Multicultural gifted education.* New York, NY: Teachers College Press.

Johnsen, S. K. (2000). What the research says about curriculum. *Tempo, 20*(3), 25–30.

Little, C. A., Feng, A. X., VanTassel-Baska, J., Rogers, K. B., & Avery, L. D. (2007). A study of curriculum effectiveness in social studies. *Gifted Child Quarterly, 51,* 272–284.

Marzano, R. (1992). *Cultivating thinking in English.* Urbana, IL: National Council of Teachers of English.

Minstrell, J., & Kraus, P. (2005). Guided inquiry in the science classroom. In J. Bransford, A. Brown, & R. Cocking (Eds.), *How students learn: History, mathematics, and science in the classroom* (pp. 475–477). Washington, DC: National Academy Press.

National Research Council. (1996). *National Science Education Standards.* Washington, DC: National Academy Press.

National Research Council. (2000). *How people learn.* Washington, DC: Author.

Paul, R., & Elder, L. (2001). *Critical thinking: Tools for taking charge of your learning and your life.* Upper Saddle River, NJ: Prentice Hall.

Perkins, D. (1992). Selecting fertile themes for integrated learning. In H. H. Jacob (Ed.), *Interdisciplinary curriculum: Design and implementation* (pp. 67–75). Alexandria, VA: Association for Supervision and Curriculum Development.

Perkins, D., & Salomon, G. (1989). Are cognitive skills context bound? *Educational Research, 18,* 16–25.

Sher, B. T. (2003). Adapting science curricula for high-ability learners. In J. VanTassel-Baska & C. Little (Eds.), *Content-based curriculum for high-ability learners* (pp. 191–218). Waco, TX: Prufrock Press.

Swanson, J. (2006). Breaking through assumptions about low-income, minority gifted students. *Gifted Child Quarterly, 50,* 11–24.

VanTassel-Baska, J. (1986). Effective curriculum and instructional models for talented students. *Gifted Child Quarterly, 30,* 164–169.

VanTassel-Baska, J. (1998). *Excellence in educating gifted and talented learners* (3rd ed.). Denver, CO: Love.

VanTassel-Baska, J., Bracken, B., Feng, A., & Brown, E. (2009). A longitudinal study of reading comprehension and reasoning ability of students in elementary Title I schools. *Journal for the Education of the Gifted, 33,* 7–37.

VanTassel-Baska, J., & Brown, E. (2007). Towards best practice: An analysis of the efficacy of curriculum models in gifted education. *Gifted Child Quarterly, 51,* 342–358.

VanTassel-Baska, J., Feng, A., Brown, E., Bracken, B., Stambaugh, T., French, H., . . . Bai, W. (2008). A study of differentiated instructional change over three years. *Gifted Child Quarterly, 52,* 297–312.

VanTassel-Baska, J., & Little, C. (2011). *Content-based curriculum for high-ability learners* (2nd ed.). Waco, TX: Prufrock Press.

VanTassel-Baska, J., & Stambaugh, T. (2006) *Comprehensive curriculum for the gifted.* Boston, MA: Pearson.

VanTassel-Baska, J., Zuo, L., Avery, L. D., & Little, C. A. (2002). A curriculum study of gifted student learning in the language arts. *Gifted Child Quarterly, 46,* 30–44.

Vygotsky, L. S. (1978). *Mind in society: The development of higher psychological processes.* Cambridge, MA: Harvard University Press.

Ward, V. (1981). *Educating the gifted: An axiomatic approach.* Ventura County, CA: Leadership Training Institute for Gifted and Talented.

CHAPTER TEN

RECOGNIZING AND NURTURING POTENTIAL ACROSS THE TIERS
U-STARS~PLUS

Mary Ruth Coleman and Sneha Shah-Coltrane

Every student comes to us as a unique individual with a set of strengths, interests, quirks, and challenges. Teachers do not get to select who their students are, but as educators, we do have the profound responsibility of helping each student become, as fully as possible, the best that he or she can be. Each interaction with a student gives us the opportunity to nurture his or her strengths and provide support in areas of challenge, but we must choose to do so. The choice is ours to make. In choosing how to interact with each child we should remember, however, that nurturing all students' potential to help them thrive in school and life is the primary role of an education. The first choice we make in interacting with our students is how to view them (Coleman, 2005). Here are two views of the same child, David, and through these we can see how important our choice can be.

A View of David as "At Risk"

David is small for his age. He is fairly manipulative and causes trouble for his peers and his teachers. He often uses his "charming" nature to make friends and get out of difficulties, but his first-grade teacher is on to this manipulation. He is always asking questions and interrupting the class for his needs. The teacher cannot get a word in edgewise with David's need to question everything. He is in constant motion. He is never able to complete anything—no writing or reading assignment is ever finished. He just can't sit in his seat and get anything done, and then he cries about it. The teacher often cannot read his papers because the handwriting is very poor and his spelling is random and not good at all. This also affects his math because his work is messy. David wants to tell the teacher the answers all the time instead of writing them down, and this takes up her class time. He loves to be the center of attention—no matter what the cost. One day, the teacher noticed David's "sneakiness" surface more than usual. David had started stealing items from the classroom to take home. David was taking home puzzles, science center materials, and nonfiction books. His teacher wanted to punish him right away to show him what was right and wrong.

A View of David as "At Potential"

David is an affectionate little boy who uses his charm to make friends and sometimes to get out of difficult situations. His thinking is advanced and his sense of social perceptiveness is high. He is incredibly curious and inquisitive. There are times when the teacher feels like she has to specifically concentrate on his questions in order to try to fulfill his curiosity about the world. Even though David does not like to do seatwork, the teacher has worked out an arrangement where certain not-so-preferred activities are completed in order to move onto more preferred activities (the "eat your spinach before dessert" principle).

David is an active learner who loves to work with his hands. Anything that has to be built or manipulated with tools or his own hands is a cherished learning activity for him. When batteries and bulbs showed up in the science center, he was the first to get his hands on them—he also enjoyed working for hours to get different light patterns to shine. He wanted to take one of his creations home to share and cried when he was not allowed to do so. After that, batteries and bulbs began slowly disappearing, and it turned out that he was gradually taking them home. His teacher wanted to find a balance between appropriate consequences for taking the materials home without permission and not suppressing his interest and excitement of learning about science. She talked with David and let him know that she understood how important it was for him to share his creation at home but that she only had so many batteries and bulbs for the class and they were expensive and had to be shared with the whole class. She then asked that he return any materials that he had at home and said that when they were back in the classroom she would allow him to recreate his masterpiece to share. She also reminded David that he was not to take things that did not belong to him. This seemed to meet both the teacher's and student's needs. Over the course of time, because of his social perceptiveness, inquisitiveness, and skill in science, David has become a leader for the class.

"At Risk" or "At Potential"?

These two views of David, at risk and at potential, are both legitimate choices. David's behavior is the same in each case; it is the teacher's interpretation of his behavior that differs. The choice the teacher makes is critical because her viewpoint will lead to very different interactions with him and will likely result in entirely different outcomes for David. The at-potential view concentrates on strengths and supports positive development while the at-risk view often leads to punitive deficit-focused interrelations. Viewing a child's behavior as at potential helps the teacher place the child on a positive trajectory toward success.

The Teacher's Observation of Potential in Students (TOPS) observation forms were designed to support teachers with an at-potential interpretation of student behavior (Coleman, Shah-Coltrane, & Harrison, 2010). TOPS was developed as part of the U-STARS~PLUS (Using Science, Talents, and Abilities to Recognize Students~Promoting Learning for Underrepresented Students), an approach for addressing the needs of young children in grades K–3 whose potential might be overlooked due to cultural/linguistic differences, economic disadvantages, or disabilities (Coleman & Shah-Coltrane, 2010a).

In this chapter, we will describe U-STARS~PLUS, show how it fits within the RtI tiers, and discuss the role of nurturing potential within gifted education. Throughout the chapter we will keep David in mind to see how this approach works for a child who is viewed as at potential instead of as at risk.

U-STARS~PLUS

U-STARS~PLUS was designed to support general education teachers, grades K–3, in the early recognition of and nurturing of potential in children from economically disadvantaged and/or culturally/linguistically diverse families, and children with disabilities. The heart of U-STARS~PLUS (as seen in the center of Figure 10.1) lies in providing a nurturing environment, recognizing potential, and responding to this potential for each child (Coleman & Shah-Coltrane, 2010a). Creating an environment that nurtures each child emotionally and intellectually, working intentionally to recognize the strengths of each child, and responding to these strengths with enriched and challenging learning activities is the foundation for U-STARS~PLUS. The five points of the star show the components of U-STARS~PLUS and each will be briefly discussed below.

High-End Learning Opportunities

U-STARS~PLUS relies on three keys to create a high-end learning environment: curriculum differentiation, dynamic assessments of students learning, and the use of flexible grouping. Providing a high-end learning environment creates intellectual nurturing that children need to thrive (Ford & Grantham, 2003; Hertzog, 2005). Although a high-end learning environment is important for all children, it is essential for children who more often find themselves viewed as at risk: children of color, students from poverty, and those who are culturally/linguistically diverse, as well as children with disabilities (Coleman Shah-Coltrane, 2010a, 2011; Ford, 2007). Furthermore, the confluence of race, culture, language, and disability with poverty can jeopardize a child's access to high-end learning opportunities (Blanchett, Klingner, & Harry, 2009).

Remember David? The school that David attended was a rural school in the middle of a cornfield in eastern North Carolina. Many of the teachers in his school grew up in the small community and had been teaching there for several years; in fact, a few of the teachers remembered teaching David's mother. The principal of the school, however, seemed to change every year or two, and the district had new superintendents 3 years in a row. David's school was ranked close to the bottom in student achievement, and it failed to show appropriate student growth for 2 years. The district was on the state's list for possible takeover, and teacher morale was very low. Unfortunately, the constant changes in leadership undermined the district's and school's ability to make the positive changes necessary to improve student growth, and so the cycle continued. The state told the district it was at risk, the district told the school it was failing, the principal told the teachers they were inadequate, and the teachers struggled to see any positive outcomes for their students. The district's energy for sev-

U-STARS~PLUS

Using Science, Talents, and Abilities to Recognize Students ~ Promoting Learning for Underrepresented Students

HIGH-END LEARNING OPPORTUNITIES

☆ Curriculum differentiation
  → curriculum compacting
  → tiered activities
  → learning centers/stations
  → independent studies/group projects
  → questioning/higher order thinking skills
☆ Dynamic assessment to inform classroom instruction
☆ Flexible grouping
☆ Classroom support materials:
  → Science and Literature Connections
  → Family Science Packets

INFRASTRUCTURE BUILDING for SYSTEMIC CHANGE

☆ Capacity building of leadership and teachers (i.e., professional development and policy)
☆ Fidelity of implementation (district, school, classroom)
☆ Accountability (district, school, classroom, child)

TEACHERS' SYSTEMATIC OBSERVATIONS

☆ "At potential" versus "at risk" mindset
☆ Teacher's Observation of Potential in Students (TOPS), a teacher tool to recognize students with outstanding potential from underserved populations
☆ Building a body of evidence, using informal and formal measures over time

HANDS-ON/INQUIRY-BASED SCIENCE

☆ Promotes thinking, achievement, and language development
☆ Captivates students' interest through real-world setting and content integration
☆ Focuses on exploration and problem solving; not solely based on traditional expository methods/verbal skills

FAMILY and SCHOOL PARTNERSHIPS

☆ Family involvement programs
☆ Effective parent conferences and communication
☆ Family Science Packets
☆ Cultural understanding (impact of poverty, diversity, and social/emotional needs)

NURTURE · RESPOND · RECOGNIZE

Figure 10.1. U-STARS~Plus big star.

eral years had been focused on figuring out who was to blame for the lack of accomplishments, and most often the blame landed on students like David!

Students whose families are economically disadvantaged often attend schools with fewer resources and higher turnover in leadership, where the "pedagogy of poverty" emphasizes deficits rather than enrichment, which is even more likely to happen for children of poverty *and* color (Blanchett et al., 2009; Coley, 2011; Kohn, 2011). The U-STARS~PLUS approach shifts the focus in classrooms, schools, and districts toward access to high-end learning opportunities that nurture strengths and provide support for the development of each child's potential. We will explore this shift as we follow how David's school implements U-STARS~PLUS.

Teachers' Systematic Observations

The second component of U-STARS~PLUS is the teachers' systematic observations to help them recognize potential areas of strength in their students. The tool used in U-STARS~PLUS to help teachers recognize potential in their students is the TOPS. The TOPS supports the systematic documentation of student strengths as observed within natural learning environments (e.g., classroom, playground, lunchroom, media center). Observations can be made in multiple settings, over time, and across different tasks. This kind of systematic observational information provides ecologically valid, authentic information about the child's strengths and learning needs (Bagnato, 2007). The nine domains on the TOPS address areas of strength that are often associated with giftedness (Coleman et al., 2010):

> ➤ learns easily, shows advanced skills;
> ➤ displays curiosity and creativity;
> ➤ has strong interest;
> ➤ shows advanced reasoning and problem solving;
> ➤ displays spatial abilities;
> ➤ shows motivation;
> ➤ shows social perceptiveness; and
> ➤ displays leadership.

Using the TOPS, teachers first observe their entire class. Areas of strengths and students observed with the whole-class TOPS show patterns that can help the teacher understand her classroom as a setting where students' potential can be nurtured. These patterns also help the teacher determine if specific student observations using the individual TOPS would be helpful. Both forms (whole class and individual) give examples of student behaviors teachers might observe if a child has strengths in one of the nine domains. These include both teacher-pleasing and non-teacher-pleasing behaviors. For example, within the domain of Learns Easily, observers might see that a child is eager to learn and has a lot of information, but they may also see that she corrects the teacher and other students in class and refuses to show her work—only wanting to share the answers. In this case, both the teacher-pleasing and non-teacher-pleasing behaviors show the teacher that the child has strengths in this domain.

By using the TOPS, David's teacher began to see his strengths and interpret his behaviors differently. Her view of David moved from at risk to at potential. After observing her whole class, David's teacher was amazed to find that his name showed up in several areas and that he had several tally marks indicating repeated observations. She smiled as she noted that the behavior she observed most frequently fell in the non-teacher-pleasing categories, and she decided to complete an individual observation for David because of the pattern of strengths she saw. Figure 10.2 shows the traits that David's teacher observed that helped her to move from an at-risk to an at-potential view of him.

Teachers self-report that through using the TOPS they are better able to recognize high-potential in students of color and plan ways to support each student's strengths (Harradine, Coleman, Winn, & Shah-Coltrane, 2012). For David, it means that his teacher sees his strengths and will work to nurture them.

Hands-On Inquiry-Based Science

The cornerstone of U-STARS~PLUS is science. Science is ideal because it has rich content that is of high interest to children, stimulating their natural curiosity and problem solving. Experiential science activities are the ideal platform for recognizing children with outstanding potential whose strengths may not be seen during didactic teaching with paper-and-pencil products (Amaral, Garrison, & Klentschy, 2002; Carlston, 2000; Simon-Dudgeon & Egbert, 2001; Worrell & Erwin, 2011). Hands-on science activities form the basis for vocabulary development while allowing learning to continue (Nyberg & McCloskey, 2008; Simon-Dudgeon & Egbert, 2001). Science can easily be integrated with other subject areas like reading, writing, and math to give students meaningful reasons to use their skills in learning about, communicating, and interpreting findings from their experiments. The U-STARS~PLUS science focus fits well with the emphasis on STEM (science, technology, engineering, and mathematics) curricula. And, because young children are natural-

Learns Easily: Eager to learn, lots of information, retains information, strong memory, appears bored with "easy work," does not show work

Shows Advanced Skills: Story telling, vocabulary, seeks out nonfiction, understands advanced number concepts, challenges teacher to go further, manipulates situations for specific purposes

Displays Curiosity and Creativity: Questions, experiments, explores, is curious, enjoys doing things in new ways, puts ideas together, offers unique responses, has an active imagination, does not follow the rules, will not wait for directions

Has Strong Interests: Is able to lose himself in his work, unusually advanced interest, recognized as an expert, resists transitions when working in areas of interest

Shows Advanced Reasoning and Problem Solving: Keen observations, makes mental connections, predicts outcomes, offers many solutions, can adapt strategies to solve problems, does not do well on tests with limited answers, can be argumentative

Displays Spatial Abilities: Good sense of direction, figures out how things work, takes things apart, creates three-dimensional structures, prefers hands-on activities, brings gadgets and toys, moves around often

Shows Motivation: Is a self-starter, is persistent in chosen tasks, is independent, does not follow a typical path, sometimes questions everything

Shows Social Perceptiveness: Displays humor, responds to needs of others, strong sense of justice, enjoys group work, easily distracted by others, overly talkative and social, is easily distracted by others' needs

Displays Leadership: Is sought out by others, can influence others, is positive and compassionate, can be manipulative and strong willed to get what he wants

Figure 10.2. Evidence of David's potential: Teacher observations using the TOPS.

born scientists working to discover their world, they love engaging in hands-on science!

Family and School Partnerships

The importance of family and school partnerships to support the success of the child has been well documented (Davis, 2003; VanTassel-Baska, Patton, & Prillaman, 1991). An integrated support system where families are engaged in the schooling of the child leads to better school attendance, stronger academic performance, and more positive school self-efficacy for the child (Cropper, 1998). The fourth component of U-STARS–PLUS looks at ways to support this engagement through family involvement programs, often focused on academics; effective family/parent conferences, using the TOPS to address the child's strengths; family science take-home activities based on the *U-STARS–PLUS Family Science Packets* (Coleman & Shah-Coltrane, 2010b); and helping teachers develop cultural competence in understanding diverse families (Coleman & Shah-Coltrane, 2010a; Villegas & Lucas, 2002).

The *U-STARS–PLUS Family Science Packets* (Coleman & Shah-Coltrane, 2010b) are designed to engage families in interesting science activities with their child. Twenty lessons, based on the National Science Education Standards (National Research Council, 1996), can be used to enhance the science curriculum and promote family engagement. Each activity is written in family friendly language (a Spanish translation is also provided) with guiding questions, data collection sheets, and follow-up activities. Students take the science activities home (all needed materials get packed into a one-gallon Ziploc bag), they complete the experiments with their families and collect the data, and the data come back to school to be compiled and analyzed in class. Engaging families through fun, nonthreatening science activities helps to build strong relationships that can support the child's academic success.

Infrastructure Building for Systemic Change

The final component of U-STARS–PLUS is different than the other four. This component focuses on the structures that need to be in place for the successful implementation of the work. Successful implementation requires intentional planning to create the capacity needed for systemic change (Wallace, Blasé, Fixsen, & Naoom, 2008). This capacity must include professional development, policy, fidelity of implementation, and accountability. A professional development kit with seven modules supports the implementation of U-STARS–PLUS (Coleman & Shah-Coltrane, 2010a). The role of high-quality professional development is central in building the knowledge and skills needed to sustain change (U.S. Department of Education, 2001). Table 10.1 shows the areas of professional development covered in the U-STARS–PLUS modules that reflect the five components of the star. Each of the U-STARS–PLUS modules has three levels: introductory, intermediate, and advanced. A needs assessment should be completed to guide the planning of professional development for individual, school, or district needs. If all the modules are completed, the professional development will likely span a 2–3-year time period supporting implementation from emerging to optimal. The

Table 10.1
U-STARS~PLUS Professional Development Modules

	Module	Level 1: Introduction	Level 2: Intermediate	Level 3: Advanced
1	Overview of U-STARS~PLUS	Overview of U-STARS~PLUS (4–5 hours)	Implementing U-STARS~PLUS (2–3 hours)	Creating Synergy (2 hours)
		Purpose, goals, and philosophy; "Big Star" components; core beliefs; classroom fidelity rubric	"Big Star" components and their interrelationship; using fidelity rubrics; creating an observable environment	"Big Star" interrelated components and synergy within the classroom; U-STARS~PLUS's fit with other initiatives at school and district levels
2	Gifted Education and "Giftedness"	Introduction to Gifted Education (3–4 hours)	Special Populations: Underrepresented Gifted Children (3 hours)	Social and Emotional Needs and Underachievement (2 hours)
		Definitions of *gifted*; young gifted children and asynchronistic development; potential and intelligence; goals of identification; challenges of underrepresentation	Special populations of gifted and high-potential learners (culturally/linguistically diverse, economically disadvantaged, and twice-exceptional students)	Social and emotional needs of gifted learners; identifying and reaching gifted learners who are underachieving
3	High-End Learning Opportunities	Overview of Differentiated Instruction (3–4 hours)	Kicking It Up a Notch (6–8 hours)	Using Assessment Effectively (3 hours)
		Differentiation for high-end learners; how to use Science and Literature Connections and Family Science Packets	Basic classroom differentiation "toolkit" (curriculum compacting, tiered assignments, learning centers/stations, independent and small-group studies, higher order thinking, effective questioning)	Making classroom learning activities even better; appropriate assessments and decision making; data-driven decision making; developing rubrics
4	TOPS (Teacher's Observations of Potential in Students)	Systematic Teacher Observations Using TOPS (2 hours)	Creating an Observable Environment (2 hours)	Building a "Body of Evidence" (3–4 hours)
		Purpose and general use of TOPS; recognizing student behaviors that indicate potential	TOPS multiple purposes and multiple settings; using TOPS for conferencing and to inform/guide instruction	Building and using a "body of evidence" for referral, planning, and placement decisions

Table 10.1, continued

	Module	Level 1: Introduction	Level 2: Intermediate	Level 3: Advanced
5	Best Practices in Science	Hands-On Science (2 hours) — Introduction to hands-on science and guided inquiry; using science as a verb; using science to help recognize potential in young children; integrating other content areas with science	Guided Inquiry (2 hours) — Integrating other content areas with science; exploring levels of inquiry and activities that promote learning	Science in the Classroom (1 hour) — "Big ideas" in science; differentiating science activities (free exploration, hands-on/lab, inquiry-based science) in the classroom
6	Family Involvement	Reaching and Connecting With All Families (1–2 hours) — Communication; reframing deficit thinking; building partnerships	Connecting With All Families Around Social and Academic Needs (1–2 hours) — Family involvement and partnerships; social needs of children; using Family Science Packets to build academic partnerships.	Strength-Based Conferencing With Parents (1–2 hours) — Engaging families through strength-based conferencing; planning to increase family involvement
7	Leadership Cadre	Systemic Change (1–2 hours) — Professional development; principles of change; U-STARS~PLUS scope and sequence; fidelity of implementation; creating a leadership cadre	Using Implementation Fidelity for Planning (1 hour) — Using fidelity for planning at school and district levels; integrating U-STARS~PLUS across district and school initiatives; classroom integration of U-STARS~PLUS; principles of change; implementation plan	Sustainability and Grant Writing (1 hour) — Sustainability of programming; integration and fit; challenges and solutions; "optimal implementation"; grant-writing strategies and tips

Note. Adapted from Coleman and Shah-Coltrane (2010a).

kit includes guidance for developing a transformational professional development plan for implementing U-STARS~PLUS at the school and district levels (Coleman & Shah-Coltrane, 2010a).

A second aspect of capacity building for implementation is policy development (Gallagher, 2006). Policy development takes place at many levels—the classroom, school, district, and state. Even federal policies will impact how resources are secured and delivered to meet student needs (Brown & Abernethy, 2011; Gallagher, 2006). Sustainability of change often hinges on seeing these changes reflected in policy (Fixsen, Naoom, Blasé, Friedman, & Wallace, 2005).

Fidelity of implementation is critical to capacity building and to keeping the quality and integrity of the work high. The approach that U-STARS~PLUS has taken is to intentionally combine fidelity with flexibility to support scale-up across multiple kinds of sites (Coleman & Shah-Coltrane, 2010a). Fidelity helps to maintain the integrity of the work while flexibility honors the range of needs, strengths, and resources across contexts. The fidelity rubric designed for U-STARS~PLUS classroom implementation describes what practice looks like as it is emerging, developing, reaching proficiency, and being optimized (see Table 10.2).

The areas described include the use of the TOPS to help teachers recognize children with high potential; classroom differentiation to respond to students' strengths; the use of hands-on, inquiry-based science; and the importance of family involvement. In the rubric, each area is defined and described across the levels of implementation setting the critical fidelity markers for *what* is expected. Yet, flexibility is also built into this approach as teachers use their judgment to guide *how* they will reach the implementation markers.

So, for example, David's teacher is developing her ability to differentiate in the classroom. She is building a stronger theoretical understanding of differentiation and why it is important, and she is also using the differentiation strategies (e.g., curriculum compacting, tiering of assignments, learning centers and stations, independent and small-group contracts, and higher level questioning) to address her students' needs. She has done some curriculum compacting for David in math and is allowing him to work on an independent science project focused on electricity and magnetism. David is currently designing an electromagnet to collect loose paperclips.

Table 10.2
Classroom Fidelity of Implementation Rubric

U-STARS~PLUS Fidelity of Implementation: Classroom Rubric

Teacher Name: _____   School/District: _____   Date: _____

Classroom Critical Components	Not Evident	Emerging	Developing	Proficient	Optimal
Teacher's Observation of Potential in Students (TOPS) • Supports "at-potential" view of all students. • Recognizes students with outstanding potential, in particular those from educationally vulnerable populations. • Informs teachers about student strengths and needs. • Informs classroom instruction and academic service options. • Provides information from a variety of settings, over time. • Supports conferencing with teachers, parents, and students. • Informs services and supports for students for the following year. • Informs a body of evidence. • Leads to referrals for GT services. • Integrates with school policies and GT program practices.	TOPS is not being used.	Beginning evidence of understanding of theoretical background and practical application of TOPS. Used for a few students, sporadically; Completed in one sitting or in retrospect.	Use of TOPS on a regular basis, beginning with the whole-class observation, which leads to some individual observations. Experimenting with guiding classroom instruction and sharing students' strengths and needs.	Consistent integration of TOPS for student observations. Entire observation process followed; students with outstanding potential are recognized. Information from observations is used to plan appropriate response for students' strengths and needs.	Significant and intentional use in classroom to see high potential in students, including those from educationally vulnerable populations. Seamless use to guide classroom instruction, share student strengths and needs with other teachers, and communicate with families. Use as a base for creating a body of evidence to document the child's strengths and needs. Helps to guide GT referrals, placement, and services in and out of the general education classroom, as well as policy issues.
Classroom Differentiation • Responds to strengths and needs of students. • Relies on dynamic assessment to inform instruction, including progress monitoring and self-assessment. • Includes differentiation strategies: compacting, tiering, centers, independent studies/small-group contracts, effective questioning/HOTS. • Varies based on readiness, interest, strengths, and needs. • Uses student-centered, open-ended product choice. • Uses a variety of materials and resources for student use. • Leads flexible grouping. • Uses U-STARS~PLUS materials.	Classroom differentiation is not being used.	Beginning evidence of understanding of theoretical background and practical application of differentiation. Few activities support appropriate challenge and interest for students at different levels.	Better understanding of the theoretical background. Some application in the classroom on a regular basis. Experimenting with ideas in a variety of ways and settings.	Consistent integration of high-end learning opportunities in the classroom. Evident in student work, curriculum planning, and classroom instruction. Used to create an optimal learning environment, which nurtures and responds to potential.	Significant and intentional integration of classroom differentiation best practices where appropriate. Clearly evident in assessment, student work, planning, and instruction. Challenging and meaningful work consistently facilitated for *all* students, seamlessly.

199

Synergy Across the Points of the Star

Each point of the star (i.e., high-end learning, teachers' observations of potential, hands-on inquiry, family and school partnerships, and infrastructure building for change) brings an important element to U-STARS~PLUS, but the real impact happens when all five aspects work together. When David's class worked on a weather project as part of U-STARS~PLUS, his teacher read the class *Come on, Rain!* by Karen Hesse and asked the class higher level questions provided in the *U-STARS~Plus Science and Literature Connections* (Coleman & Shah-Coltrane, 2010c) lessons. She was pleasantly surprised to see how many students gave thoughtful answers to what she considered to be fairly difficult questions, and she noted her observations on the whole-class TOPS (Coleman et al., 2010).

After doing the family science activity "Weather Watch" (Coleman & Shah-Coltrane, 2010b), David and a few classmates showed an interest in how weather is predicted. Their teacher helped them create a classroom chart to monitor the weather using the chart in the U-STARS~PLUS family science activity. She found that the weather data in the chart was very useful during math to help children learn how to interpret meaningful patterns of numbers. She also added a weather report to their morning class announcements and put the group in charge of organizing this. The class seemed to enjoy the hands-on science and the teacher liked seeing the strengths of her students.

U-STARS~PLUS Within RtI

Response to Intervention (RtI) uses a tiered approach to arrange supports and services. Tiered services scaffold support as needed to meet the increasing intensity or complexity of student needs (Kirk, Gallagher, Coleman, & Anastasiow, 2012). The tiered supports and services are activated, as needed, to help students meet with success in school. From a gifted education perspective, these supports and services address students' strengths. Tier 1, universal interventions for all learners, provides a focus on nurturing potential/talent development. Tier 2, targeted interventions and enhancements, addresses learners with more intense strengths, interests, and needs. Tier 3, individualized interventions and enhancements, is available for students who need comprehensive intervention. The key to delivering supports across the tiers is collaborative teaming. General classroom teachers are primarily responsible for Tier 1 supports, greater collaboration is needed for targeted supports at Tier 2, and a

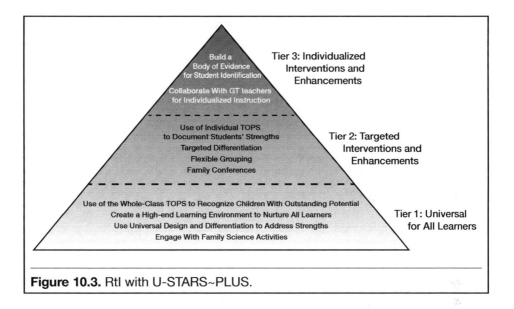

Figure 10.3. RtI with U-STARS~PLUS.

collaborative team is often required for Tier 3 supports. At all tiers, the child's family is included as key members of the team.

U-STARS~PLUS fits within the tiered structure of RtI with a focus on nurturing, recognizing, and responding to a child's potential. Figure 10.3 shows how the components of U-STARS~PLUS fit within each tier.

Tier 1 supports and services are often delivered within the general education classroom with the classroom teacher taking the lead. In Tier 1 U-STARS~PLUS we can see the use of the whole-class TOPS to spot potential and the creation of a high-end learning environment to nurture all students. Through the use of universal design principles, teachers provide multiple representations of the content to be learned, multiple ways to engage in learning, and multiple ways for the students to show what they have learned. The emphasis on hands-on approaches to science fit within the universal design framework. Tier 1 U-STARS~PLUS also focuses on engaging families through the family science activities, establishing the foundation for strength-based partnerships.

Tier 2 supports often require greater collaboration between general education instructors and specialists (in this case, gifted education teachers). The targeted support provided in Tier 2 responds to specific students' strengths and interests with differentiated instruction. The individual TOPS helps teachers recognize the strengths of students so that these can be addressed. The TOPS also supports family conferencing with the focus on the child's strengths. No formal identification as gifted is required to receive supports within Tiers 1 and 2; these supports are offered based on evidence of need.

Tier 3 services are individualized for students with more intense and/or complex needs. Depending on the school or district, Tier 3 services may require formal identification (or they may not). U-STARS~PLUS Tier 3 focuses on a body-of-evidence approach to showing students' strengths, collaboration for individualize planning for the student, and strong family partnerships to look at how the needs of the child can be met.

U-STARS~PLUS Across the Tiers in David's School

Looking at David's school, one can see that supports and services are available across the three tiers.

Tier 1: Universal Interventions for All Learners

David was allowed to do much of his written work on the computer. This seemed to help him, and he quickly learned how to use the computer effectively. His spelling and handwriting skills no longer hindered his thinking or learning process.

Through a more varied curriculum, David became known as a really good problem solver and considered himself to be an inventor. He also asked if he could be released from morning work so he could work on his experiment. Morning work involved coloring a concept paper with a shape, a letter, or a fact and drawing a picture to go along with it. This was primarily designed to help the kids who needed practice with fine motor skills—in other words, David. But, as it involved writing and coloring, David did not want to do it. This often led to a battle as school began, with David shuffling the paper around until he was out of time and then having to stay in at recess to complete the page. Again, a discussion was held and a solution was developed together. David would complete his science notes and draw his picture for his experiment some mornings and then he would be allowed to work in the science center. Other mornings, however, he would have to do the assigned morning work. This decision would be the teacher's, and he would know what he was expected to do based on what was on his desk (this also prompted the teacher to start differentiating the morning work for other students).

Tier 2: Targeted Interventions and Enhancement

David and a small group of classmates worked together to create a weather station to collect and analyze weather patterns. The group worked with a parent volunteer who came in one afternoon per week to meet with them. The gifted education teacher also set up some enrichment activities for the group to learn what a meteorologist does and how weather is predicted. David's classroom teacher used curriculum compacting to "buy" time for these students to participate in the enhancement activities. She also supported their work on the days that they do not have the parent volunteer and gifted education activities.

Tier 3: Individualized Interventions and Enhancements

David's classroom teacher, the gifted education teacher, the school psychologist, and his parents met to look at a portfolio that shows a body of evidence for David's strengths and accomplishments. Included in this portfolio are the TOPS showing the teacher's observations over time, his progress monitoring chart showing mastery in math, and work samples (from his science experiments) that demonstrate high levels of thinking and creativity. The team considered nominating David for formal identification as gifted.

Concluding Thoughts

Nurturing potential is a key responsibility of gifted education (Subotnik, Olszewski-Kubilius, & Worrell, 2011). U-STARS~PLUS is a nurturing model for students in grades K–3. The focus is on helping classroom teachers recognize children's strengths through systematic observation and documentation so that they can respond to these strengths though differentiated instruction. Using hands-on science activities, teachers are better able to recognize strengths in children from culturally/linguistically diverse and/or economically disadvantaged families (Harradine et al., 2012). Although U-STARS~PLUS was not designed specifically for implementation within RtI, it fits well within the collaborative, multi-tiered framework that RtI provides. For students like David, the focus on nurturing, recognizing, and responding to strengths has made all the difference in the world.

References

Amaral, O. M., Garrison, L., & Klentschy, M. (2002). Helping English learners increase achievement through inquiry-based science instruction. *Bilingual Research Journal, 26,* 214–239.

Bagnato, S. J. (2007). *Authentic assessment for early childhood intervention best practices.* New York, NY: Guilford.

Blanchett, W. J., Klingner, J. K., & Harry, B. (2009). The intersection of race, culture, language, and disability: Implications for urban education. *Urban Education, 44,* 389–409.

Brown, E. F., & Abernethy, S. H. (2011). RtI for gifted students: Policy implications. In M. R. Coleman & S. K. Johnsen (Eds.), *RtI for gifted students* (pp. 87–102). Waco, TX: Prufrock Press.

Carlston, C. (2000). Literacy for all: Helping English language learners make sense of academic language. In J. Green (Ed.), *Science learning for all, celebrating cultural diversity* (pp. 68–72). Arlington, VA: NSTA Press.

Coleman, M. R. (2005, Fall). With the eyes of a teacher. *Teaching for High Potential,* 1–2.

Coleman, M. R., & Shah-Coltrane, S. (2010a). *U-STARS~PLUS professional development kit.* Alexandria, VA: Council for Exceptional Children.

Coleman, M. R., & Shah-Coltrane, S. (2010b). *U-STARS~PLUS family science packets.* Alexandria, VA: Council for Exceptional Children.

Coleman, M. R., & Shah-Coltrane, S. (2010c). *U-STARS~PLUS science and literature connections.* Alexandria, VA: Council for Exceptional Children.

Coleman, M. R., Shah-Coltrane, S., & Harrison, A. (2010). *Teacher's observation of potential in students: Whole class form.* Arlington, VA: Council for Exceptional Children.

Coleman, M. R., & Shah-Coltrane, S. (2011). Remembering the importance of potential: Tiers 1 and 2. In M. Coleman & S. Johnsen (Eds.), *RtI for gifted students* (pp. 43–61). Waco, TX: Prufrock Press.

Coley, R. J. (2011). *A strong start: Positioning young Black boys for educational success: A statistical profile.* Retrieved from http://www.ets.org/s/sponsored_events/pdf/16818_BlackMale_trifold3_WEB.pdf

Cropper, C. (1998). Fostering parental involvement in the education of the gifted minority student. *Gifted Child Today, 21*(1), 20–24.

Davis, J. E. (2003). Early schooling and academic achievement of African-American males. *Urban Education, 38,* 515–537.

Fixsen, D. L., Naoom, S. F., Blasé, K. A., Friedman, R. M., & Wallace, F. (2005). *Implementation research: A synthesis of the literature.* Unpublished manuscript, University of Florida National Implementation Research Network, Gainesville, FL.

Ford, D. (2007). Diamonds in the rough: Recognizing and meeting the needs of gifted children from low SES backgrounds. In J. VanTassel-Baska & T. Stambaugh (Eds.), *Overlooked gems: A national perspective on low-income promising learners* (pp. 37–41). Washington, DC: National Association for Gifted Children.

Ford, D., & Grantham, T. (2003). Providing access for culturally diverse gifted students: From deficit to dynamic thinking. *Theory Into Practice, 42,* 217–225.

Gallagher, J. (2006). *Driving changes in special education.* Baltimore, MD: Brookes.

Harradine, C. C., Coleman, M. R., Winn, D. C., & Shah-Coltrane, S. (2012). *Teacher identification of students of color with academic potential: Findings of the U-STARS~PLUS project.* Manuscript submitted for publication.

Hertzog, N. B. (2005). Equity and access: Creating general education classrooms responsive to potential giftedness. *Journal for the Education of the Gifted, 29,* 213–257.

Kirk, S., Gallagher, J. J., Coleman, M. R., & Anastasiow, N. (2012). *Educating exceptional children* (13th ed.). Belmont, CA: Cengage.

Kohn, A. (2011, April 27). Poor teaching for poor children . . . in the name of reform. *Education Week, 30,* 32–34.

National Research Council. (1996). *National Science Education Standards.* Washington, DC: National Academy Press.

Nyberg, L., & McCloskey, S. (2008). Integration with integrity. *Science & Children, 46*(3), 46–49.

Simon-Dudgeon, C., & Egbert, J. (2001). Science as a second language: Verbal interactive strategies help English language learners develop academic vocabulary. In J. Green (Ed.), *Science learning for all, celebrating cultural diversity* (pp. 62–67). Arlington, VA: NSTA Press.

Subotnik, R. F., Olszewski-Kubilius, P., & Worrell, F. C. (2011). Rethinking giftedness and gifted education: A proposed direction forward based on psychological science. *Psychological Science in the Public Interest, 12*(1), 3–54.

VanTassel-Baska, J., Patton, J., & Prillaman, D. (1991). *Gifted youth at risk.* Reston, VA: Council for Exceptional Children.

Villegas, A. M., & Lucas, T. (2002). Preparing culturally responsive teachers: Rethinking the curriculum. *Journal of Teacher Education, 53,* 20–32.

Wallace, F., Blasé, K., Fixsen, D., & Naoom, S. (2008). *Implementing the findings of research: Bridging the gap between knowledge and practice.* Alexandria, VA: Educational Research Service.

Worrell, F. C., & Erwin, J. O. (2011). Best practices in identifying students for gifted and talented education programs. *Journal of Applied School Psychology, 27,* 319–340.

U.S. Department of Education. (2001). *Building bridges: The mission & principles of professional development.* Retrieved from http://www.eric.ed.gov/PDFS/ED404322.pdf

SECTION IV

SPECIAL ISSUES AND CONCERNS

CHAPTER ELEVEN

CULTURALLY RESPONSIVE RESPONSE TO INTERVENTION

Meeting the Needs of Students Who Are Gifted and Culturally Different

Donna Y. Ford and Michelle Trotman Scott

Response to Intervention (RtI) has been studied and applied widely in special education, and only recently has it received attention in gifted education. RtI's focus on learning difficulties, such as learning disabilities and poor achievement, has much to offer the field of gifted education when students are underrepresented, low achievers, and/or underachievers. In addition to using RtI with students who have learning difficulties, it is timely and appropriate to apply the model to students who have learning differences associated with culture. Stanovich's (2005) intriguing line of thought in his article, "The Future of a Mistake: Will Discrepancy Measurement Continue to Make the Learning Disabilities Field a Pseudoscience?" is apropos here. Education must not only accurately differentiate between a learning disability and a learning difference, but also between these and cultural differences. The purpose of this chapter is to examine RtI through three lenses: culture, giftedness, and poor achievement. We argue that RtI will be most effective with culturally different (e.g., African American and Hispanic American) gifted underachieving students when it is culturally responsive.

For several decades, gifted education has been criticized for having too few African American and Hispanic American students identified as gifted. As of 2006, African American students were underrepresented by almost 50% in gifted programs nationally, and Hispanic American students were underrepresented by some 40% (Ford, 2011b; U.S. Department of Education, 2006). Combined, slightly more than 500,000 gifted Black and Hispanic students are not receiving gifted education services. It cannot be denied that there is no group as underrepresented in gifted education as African American students, with Black males being the least likely of all racial and gender groups to be represented in gifted education.

Also troubling is that gifted students can and do underachieve, with far too many Black students failing to reach their potential (Ford, 2011a). Including ourselves, several scholars have presented data, developed theoretical and conceptual frameworks, developed gifted education models, and created and modified instruments and assessment models to reduce (and ideally) eliminate underrepresentation and underachievement (e.g., Alexinia Baldwin, Mary Frasier, Ernesto Bernal, Joseph Renzulli, Sally Reis, Tarek Grantham, Joy Davis, Mary Ruth Coleman, Jack Naglieri). Despite decades of work, our field has seen too little progress with underrepresentation, as doors to gifted education remain closed. Response to Intervention holds promise for preventing academic failure by providing support for culturally and linguistically different students who are underachieving (García & Ortiz, 2008; Klingner & Edwards, 2006). Further, RtI—when culturally responsive—holds promise for opening doors to gifted education. This chapter focuses on Response to Intervention that is responsive to cultural differences and the needs of gifted African American and Hispanic American students (see Figure 11.1).

At this point, it is important to distinguish between the terms "response" and "responsive." A response is an answer or reply to a treatment, action, or words, for example. For us, to be responsive is to respond at a deeper level—to respond readily, compassionately, and empathetically to a need.

This chapter focuses on culture and culturally different students. Culture is defined herein as the beliefs, attitudes, values, customs, and traditions shared by a group of people (Ford, 2011a). *Everyone* has a culture; our focus is on culturally different students, defined as those whose culture differs from the mainstream and from educators, the vast majority of whom are White (85%; U.S. Department of Education, 2011). Countless reports reveal that as our teaching population remains stubbornly White, our student population grows increasingly culturally different, with African American, Asian American, Hispanic American, and Native American students comprising 45% of students in public schools in 2009 (U.S. Department of Education, 2011). This inverse relationship of the demographics of students and teachers carries important implications.

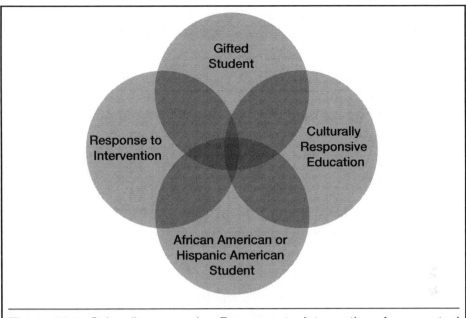

Figure 11.1. Culturally responsive Response to Intervention: A conceptual perspective.

Culture is learned and is mostly out of our awareness. We believe that culture is in all that we think, believe, and do: communication styles (verbal and nonverbal), learning styles, assessment styles, social skills, social relationships, likes and dislikes, behaviors, and much more. When the cultural styles of individuals and/or groups are incompatible, cultural clashes and shock are likely (Oberg, 1954). Thus, when the cultural styles of students and educators clash, misunderstandings, poor relationships, and low or negative expectations are likely. This contributes to underreferrals for gifted education screening and placement and culturally assaultive educational settings (Ford, 2011a, 2011b; Ford, Grantham, & Whiting, 2008).

RtI That Is Culturally Responsive

We are concerned that if we do not engage in dialogue about how culture mediates learning, RtI models will simply be like old wine in a new bottle, in other words, another deficit-based approach to sorting children, particularly children from marginalized communities. (National Center for Culturally Responsive Educational Systems [NCCRESt], 2005, p. 1)

RtI is the practice of providing high-quality instruction and intervention matched to students' needs and using data from screenings, assessments, and progress monitoring to make important educational decisions (García & Ortiz, 2008; National Association of State Directors of Special Educators [NASDSE], 2005). Effective RtI results in "an inadequate change in target behaviors as a function of intervention" (Gresham, 2005, p. 331). "It is a decision-making method that uses graduated increases or decreases in intensity to demonstrate the initial and ongoing need for special services" (Barnett, Daly, Jones, & Lentz, 2004, p. 68). As a student's needs increase, the amount of educational resources increases as well.

In 2009, The Association for the Gifted (TAG), a division of the Council for Exceptional Children (CEC), highlighted several aspects of RtI that were critical to its implementation and effectiveness, including (a) universal screening, assessments, and progress monitoring; (b) established protocols for students who need additional supports and services; (c) problem solving that includes involving caregivers to determine the student's needs; and (d) a tiered system of intervention, based on level of need and support.

CEC-TAG (2009) recommended that the Response to Intervention model be expanded in its implementation to include the needs of gifted students. Specifically, its position paper asserted, "The use of the RtI framework for gifted students would support advanced learning needs of children in terms of a faster paced, more complex, greater depth and/or breadth with respect to their curriculum and instruction" (p. 1).

The position paper mentioned the issue of implementing RtI with gifted students who are underachieving and/or who are culturally different. As Ford (2011b) delineated, for a number of reasons associated with underreferrals for gifted education screening, identification, and services and eventual underrepresentation, a disproportionate percentage of gifted underachievers will be African American and Hispanic American. Likewise, when identified as gifted, many of these students underachieve for social-emotional reasons (e.g., negative peer pressures from African American peers, feeling isolated in predominantly White gifted classes), curricular reasons (e.g., find little personal and cultural relevance in what is taught), and instructional reasons (e.g., mismatch between learning preference and teaching style). For these and other reasons, NCCRESt (2005) contended that RtI must be addressed within the context of cultural learning. RtI must consider interpersonal, social, and institutional factors that contribute to and prevent students' academic and social-emotional difficulties. Stated differently, culturally responsive RtI "expands the unit of analysis and considers students' strengths and needs within educational and cultural contexts" (Harris-Murri, King, & Rostenberg, 2006, p. 780).

We concur with Harris-Murri et al. (2006) that "arguably, the most relevant factors to consider are related to culture: the culture of individuals and institutions and the interactions that take place between and within them" (p. 780). When the RtI method is implemented in a color-blind/culture-blind fashion—without consideration of how culture mediates and influences all that we believe, value, and do—the potential for inaccurate eligibility decisions is ever present. According to Klingner et al. (2005):

> Culturally responsive educational systems are grounded in the beliefs that all culturally and linguistically diverse students can excel in academic endeavors when their culture, language, heritage, and experiences are valued and used to facilitate their learning and development, and they are provided access to high quality teachers, programs, and resources. (p. 8)

Further, NCCRESt (2005) noted that it is also clear that the

> opportunity to learn is a complex construct that includes not only *access to key resources* (qualified teachers, funding, relevant and rigorous curriculum and instruction), but also factors related to the *nature and implementation of school activities* (e.g., culturally meaningful tasks and activities, teacher-student shared understandings of the purpose of tasks and activities, culturally inclusive participation frameworks in classroom discourse, school deficit ideologies about low-income racial minority students used in referral and placement practices). (p. 1)

In sum, without consideration of culture, cultural differences, and culturally responsive interventions throughout *all stages* of the RtI decision-making model, the probability of cultural misunderstandings and misinterpretation of performance and achievement exists, as described next.

Possible Challenges to Implementing a Culturally Responsive RtI Model

It goes without saying that all interventions, even when guided by research, can and do suffer from generalizability or validity errors. What works with one student or a group of students may not work effectively or as well with another student or second group of students. And when cultural differences are considered, the problems and solutions become even more questionable. In this section, we consider challenges associated with screening and assessment, tiered supports and services, established protocols, problem solving and research, and curriculum and instruction.

Screening and Assessment

Universal screening is essential—all students and their educational performance must be examined to ensure that *every* student has an equitable opportunity to receive support. Universal screening must be applied with the goal of developing a profile of each student's weaknesses and strengths as a means to provide an appropriate education to gifted culturally different underachievers—students whose development is advanced but who are struggling.

For gifted underachieving students, who learn more efficiently in their areas of strength and interests, progress monitoring should be used to document mastery. Once mastery has been documented, students must be given opportunities to continue learning with enriched and advanced materials related to their area(s) of strength and interests (CEC-TAG, 2009).

Equally important, all assessment instruments and procedures must be culturally and linguistically fair and reduced in bias. Given the ongoing discussions, debates, and litigation about African Americans and test bias (too many to discuss in this chapter), such issues must be considered and addressed in RtI. Is the assessment valid for African American and Hispanic American students? Have these students been included in the norming sample? Is the sample representative? Does the measure contain language that is biased or discriminatory or offensive? Are assessment policies and procedures culturally responsive? Are scoring criteria (e.g., cutoff scores) appropriate for this student and his or her cultural group? Have within-group differences been examined to avoid homogenizing African Americans and Hispanic Americans (e.g., various income levels, gender differences, geographic/regional differences, language differences[1]). Additional considerations for Hispanic Americans include whether they are immigrants or U.S. born, acculturation level (first or other generation in the U.S.), bilingual or non-English speaking, and Hispanic membership (e.g., Mexican, Puerto Rican, Cuban).

Tiered Supports and Services

As previously indicated, RtI consists of multiple levels of intervention, with the most significant level of intensive intervention (Tier 3) serving the fewest numbers of students having the most intense and greatest needs. Typical models have three levels of intervention, with Tiers 1 and 2 focused on universal and small-group interventions, respectively. When applied to gifted students, each tier is governed by the intensive services required for students whose achievement is greater than typical students in specific areas (CEC-TAG, 2009). RtI for gifted students must be differentiated in the depth, breadth, pace, and complexity of content for students through acceleration and enrichment opportunities. Gifted students who need more intensive services beyond the general education differentiated curriculum will move into different tiers (CEC-TAG, 2009). As stated and clarified in the previous pages, RtI must not and cannot be implemented in a culture-free manner.

Established Protocols

Established protocols are evidence-based (Eisenhart & Towne, 2003). They are also based on theoretical models used to understand and explain students' performance and outcomes. Established protocols, guided by evidence-based studies found to be successful with gifted students who are culturally different, must be adopted. As we focus on finding evidence for what works and why it works, it is essential to find out what works and does not work *with whom*. When deciding if a practice or strategy is appropriate for implementation as part of an RtI model, it must have been validated with students like those with whom it will be applied. As noted by Pressley (2003), "experiments should include students who are the intended targets of the instruction being evaluated" (p. 68).

In the context of ensuring that studies and interventions are culturally focused, NCCRESt (2005) raised five population validity/generalizability

1   When assessing English language learners (those not yet proficient in English), few debate the efficacy of making modifications to address language. We argue that modifications must also be made with Black students who do not speak mainstream English (i.e., those who speak African American English).

questions that ought to be considered. The authors of this chapter raise the sixth question.

> ➢ What should RtI's Tier 1 look like for culturally different students?
> ➢ What should Tier 2 look like? Should it be the same for all students? If not, how should it vary?
> ➢ When population validity is violated, what assumptions need to be interrogated about the student and intervention?
> ➢ How can cultural theories inform sampling strategies that acknowledge the limits of representativeness and generalizability?
> ➢ What sampling guidelines can be used to improve population validity?
> ➢ How can researchers use their understanding of experiences lived by their students in designing interventions? What is lost when the data and findings homogenize the lives and experiences of culturally different students?

Problem Solving, Data Collection, and Interpretation

The problem-solving model of the RtI framework is grounded in literature connected with behavioral consultation, which is inductive, empirical, and focused on the problem behavior (Harris-Murri et al., 2006). Due to its inductive nature, this model seemingly rejects the idea that specific student characteristics dictate what intervention will work and assumes, instead, that specific interventions will be effective for all students belonging to a specific group in terms of race, ethnicity, gender, socioeconomic status, income, and ability (Vaughn & Fuchs, 2003). RtI is not culturally responsive if it lacks ecological validity and if it is grounded in decontextualized generic practices and research (NCCRESt, 2005).

The problem-solving approach, like differentiation, is tailored to a student's individual learning needs and profiles. Individualized adaptations are necessary when a student is not responding to effective curriculum and instruction. We interpret *effective* as producing intended or desired results. CEC-TAG (2009) advised that although problem-solving approaches primarily consider students who are not progressing when compared with their same-age peers, they must also address gifted students who are not progressing at the level commensurate with their abilities and skills. These accelerated interventions allow students to increase their levels of knowledge and skills in their area(s) of strengths; they include advanced or accelerated educational options (e.g., continuous progress learning, curriculum compacting, Advanced Placement classes, grade skipping, subject skipping, and postsecondary enrollment).

While sharing the same goals, several RtI approaches exist. However, the standard protocol approach uses a core, standardized curriculum in Tier 1. Teachers and other educators monitor students to identify those who fail to make expected progress, to provide for collaboration among all professionals (e.g., general education teachers, special education teachers, gifted education teachers, school psychologists, reading and math specialists, health professionals, speech pathologists, community organizations) in partnership with primary caregivers, and to make referrals to specialized services in Tier 2 or 3 if students do not respond or achieve as desired and expected. Although the standard protocol approach is used primarily for students who may need additional support for success to meet grade-level standards, it must be differentiated and used with students who perform or are capable of performing beyond grade level (CEC-TAG, 2009).

To repeat, in need of attention are established protocols that have not considered with whom they are effective. On whom was the protocol established? Too often, culturally different students are underrepresented or omitted from research samples, and/or their demographic characteristics are inadequately described (Whiting, Ford, Grantham, & Moore, 2008). How culturally responsive to African American and Hispanic American students is the study and intervention design? Are the research questions, terms, and wording culturally responsive? Are African Americans, Hispanic Americans, and other culturally and linguistically different individuals on the research team, and did they help to design the study and assessments? Are they involved in interpreting the results and designing the intervention(s)? A more in-depth discussion of culturally responsive research considerations and recommendations appears in Whiting et al. (2008).

Curriculum and Instruction

Classroom curriculum and instruction go hand in hand and must be rigorous or of high quality. High-quality education must include curriculum, materials, and instruction that (a) are differentiated and respond to students who are ready to learn curriculum that is beyond their current grade level and (b) are relevant and responsive to students' culture (recall Figure 12.1). Gifted students must be able to access a flexibly paced and advanced curriculum that provides depth and breadth in their area(s) of strength (CEC-TAG, 2009), as well as curriculum and instruction that is of interest and relevant to their lives (i.e., culturally responsive education). Following these protocols will eliminate ineffective curriculum and instruction as a reason for poor performance. On this last note, Ford (2011a) defined a culturally responsive education as having at least five components:

> ➢ an educational philosophy among teachers/educators that is not color-blind but instead appreciates and values cultural differences and culturally different students;
> ➢ a learning environment/context that is nurturing and welcoming to students from all cultural backgrounds;
> ➢ curriculum that is multicultural (at the highest levels of Banks's multicultural model);
> ➢ instruction that addresses culturally different ways of learning and understanding (e.g., using Boykin's Afro-Centric cultural style model); and
> ➢ assessment and testing/evaluation that is linguistically and culturally fair.

Current school practices and the normative curriculum are responsive to the dominant culture in society, yet they are generally not responsive to communities whose cultural styles and practices differ from mainstream culture (NCCRESt, 2005). Merging the models of Banks (2006) and Bloom (1956), Ford and Harris (1999), and Ford (2011a) created a 4 x 6 matrix that combines the four levels of multicultural curriculum by Banks with the six levels of critical thinking by Bloom (see Table 11.1). More so than special and general education, gifted education espouses the importance of critical thinking and problem solving to meet the advanced learning needs of students. Many teachers rely on Bloom's analysis, synthesis, and evaluation levels to challenge gifted students.

The Bloom-Banks Matrix (also known as the Ford-Harris Matrix) was developed to guide teachers in designing curriculum that is multicultural (relevant and responsive) and to promote critical thinking and problem solving. The matrix was developed to respond to the complaints, interests, and needs of gifted and other African American students who find the curriculum unchallenging and irrelevant from a cultural perspective in particular.

As described in detail by Ford (2011a), the four levels of Banks's multicultural model, from the lowest (most basic) to the highest (most substantive) are: (a) contributions, (b) additive, (c) transformation, and (d) social action. With *all* students, educators are urged to reach the two highest levels. Stated in a different way, multicultural education is necessary for all students. However, as we

Table 11.1
Ford-Harris Matrix of Culturally Responsive Gifted Education: Definition of Categories

	Knowledge	Comprehension	Application	Analysis	Synthesis	Evaluation
Contributions	Students are taught and know facts about cultural artifacts, events, groups, and other cultural elements.	Students show an understanding of information about cultural artifacts, groups, and so forth.	Students are asked to and can apply information learned on cultural artifacts, events, and so forth.	Students are taught to and can analyze (e.g., compare and contrast) information about cultural artifacts, groups, and so forth.	Students are required to and can create a new product from the information on cultural artifacts, groups, and so forth.	Students are taught to and can evaluate facts and information based on cultural artifacts, groups, and so forth.
Additive	Students are taught and know concepts and themes about cultural groups.	Students are taught and can understand cultural concepts and themes.	Students are required to and can apply information learned about cultural concepts and themes.	Students are taught to and can analyze important cultural concepts and themes.	Students are asked to and can synthesize important information on cultural concepts and themes.	Students are taught to and can critique cultural concepts and themes.
Transformation	Students are given information on important cultural elements, groups, and so forth, and can understand this information from different perspectives.	Students are taught to understand and can demonstrate an understanding of important cultural concepts and themes from different perspectives.	Students are asked to and can apply their understanding of important concepts and themes from different perspectives.	Students are taught to and can examine important cultural concepts and themes from more than one perspective.	Students are required to and can create a product based on their new perspective or the perspective of another group.	Students are taught to and can evaluate or judge important cultural concepts and themes from different viewpoints (e.g., racially and culturally different groups).
Social Action	Based on information on cultural artifacts, students make recommendations for social action.	Based on their understanding of important concepts and themes, students make recommendations for social action.	Students are asked to and can apply their understanding of important social and cultural issues; they make recommendations for and take action on these issues.	Students are required to and can analyze social and cultural issues from different perspectives; they take action on these issues.	Students create a plan of action to address a social and cultural issue(s); they seek important social change.	Students critique important social and cultural issues and seek to make national and/or international change.

Note. Based on the models of Banks (culturally responsive) and Bloom (thinking skills). Actions taken on the social action level can range from immediate and small scale (classroom and school levels) to moderate (community and regional levels) to large scale (state, national, and international levels). Likewise, students can make recommendations for action or actually take social action. From *Multicultural Gifted Education* (2nd ed., p. 116), by D. Y. Ford, 2011, Waco, TX: Prufrock Press. Copyright 2011 by Prufrock Press. Reprinted with permission.

have discussed in numerous venues, African American students in particular are often desperate for a multicultural/culturally responsive education.

In Quadrant 1 of the Bloom-Banks Matrix (Ford, 2011a), the curriculum is low level in both multicultural content and critical thinking; in Quadrant 2, the curriculum is low level in critical thinking and problem solving but high level in multicultural content; in Quadrant 3, the curriculum is low level in multicultural content but high level in critical thinking and problem solving; and in Quadrant 4, the curriculum is the highest level of both models—students are thinking critically, solving problems, and delving deeply into substantive multicultural topics, issues, and themes—and, importantly, they seek to make social change in some way. Gifted students must work at all levels (Quadrants 1–3), which sets important foundations in critical thinking and problem solving, along with deep multicultural content; teachers must work to challenge and engage gifted students in their thinking and multiculturalism (i.e., Quadrant 4).

Ford-Harris Matrix in an RtI Framework

In Tier 1 of RtI, student progress is measured weekly. It consists of effective, research-based instruction that takes place in the general classroom setting. When applying RtI to gifted students, students' responses should be reversed. In other words, using the Ford-Harris Matrix of multicultural gifted education, students' progress can be monitored using a culturally responsive analytical model of teaching. Students can begin in Quadrant 1, which is low on Bloom's taxonomy (knowledge, comprehension, and application) and low on Banks's multicultural levels (contributions and additives), or on Quadrant 2, which is low on Bloom's taxonomy and high on Banks's multicultural levels (transformation and social action).

If a student progresses favorably in Tier 1, she should be recommended to Tier 2. This tier provides students with targeted interventions, but they are still monitored. Quadrant 3 of the Ford-Harris Matrix can be used on this level to meet the individual needs of the aforementioned students. Students are serviced on the higher levels of Bloom's taxonomy (analysis, synthesis, and evaluation) and are able to work on the lower Banks's multicultural levels (contributions, additives) in Quadrant 3.

Students who progress sufficiently in Tier 2 may receive even more intensive instruction in Tier 3. Quadrant 4 of the Ford-Harris Matrix provides instruction high on Bloom's taxonomy and high on Banks's levels. This quadrant provides students with academic rigor and differentiates curriculum in a way that provides meaning and relevance to culturally different gifted students. Because progress has been monitored at each tier, data can be used to evaluate students' academic performance and possibly be used to help students qualify for gifted education services.

Summary of Culturally Responsive RtI

In the above sections, we described potential shortcomings with RtI when it is not culturally responsive. We questioned and challenged the utility of RtI that is culture-blind.

Although it is important to design interventions specific to every student referred to the RtI team or committee, it can be uncomfortable and difficult for decision makers to consider and then address cultural factors that influence students' behavior and achievement, as well as their response to interventions. Pertinent questions are: What is the student's culture? How does the culturally different student learn best? What does the culturally different student find relevant and interesting? What is the culturally different student's dominant or preferred language? What is the teacher's philosophy about culture and how culture influences learning and testing? What institutional factors influence the learning environment? What social factors influence the learning environment?

The scholarship of advocates of multicultural or culturally responsive education is informative here. Curricular works and models by James Banks, Geneva Gay, Jacqueline Irvine, and Gloria Ladson-Billings, as well as the instructional model of A. Wade Boykin are all highlighted in Ford (2011a). Their approaches are in reaction (i.e., opposition) to the use of a standard or Procrustean curriculum that is the same for all students, delivered in the same manner, and over the same amount of time, thereby ignoring the individual and cultural interests and needs of those for whom it is designed. This homogenized curriculum merely reproduces socio-cultural-historical hierarchies within schools and serves to continue the disenfranchisement of Black and other culturally different students (Harris-Murri et al., 2006).

Central to a culturally responsive RtI approach "is the belief that instructional methods do not work or fail as decontextualized generic practices but work in relation to the sociocultural contexts in which they are implemented" (NCCRESt, 2005, p. 3). In essence, culturally responsive connections must be applied to all tiers of RtI, beginning clearly with Tier 1, which considers the quality of instruction within general and gifted education classrooms, complemented by continuous monitoring of progress.

Another challenge is the need to consider the context or learning environment. When viewed through this lens, the exclusive focus on the problem or issue deemed as resting *within* the student is relocated and broadened to include the teacher, classmates, and other aspects of the classroom. In other words, there must be a greater focus on teachers' and classmates' behaviors than has been traditionally considered in the problem definition and problem-solving process. It is undeniable that behavior is a function of the student, the teacher, the curriculum and instruction, and the classroom learning environment. Thus, the learning difficulty does not rest solely or exclusively within the student. With this said, the RtI committee must broaden the scope of the defined problem to include other factors related to students' behavior, assessment performance, achievement, and learning (Harris-Murri et al., 2006).

Although RtI is more concerned with academic performance and outcomes, we cannot ignore identification. Thus, another challenge associated with the use of a culturally responsive model of RtI with African American and Hispanic American students is to understand the reason behind their low referral rates (and subsequent underidentification) for gifted education evaluation and services. Teachers frequently begin this referral process, and all studies indicate that they significantly underrefer African American students for gifted education (Ford et al., 2008). About half of studies report underreferrals for Hispanic Americans. Teachers must acknowledge and own up to their prejudices and biases about cultural differences in order to improve the experience of African American and Hispanic American students who are underrepresented in gifted education and/or who are underachieving. Thus, teacher expectations—beliefs, attitudes, values, perceptions, and biases—and knowledge must be considered and interrogated. A case in point: African American males are significantly underrepresented in gifted education, as already noted. Why are they underrepresented and why are they underachieving? We must question why such recommendations are not being made to determine the appropriateness and validity of referrals by teachers and by the screening, identification, and placement process in general.

The last challenge we considered concerns the RtI problem-solving model relative to determining appropriate assessment(s). Criticisms abound regarding test bias and unfairness with African American and Hispanic American students and they will not be reiterated herein due to space limitations. A pervasive issue with assessment is the misuse of instruments and the misinterpretation of the resulting scores. Are the tests and instruments valid and reliable for the culturally different student or groups? Is the test or instrument biased and/or unfair? Is the test or instrument culturally fair? Does the test or instrument have a disparate impact on the representation of African Americans and Hispanic Americans in gifted education?

A Final Word

Yates (2005) asserted that schooling as the broader "intervention" provided to all students has not been responsive to the educational needs of culturally different students—and, by extension, gifted students who are culturally different. For RtI to be implemented in culturally responsive ways, educators must be trained in *both* gifted education and multicultural education. To implement RtI in a culturally responsive way, formal preparation is required. Educators need to become aware and capable of progress monitoring between and within all cultural groups.

Teacher preparation in the form of education and professional development is necessary to help educators to become culturally competent. Professional development must focus on culturally specific essential knowledge, skills, beliefs, and attitudes. Diversity standards by professional organizations such as the National Association for Multicultural Education and The Association of Black Psychologists are useful. In higher education, accredited institutions are guided by diversity Standard 4 of the National Council for the Accreditation of Teacher Education (NCATE) preparation standards. In gifted education, such knowledge, skills, and attitudes are clearly noted in the standards established through collaboration with CEC-TAG and the National Association for Gifted Children (NAGC; Johnsen, VanTassel-Baska, & Robinson, 2008). Other recommendations and resources appear in Ford (2011a), who maintained that culturally competent teachers have the dispositions, knowledge, and skills to work effectively with culturally different gifted students. "Culturally responsive teachers make connections with their students as individuals while understanding the socio-cultural-historical contexts that influence their interactions and practices" (NCCRESt, 2005, p. 2). In addition:

> Schools and school systems that are predicated on continuous improvement and responsiveness to the changing needs of

new generations of students work to deepen their understandings of race, class, gender, language, culture, and democracy
and develop practices that promote the success of all students.
(NCCRESt, 2005, p. 2)

Throughout this chapter, we contended that RtI models should be based on
a theory of how culture mediates learning processes. As Moje and Hinchman
(2004) noted, "All practice needs to be culturally responsive in order to be
best practice" (p. 321). This view is especially relevant when considering the
cultural nature of human development and learning. Culture is dynamic rather
than being a static set of characteristics located within individuals (e.g., ethnicity, social class), but is instrumental and indexed in practice (Gutiérrez &
Rogoff, 2003). Discussions and debates about effective instructional methods
and considerations of student performance should be framed within the larger
context of how such practices interrelate with issues of social practice, culture,
and power across these levels (NCCRESt, 2005).

Collaboration will also be necessary. An African proverb states that "It takes
a village to raise a child." On this note, collaboration between professionals and
families is an essential RtI component. If the general or gifted education curriculum is ineffective, then professionals and caregivers work together to develop
intervention strategies and plans. If the general or gifted education classroom
cannot effectively improve students' achievement or performance, then special
services could be warranted. This collaboration is extremely important for students from culturally different backgrounds and students who are underachieving (CEC-TAG, 2009) to decrease false positive identification for special education and false negative identification for gifted education. For example, much
debate exists regarding the difficulties associated with distinguishing a learning
disability from a learning difference (e.g., cultural difference) and from underachievement. Both a learning disability and underachievement are grounded
in a discrepancy framework in which there is a gap between potential and per-
formance/achievement. Further, when educators discount, do not understand,
or do not value the culture of their students, misinterpretations of behaviors
are likely to occur. Given that interpretations of behavior are subjective, how
behaviors are labeled and addressed vary across educators and settings. Teacher
beliefs and behaviors regarding school and education are sometimes incompatible with culturally different students' beliefs and behaviors. To wit, "teachers
often do not take into account their own contributions to students' behavioral
and learning patterns" (Harry & Anderson, 1994, p. 611). As we move into the

future, no time is better than now to be responsive to our culturally different gifted students.

References

Banks, J. J. (2006). *Cultural diversity and education: Foundations, curriculum and teaching.* Boston, MA: Allyn and Bacon.

Barnett, D. W., Daly, E. J., III, Jones, K. M., & Lentz, F. E. (2004). Response to Intervention: Empirically based special service decisions from single-case designs of increasing and decreasing intensity. *The Journal of Special Education, 28,* 66–79.

Bloom, B. S. (Ed.). (1956). *Taxonomy of educational objectives: The classification of educational goals—Handbook I: Cognitive domain.* New York, NY: McKay.

Council for Exceptional Children, The Association for the Gifted. (2009). *Response to Intervention for gifted children.* Retrieved from http://cectag.com/wp-content/uploads/2012/04/RTI.pdf

Eisenhart, M., & Towne, L. (2003). Contestation and change in national policy on "scientifically based" education research. *Educational Researcher, 32,* 31–38.

Ford, D. Y. (2011a). *Multicultural gifted education* (2nd ed.). Waco, TX: Prufrock Press.

Ford, D. Y. (2011b). *Reversing underachievement among gifted Black students* (2nd ed.). Waco, TX: Prufrock Press.

Ford, D. Y., Grantham, T. C., & Whiting, G. W. (2008). Culturally and linguistically diverse students in gifted education: Recruitment and retention issues. *Exceptional Children, 74,* 289–308.

Ford, D. Y., & Harris, J. J., III. (1999). *Reversing underachievement among gifted Black students.* New York, NY: Teachers College Press.

García, S. B., & Ortiz, A. A. (2008). A framework for culturally and linguistically responsive design of Response-to-Intervention models. *Multiple Voices for Ethnically Diverse Exceptional Learners, 11,* 24–41.

Gresham, F. M. (2005). Response to Intervention: An alternative means of identifying students as emotionally disturbed. *Education and Treatment of Children, 28,* 328–344.

Gutiérrez, K. D., & Rogoff, B. (2003). Cultural ways of learning: Individual traits or repertoires of practice. *Educational Researcher, 32,* 19–25.

Harris-Murri, N., King, K., & Rostenberg, D. (2006). Reducing disproportionate minority representation in special education programs for students with emotional disturbances: Toward a culturally responsive Response to Intervention model. *Education and Treatment of Children, 29,* 779–799.

Harry, B., & Anderson, M. G. (1994). The disproportionate representation of African-American males in special education programs: A critique of the process. *Journal of Negro Education, 63,* 602–619.

Johnsen, S., VanTassel-Baska, J., & Robinson, A. (2008). *Using the national gifted education standards for university teacher preparation programs.* Thousand Oaks, CA: Corwin Press.

Klingner, J. K., Artiles, A. J., Kozleski, E., Harry, B., Zion, S., Tate, W., . . . Riley, D. (2005). Addressing the disproportionate representation of culturally and linguistically diverse students in special education through culturally responsive educational systems. *Education Policy Analysis Archives, 13*(38), 1–39.

Klingner, J. K., & Edwards, P. A. (2006). Cultural considerations with Response to Intervention models. *Reading Research Quarterly, 41,* 108–117.

Moje, E. B., & Hinchman, K. (2004). Culturally responsive practices for youth literacy learning. In J. Dole & T. Jetton (Eds.), *Adolescent literacy research and practice* (pp. 321–350). New York, NY: Guilford Press.

National Association of State Directors of Special Educators. (2005). *Response to Intervention: Policy considerations and implementation.* Alexandria, VA: Author.

National Center for Culturally Responsive Educational Systems. (2005). *Cultural considerations and challenges in Response-to-Intervention models: An NCCRESt Position Statement.* Retrieved from http://www.nccrest.org/publications/position_statements.html

Oberg, K. (1954, August 3). *Culture shock.* Presentation to the Women's Club of Rio de Janeiro, Brazil.

Pressley, M. (2003). A few things reading educators should know about instructional experiments. *The Reading Teacher, 57,* 64–71.

Stanovich, K. (2005). The future of a mistake: Will discrepancy measurement continue to make the learning disabilities field a pseudoscience? *Learning Disability Quarterly, 28,* 103–106.

U.S. Department of Education. (2006). *2006 Elementary and Secondary School Survey.* Washington, DC: Office for Civil Rights.

U.S. Department of Education. (2011). *The condition of education 2011.* Washington, DC: Author.

Vaughn, S., & Fuchs, L. (2003). Redefining learning disabilities as inadequate response to instruction: The promise and potential. *Learning Disabilities: Research & Practice, 18,* 137–146.

Whiting, G. W., Ford, D. Y., Grantham, T. C., & Moore, J. J., III. (2008). Considerations for conducting culturally responsive research in gifted education. *Gifted Child Today, 31*(3), 26–29.

Yates, J. R. (2005, April). *The demographic context of education reform.* Paper presented at the annual convention of the Council for Exceptional Children, Baltimore, MD.

CHAPTER TWELVE

TWICE-EXCEPTIONAL LEARNERS AND RTI

Targeting Both Sides of the Same Coin

Cheryll M. Adams, Nina Yssel, and Heidi Anwiler

Until the 1970s, educators conceptualized gifted and special education at opposite sides of an educational spectrum because they did not realize that gifted children could also have disabilities (Trail, 2011). During the last two decades, the body of literature on twice-exceptional (2e) students has certainly increased, documenting improved identification procedures and programming. However, the baffling phenomenon of finding both exceptionalities in one person is still likely to be misunderstood or overlooked. Gallagher noted that twice-exceptional students are gifted in one area, but they also have a disability (as cited in Coleman, Harradine, & King, 2005). Generally referred to as gifted/LD in the past, the more current term, *twice-exceptional*, has broadened the concept to include all students with disabilities who also demonstrate giftedness or talent (Yssel, Prater, & Smith, 2010).

Twice-exceptional students had been estimated to make up 2–9% of students with disabilities (Dix & Schafer, 1996). More current reports made available in 2006 estimated that 2–5% of students with learning disabilities are gifted (Bracamonte, 2010). One major problem with these estimates is that without an appropriate and more inclusive federal definition of twice-exceptionality that includes children with not only specific learning disabilities but also students with physical or behavioral disabilities, we cannot be confident that those estimates are accurate. Furthermore, not all school districts recognize twice-exceptionality, and those that do may not participate in reporting these data (Bracamonte, 2010). Considering these unresolved issues, it stands to reason that the actual numbers of 2e children are higher than previously reported estimates.

Again, contributing to the limited number of gifted students with disabilities being identified is the lack of an appropriate federal definition. The only part of the definition of specific learning disabilities included in IDEA (2004) that alludes to 2e students is found in the operational definition: A student has a specific learning disability if "the student does not achieve at the proper age and ability levels . . . when provided with appropriate learning experiences" (Sec. 300.311[a]). Weinfeld, Barnes-Robinson, Jeweler, and Shevitz (2006) considered the inclusion of "ability levels" in the regulations as an important step, specifically "that students' performance should be compared not just to their age level, but to their ability level, as well" (p. 51).

A report by the National Joint Committee on Learning Disabilities (NJCLD, 2011), of which the Division of Learning Disabilities of the Council for Exceptional Children (CEC) is a member, addressed the issue:

> Individuals identified as intellectually gifted may also have LD. Although twice-exceptional individuals may appear to be functioning adequately in the classroom, their performance may be far below what they are capable of, given their intellectual ability. As a consequence of the students' ability to compensate for their LD-related challenges until the volume or intensity of work or assessment and grading procedures pose barriers to demonstrating their learning or accomplishing required tasks, educators often overlook these students until late in their academic careers. (p. 2)

Characteristics

Common areas of giftedness in 2e children include superior vocabulary, specific talent or area of interest, tendency toward abstract thinking, high degree of creativity, advanced sense of humor, unrelenting curiosity, penetrating insights into complex issues, interest in the "big picture" rather than minute details, and an ability to compensate for their disability (Nielsen & Higgins, 2005). Twice-exceptional children also typically have a high level of problem-solving and reasoning ability (Nielsen & Higgins, 2005). They may appear to be divergent thinkers, and their sense of humor can, at times, even be viewed as bizarre (Trail, 2011). The most common challenge areas for 2e children are reading and language processing (Baum & Owen, 2004).

Another characteristic of 2e students noticed by trained teachers is the "reverse hierarchy" of learning that many of these students experience (Hughes, 2011). For example, they may find it easier to learn the concept of multiplication before they have a complete memory of addition facts (Tannenbaum & Baldwin, 1983). They often have a need or preference for understanding global information and then later connecting discrete facts to larger concepts (Hughes, 2011), whereas traditional school curriculum generally moves from small, discrete facts and then expands to large, global concepts (Anderson & Krathwohl, 2001).

Other common areas of challenge in 2e children are high levels of frustration or emotional disturbance, extremely uneven academic skills that may result in avoidance of schoolwork or appear as a lack of initiative, memory difficulties, gross or fine-motor difficulties, lack of organizational or study skills, and a difficulty with linear thinking (Nielsen & Higgins, 2005). Low self-esteem is often masked by inappropriate and disruptive behaviors. Examples of behaviors that may manifest are teasing, clowning, denial of problems, withdrawal, anger outbursts, apathy, stubbornness, impulsiveness, antisocial behaviors, poor social skills, and a high level of distractibility (Nielsen & Higgins, 2005).

Twice-exceptional students may initially feel that they can relate to their gifted peers because they have similar ideas, only to realize that they fall behind them academically. Likewise, they may feel that they relate to students with behavioral and learning disabilities in that they share these areas of challenge, but this group of students may be puzzled by their advanced sense of humor and their superior vocabulary (Nielsen & Higgins, 2005). Because of these issues, 2e children often feel pushed aside and/or isolated (Nielsen & Higgins, 2005).

If these students are not identified early, disengagement in learning may take place and sometimes there may even be a loss of talent (Rollins, Mursky, Shah-Coltrane, & Johnsen, 2009). Their unique characteristics contribute to the "emotional storm" into which 2e students are thrust when they enter school and are faced with a standard curriculum that does not meet their needs (Nielsen & Higgins, 2005). This, in turn, contributes to their emotional instability and the behavior problems that often mask their giftedness.

There is frustration on the part of children who are twice-exceptional when they are unable to meet not only their own expectations but also the academic expectations of their teachers and the social expectations of their peers. The difficulty they have forming relationships and interacting with their peers can also result in becoming the target of peer bullying, which further interferes with academic success and contributes to emotional disturbances and low self-esteem (Trail, 2011). Problems with social interactions contribute greatly to feelings of isolation and failure (Nielsen & Higgins, 2005). Baum and Owen (2004) noted that these children often have an external locus of control, blaming external sources, such as other people, for their problems and failures.

Identification of Twice-Exceptional Students

Identification of 2e children has been fraught with difficulty. These students often get lost in the system because they do not fit neatly into the category of either exceptionality (Pereles, Omdal, & Baldwin, 2009). Nielsen (2002) explained the difficulties based on state criteria for giftedness and for learning disabilities: These students either fail to meet gifted criteria because their disabilities could affect testing performance, or they do not qualify for the LD label because they are performing at grade level. In the past, 2e students were often overlooked, unless they were referred for testing due to behavior problems (Brody & Mills, 1997).

An additional barrier is often referred to as the masking phenomenon: one exceptionality masks the other, resulting in students remaining unnoticed and thus unidentified (Baum, 1994). Silverman (2009) explained, "Giftedness masks disabilities and disabilities depress IQ scores" (p. 116). When exceptionalities are masked, or when students compensate for their weaknesses, they might function at grade level, and students functioning at grade level seldom raise a red flag. For example, a student may have an advanced vocabulary but difficulty with reading words; in this case, the child gets remediation for the reading disability but no recognition for the need for enrichment or acceleration for having an advanced vocabulary. This can work in the other direction as well. When 2e students use their intelligence to compensate for their weakness, their struggle remains hidden; thus, the student whose struggle remains hidden may appear to be at grade level rather than gifted. In most cases, an evaluation for special services is initiated because of the student's low academic performance and/or behavioral problems and rarely because of the child's giftedness (Nielsen & Higgins, 2005).

Many 2e students fail to meet the criteria for gifted or remediation services because identification protocols do not consider the unique characteristics of this special population (Brody & Mills, 1997). Their characteristics are atypical of gifted students and also atypical of students with disabilities (Trail, 2011). Nielsen (2002) provided guidelines for assessment and identification of 2e students. Some of her recommendations included (a) charging a multidisciplinary task force with establishing and implementing the identification process and program implementation; (b) examining records of students who might have been evaluated for learning and behavioral problems, specifically whether such students might have scored at or above 120 on an IQ measure; (c) using multiple data sources and examining tests to determine discrepancies in performance, such as extreme scatter on subtests of intelligence measures, and (d) paying particular attention to coding and digit span subtest information. These recommendations clearly highlight the complexity of identifying 2e students.

The role of the school psychologist in the RtI process cannot be underestimated. He or she can be particularly helpful in terms of providing suggestions for various behavior management techniques as well as recognizing and differentiating between specific learning disabilities and ADHD and Autism Spectrum Disorders (ASD; Assouline & Whiteman, 2011). Some of the assessment factors that can lead to erroneous conclusions include similar behaviors that stem from different causes for different children. For example, children might display maladaptive behaviors because they are not being presented with appropriately advanced material or they might have a diagnosable attention disorder (Assouline & Whiteman, 2011). Assouline and Whiteman (2011) discussed the importance of using appropriate diagnostic tools in comprehensive evaluations that identify the suspected disability. For example, if ASD is suspected, a school psychologist who is knowledgeable about specific disorders might use the Autism Diagnostic Observation Schedule (ADOS; Assouline & Whiteman, 2011).

Identification and RtI

How will Response to Intervention (RtI) change identification procedures that have been often controversial? Any discussion of RtI and how it might affect 2e students should probably start by considering the discrepancy model as the foundation for identifying students with specific learning disabilities (SLD).

Overview of the Discrepancy Model

The discrepancy model (i.e., discrepancy between achievement and intellectual ability) had been used as a criterion to identify students with SLD, albeit as one component in the comprehensive evaluation (Lerner & Johns, 2009), since PL 94-142 was passed in 1975. Although most states allow for the continued use of the discrepancy model, some states no longer permit its use. According to Schultz and Stephens (2008), 11 states prohibited the use of the discrepancy model when determining eligibility for SLD. IDEA 2004 does not prohibit its use; it is simply no longer required. The discrepancy model compares a student's achievement (what he or she has learned) to the student's intellectual ability (the student's potential for learning). If the difference between the two standard scores exceeds one or two standard deviations, the student could be identified as having a SLD (Lerner & Johns, 2009). Criticisms against this model included concerns about the use of an IQ score, the fact that qualitative information is not considered, the issue of low achievers who might show the same characteristics, and discrepancy formulas that differed from state to state.

Referring to the discrepancy model, Lovett and Levandowski (2006) stated that

> Within the discrepancy paradigm, it is easy to imagine an individual whose measured general ability is significantly above average . . . but whose achievement in some academic subject area is squarely in the below-average range. Such an individual would seem to simultaneously possess giftedness and a specific learning disability, at least by definition. (p. 515)

McCoach, Kehle, Bray, and Siegle (2001) also endorsed this discrepancy conceptualization, with IQ tests differentiating between LD students and gifted/LD students; they, however, were not in favor of scatter and profile analysis.

Identifying 2e Students Within the RtI Framework: Pros and Cons

McKenzie (2010) discussed the discrepancy model and the criticism against it, specifically the incidences of false positives. Citing Kauffman, who argued that prevention models (e.g., RtI) increased false positives, McKenzie pointed out that the incidence of false negatives had not been addressed and provided compelling arguments for the possibility that students with SLD would be excluded from special education services as a result of flawed or incomplete assessment. Twice-exceptional students, according to McKenzie, are also "less likely to be identified as such using RtI as an alternative to discrepancy-based approaches" (p. 162). Generally, the masking effect, where one exceptionality masks the other, contributes to the difficulty of identifying 2e students, as discussed previously. McKenzie admitted the limitations of the discrepancy model to accurately identify gifted/LD students but felt it "unreasonable to assume, however, that those limitations constitute justification for abandoning that scheme in favor of the emerging RtI model of SLD identification" (p. 164). In spite of its shortcomings, the discrepancy model hinged upon a framework for establishing general intellectual and academic skill levels, and the absence of this in RtI needs to be examined (McKenzie, 2010). McKenzie argued that the failure to establish general intelligence within a gifted/LD student's psychometric profile increases the probability of false negatives. He used the example of a student with a standard score of 97 on a reading measure: Such a student is considered responsive (R) in the RtI model based on the criterion of 90 or above that was adopted by the school district. This student's IQ might be 130, unbeknownst to her teachers. Under the discrepancy model, this student, when assessed, would be eligible for dual services. "However, without an authenticated IQ score, this student will be determined R [responsive] when in fact she is NR [nonresponsive], remain in the same RtI tier, and not be eligible for either of the categories" (McKenzie, 2010, p. 165). Table 12.1 shares additional examples.

The joint paper from the National Association of State Directors of Special Education and the Council of Administrators of Special Education (2006) explicated that RtI "challenges the assumptions that separate, often disconnected 'silos' are the best method to address the learning needs of students" (p. 4). These silos are a result of labeling and placing students in an established program associated with the label rather than the identified educational need. Twice-exceptional students have never quite fit into any of the usual programs in our schools (see Figure 12.1). Pereles et al. (2009) argued that RtI could usher in the move away from labeling; moreover, the core principles of RtI could result in the needs of all students, including twice-exceptional students, being met. Access to a rigorous, standards-based curriculum and research-based instruction, early intervention, tiered interventions, use of data, collaboration,

Table 12.1
An Illustration of False Negative With and Without the Additional IQ Score

Name	Reading Score	Responsive (R)/ Nonresponsive (NR)	IQ Verbal Score (Given Later)	False Negative
Ashley	97	R	135	Yes (NR)
Barron	80	NR	105	No (NR)
Carmen	43	NR	93	No (NR)
Derrick	95	R	110	No (R)

and family engagement are the principles that should provide an environment with clear expectations and support in which 2e students would thrive, according to Pereles et al. (2009).

Heitin (2008) reacted positively to the new direction that RtI promises with regard to identification and programming of 2e students. She noted that IDEA 2004 has expanded the definition of SLD by including reading fluency as an area of underachievement. Revised verbiage—that a student may be determined to have a SLD if he or she does not achieve adequately for age- or grade-level standards—leaves room for interpretation, "suggesting a broader scope of consideration" (Heitin, 2008, p. 2).

Some of Nielsen's (2002) recommendations for effective identification included convening a multidisciplinary task force and examining discrepancies in performance. A multidisciplinary team is implicit in RtI and could potentially address identification of 2e children effectively. School psychologists can play an important role in the multidisciplinary team because they have the experience necessary to provide a range of services to students, from testing, prevention, and individual counseling, to collaboration with other professionals (King, Coleman, & Miller, 2011). Using the Colorado Department of Education as an example, King et al. (2011) emphasized the importance of discussions to clarify roles in the RtI process, which were considered a very valuable and helpful experience.

However, given the compensatory strategies of 2e children, the possibility of early intervention still remains. Silverman (2009) explained the nature of compensation and the resulting conundrum well: It allows a person to adapt and is truly a "miracle of the mind" (p. 116); yet, compensation also prevents identification and accurate diagnosis. Scatter on subtests of cognitive measures has been considered in identification (Nielsen, 2002; Schiff, Kaufman, & Kaufman, 1981; Silverman, 2009), but without a cognitive measure, this

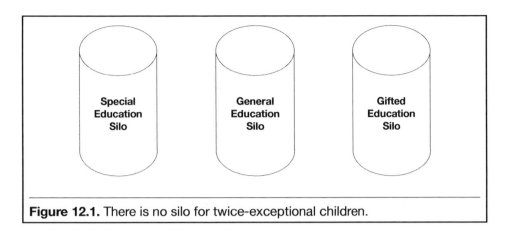

Figure 12.1. There is no silo for twice-exceptional children.

information is not available. Using multiple data sources (Nielsen, 2002) that can provide information about strengths is a recommended practice for identifying giftedness. Nielsen (2002) cited the use of the Torrance Tests of Creative Thinking (Torrance, 1966), which is often included as a measure of creative abilities as part of an identification plan for gifted students. However, if the child is functioning at grade level and giftedness is not suspected, then the child will not be administered these additional measures whose scores are used for identifying gifted students (see Figure 12.2).

Serving Twice-Exceptional Students Through RtI

Twice-exceptional learners are underserved in an academic environment that does not understand their needs (Trail, 2011). Warshaw (2006) noted that 2e students often feel like schoolwork is either "too hard" or "too easy" but rarely "just right." These students need specialists in both gifted and special education in order to reach their full potential and succeed academically (Trail, 2011). Emma may have primarily academic challenges, but Jerry may have primarily attention and behavior problems (Nielsen & Higgins, 2005). Each twice-exceptional student has a unique combination of gifts and challenges; thus, a one-size-fits-all approach to education is simply not sufficient (Hughes & Rollins, 2009). When and if these students are identified, their complex needs often lead to fragmented interventions and services (Hughes & Rollins, 2009).

The Council for Exceptional Children's (CEC, 2008) position paper on RtI explains that an RtI process

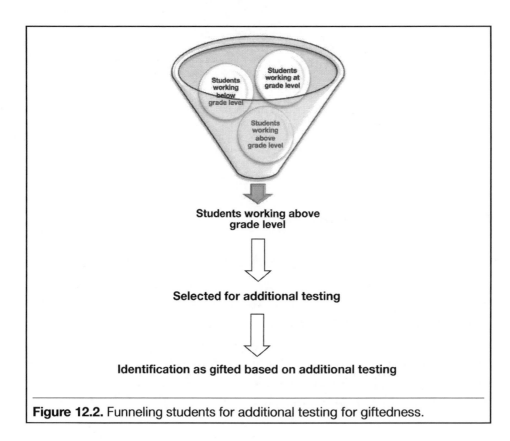

Figure 12.2. Funneling students for additional testing for giftedness.

shall consider the educational needs of children with gifts and talents and their families, particularly related to the identification of children considered to be twice exceptional because they have gifts and talents as well as a disability. These advanced learners shall be provided access to a challenging and accelerated curriculum while also addressing the unique needs of their disability. (p. 2)

Thus, CEC situates twice-exceptional students within the RtI framework and underscores these students as having both gifts and talents *and* a disability. Clearly, at least from CEC, the expectation is that both exceptionalities will be recognized and addressed through RtI. With that in mind, a search of the National Center on Response to Intervention's website (NCRtI; http://www. rti4success.org) indicates only one reference to the word "gifted" (although not in the context of RtI) and none for "twice-exceptional." If this is a major source of information on RtI, it is no wonder that schools seem to ignore gifted students in general and twice-exceptional students in particular when implementing RtI. As mentioned previously, identification and services are based on weaknesses that must be remediated, often without any attempt to view the child as possibly 2e. If the focus is remediation, then access to a challenging and accelerated curriculum will be difficult to institute at best.

According to Bianco (2010), ideally RtI is a flexible and fluid tiered system that can be adjusted to all learners. The essential components of RtI are screening, progress monitoring, data-based decision making, and implementing the multilevel prevention system (NCRtI, n.d.). All of these components can be used successfully to identify and serve 2e students provided that schools and parents approach the process with the notion that students can be both gifted and have an SLD. The varied services and interventions provided through RtI have the potential to meet the needs of 2e students whose SLD may run the gamut from very mild to severe.

Screening

The purpose of screening is to identify students who are academically at risk; these students have generally had poor learning outcomes. A universal assessment that is brief and has been shown to be both reliable and valid in identifying learning problems is given to all students. A target score is used to separate those who are and those who are not at risk in a particular subject area such as reading. It is at this initial stage that educators run the risk of missing twice-exceptional students. For example, Stephanie's score on the screening measure does not indicate that she has any reading difficulties. As a third grader, she is right at grade level. However, when she is at home where her parents expose her to books and print materials 2–3 years above grade level, she can comprehend the material easily. She has difficulty with the process of reading, not with the comprehension; because her reading score indicates she is at grade level, she is not identified as a gifted reader with a SLD. Thus, her placement at Tier 1 with grade-level materials allows her to underachieve in reading. Stephanie's case is a good example of the masking effect mentioned earlier: Her giftedness is masking her SLD.

It is at the screening level that the twice-exceptional student is often missed or misidentified. Although the discrepancy model is no longer used in many states with the advent of RtI, this model did have the advantage at looking at IQ first. We had the potential to see that Stephanie had a 135 expectancy IQ and a 96 reading score. With that information, Stephanie would work at Tier 1 with material to assist her reading fluency while working with more advanced material in comprehension. Without this additional information, Stephanie will continue to complete all reading work at the third-grade level. It would be beneficial at the screening level to gather information from parents and teachers in addition to the scores on the screening measures. A sample form is shown in Figure 12.3.

If educators were to gather these additional data from all students, they would have multiple pieces of data to examine beyond just the universal screening score. When data gathered from parents or teachers provide information that conflicts with the score on the universal screening measure, then an IQ test may be warranted. Taken together, these multiple sources of data provide a clearer picture of the needs of twice-exceptional learners. For example, Figure 12.4 shows Stephanie's mother's completed form.

In looking at the answers, Mrs. Cladwell has indicated that Stephanie enjoys literature that is well above her grade level. She also stated that when reading aloud to Stephanie, she makes sure Stephanie comprehends the material by asking high-level questions based on what is being read. Mrs. Cladwell mentioned that Stephanie's vocabulary development seems to be above even that of her fifth-grade sister. She has a high interest in math and science and has received awards for projects completed in both areas. One of Stephanie's favorite pastimes is listening to audiobooks. The answers provided by Mrs. Cladwell point to a child who has a keen interest in reading above-grade-level books and an advanced vocabulary. To compensate for her struggle with reading fluency at these levels, she uses audiobooks or asks to be read to. Clearly the best placement for Stephanie would be using grade-level materials to assist her with reading fluency while allowing her to work with gifted learners who are doing advanced work in vocabulary and reading comprehension. Until Stephanie's reading fluency catches up with her vocabulary and comprehension, she can use audiobooks and earphones to gain the content necessary for the advanced vocabulary and reading comprehension activities. Thus, she is working at appropriate levels to remediate the weakness while still advancing her strengths.

Progress Monitoring

During this stage, the progress of all students is monitored to determine who should be provided with more intense intervention, who is making good progress at the current level, and who needs more advanced material or a faster pace. Daily formative assessments embedded within the lesson, exit cards, or other quick assessments are used as checkpoints to be sure the current level of

Child's Name: _____ Child's Grade: _____

Name of Parent/Guardian Completing This Form:

_____

Prompt	Comments
List three or four books that your child has read for pleasure recently.	
List any books your child has asked you or another family member to read to him or her.	
List the afterschool activities in which your child participates.	
List any sports that your child plays.	
List any awards or honors your child has received.	
What is your child's favorite subject?	
What has your child done at home to learn more about his or her favorite subject?	
Is your child passionate about a particular topic? If so, what?	
Compared to your child's age-mates, does your child have a more advanced vocabulary?	
Does your child ask questions that you have trouble answering?	
Does your child have any unique talents?	
What does your child like to do during his or her free time?	

Figure 12.3. Sample data-gathering chart to supplement test scores.

Child's Name: __Stephanie Cladwell__   Child's Grade: __3__

Name of Parent/Guardian Completing This Form:
__Marianne Cladwell__

Prompt	Comments
List three or four books that your child has read for pleasure recently.	Stephanie has difficulty reading, but she has listened to all of the <u>Harry Potter</u> books on CDs.
List any books your child has asked you or another family member to read to him or her.	The Chronicles of Narnia, The Door in the Wall, A Swiftly Tilting Planet, The Saturdays, and The Mysterious Benedict Society. We ask her questions at a high level while we are reading, and she shows good comprehension and insight.
List the afterschool activities in which your child participates.	Ballet, science club, Math Bowl
List any sports that your child plays.	Soccer, gymnastics
List any awards or honors your child has received.	First place in school science fair in second grade; first place, Math Bowl team
What is your child's favorite subject?	Science
What has your child done at home to learn more about his or her favorite subject?	Particularly likes marine science; checked out books from the library (we had to read most of them to her)
Is your child passionate about a particular topic? If so, what?	Yes, humpback whales
Compared to your child's age-mates, does your child have a more advanced vocabulary?	She has a very advanced vocabulary. Her sister is in fifth grade, and Stephanie uses more complex words than her sister does.
Does your child ask questions that you have trouble answering?	Yes. She wants to know the latest facts and figures about humpback whales. She is curious about their life cycle. We have shown her how to find material at appropriate websites.
Does your child have any unique talents?	No
What does your child like to do during his or her free time?	Listen to audiobooks, play math games, watch videos of gymnastics meets

Figure 12.4. Stephanie's data-gathering chart.

instruction is meeting the needs of all students. Weekly or monthly benchmark testing aimed at determining how well the program is working makes data available to determine next steps for each child to ensure continuous progress. For some, it may mean moving to more intense one-on-one or small-group interventions. For others, it may mean compacting the curriculum (i.e., providing opportunities for enrichment or acceleration when students have already mastered grade-level material that is getting ready to be presented to the rest of the class). For 2e students, it is critical that educators understand the importance of working on these students' strengths as well as their weaknesses.

In Stephanie's case, she may be working on a particular aspect of reading fluency at grade level while at the same time participating with the most advanced students on new reading comprehension strategies. Quite often reading occurs in a 90-minute block with many different groups and activities occurring simultaneously. It would be important for Stephanie's teacher to ensure that the advanced group is working on fluency when Stephanie's fluency work is occurring so that she is not missing the advanced work in comprehension that is critical for her continuous progress in that area. When Stephanie's fluency improves, she should work with material that allows her to continue being challenged rather than languish in an intervention where her progress neither declines nor advances.

For 2e students whose learning disabilities impact nonverbal areas or whose challenges are with fine/gross motor tasks such as dysgraphia and dyspraxia, our most critical task involves efforts to mitigate these difficulties, thereby allowing the students to continue to learn and express themselves in a manner commensurate with their cognitive level. Assistive devices such as the Dragon Dictation application for the iPad (and computer) allow twice-exceptional students to speak their thoughts and capture them in a document rather than using a keyboard. Computers can help as well by providing a means to edit and organize written products. An inability to write legibly with a pencil or pen is not a reason for placing a child in an intense intervention when his or her ability to express thoughts coherently and fluently is not the issue.

Data-Based Decision Making

Teachers constantly gather data as they move through the daily lessons in their classrooms. Asking questions, moving around the room to observe students at work, gathering prior knowledge through a KWL chart, having students complete a graphic organizer about a particular topic, and gathering exit cards at the end of an activity are ways that teachers gather data about their students. Whether or not we have previously considered these normal classroom activities as a means to collect data, they are all legitimate ways for a teacher to determine who has mastered a concept or skill, who needs just a little more work, and who still is struggling with the material. These data pieces can provide important information to indicate whether or not a particular intervention is helping a student make progress. End-of-unit assessments, benchmark testing, and standardized tests provide additional sources of data that may give a global picture of progress over time.

Generally, schools have established routines and procedures for making decisions based on formative, ongoing, and summative assessments. For example, there will be established criteria that students must meet before they can be considered to have made appropriate progress. Not meeting the criteria can result in a more intense intervention based on the data that were gathered. Students who make progress and show continuous growth may eventually resume grade-level work. For the 2e child, it is vital that an appropriate pace is kept in all areas, not just the area that needs attention. For Stephanie, an accelerated pace with complex material should continue in her areas of strength even if a slow pace with less complex material is indicated in her area of weakness. Taking her out of her accelerated work to concentrate more on her area of weakness should not be considered.

Multilevel Prevention System

The bases for implementing the RtI framework are integration of screening, progress monitoring, and data-based decision making within a multilevel prevention system. To ensure continuous progress for all students, a clearly articulated rigorous curriculum aligned to state standards and taught using evidence-based instructional practices is key. Differentiating the instruction to meet the needs of all learners using multiple ways to indicate learning and mastery allows accommodations for learners who may be culturally, linguistically, or economically diverse; lack prior exposure to basic material; or have advanced understanding or learning disabilities.

Because classrooms are generally quite diverse, it is essential that teachers, specialists, support personnel, and parents work collaboratively to meet the needs of these learners within the RtI framework. This collaboration of experts is vital so that appropriate interventions and services can be chosen to meet the needs of 2e learners. As we have seen from Stephanie's case described above, information from her mother assisted in determining Stephanie's need for advanced work in one area while remediation occurred in another. To the general education teacher, Stephanie appeared to be an average third-grade student. Without additional information that indicated some of Stephanie's knowledge and skills were actually above grade level, she ran the risk of under-achieving. Because the universal screening measure indicated she was at grade level, it was not apparent that her SLD was masking her giftedness. To meet Stephanie's range of needs, her third-grade teacher, the special education teacher, and the gifted education teacher collaborated to develop appropriate evidence-based interventions that would provide Stephanie with the support she needed to become a fluent reader while allowing her to work with advanced material in reading comprehension.

The amount of data gathered, the intervals at which it is gathered, and the frequent progress monitoring to reach the goal of continuous progress for all students can be an arduous task for any one person. The collaboration of all those who have responsibility for the education of children is crucial for the RtI model to prevent negative learning outcomes for all students in general and twice-exceptional students in particular. In the past, the traditional role of school psychologists mainly consisted of making decisions based upon testing (discrepancy model) and deciding whether students qualified for services (King et al., 2011). In the RtI framework, school psychologists will be spending less time with standardized testing and placement and more time working with parents and teachers to ensure the child is getting services necessary to succeed (King et al., 2011).

Organizational skills can be an area of weakness for many 2e students, as parents and teachers would testify. They might complete assignments at home but those often get lost in the locker or on the way to the classroom. Other problems might include poor time management, an inability to plan and organize, and struggles with study skills and note-taking. These difficulties not only result in much frustration for the student, parents, and the teacher, but also have a direct effect on the student's academic performance. The RtI team should take all of these into consideration when planning a student's intervention.

Two Case Studies

Joe, an Elementary Student

Joe is a fourth grader with a suspected learning disability in reading. His performance in math and science is superior when compared with peers. Since the middle of his third-grade year, Joe has struggled in language arts, performing in the 40th percentile on the statewide test administered in the fall of this year. Joe's current teacher, Ms. Anderson, is puzzled by his poor reading skills. She reports that Joe is very attentive when she reads to the class and often asks questions that are very thoughtful and intuitive for a fourth grader; however, "he just shuts down when he has to read." It is clear to Ms. Anderson that listening comprehension is not an area of concern. Ms. Anderson believes Joe's excellent memory and reliance on context clues enabled him to compensate for poor decoding skills, but as the reading material became more advanced, this compensatory skill was no longer effective.

Lack of organizational skills is another area of concern. Joe's mother noted that he had always lost items (e.g., pens, books, gloves). She did not seem to think it was much of a problem and shrugged it off as, "Joe needs a personal assistant to pick up the things he loses." However, when Joe's fourth-grade teacher explained the impact of his forgetfulness and poor organizational skills, his mother realized that something had to be done. Joe would, for example, claim to do his homework but lose it on the way to the classroom. This had resulted in lowered grades and much frustration for Joe and his teacher. The RtI team understood that this problem could eventually culminate in difficulties with note-taking, study, and time management skills and that Joe needed help in this area along with reading intervention. The team proposed the following plan for Joe: Tier 2 intervention for 20 minutes daily in addition to reading instruction in the general fourth-grade classroom. A reading specialist would teach reading remediation to Joe and three other students using an intensive phonics-based reading program. In 6 weeks, Joe would be assessed on reading fluency to determine whether he is making progress. To remedy the problem with organizational skills, Joe's teacher and mother are collaborating to ensure the same skills are reinforced at school and at home. They have proposed a simple folder system for completed assignments and ongoing assignments; Joe is also learning a time management strategy with a to-do list to help him prioritize assignments.

Ms. Anderson will continue to build on Joe's strengths in science and math through differentiated instruction in her classroom. Joe is one of the top-performing students in these classes because of his ability to think critically in these areas and often works with a small group of students on more advanced content.

Lydia, a High School Student

Lydia attends a residential high school for gifted students and enjoys the challenge presented by a rigorous curriculum and highly effective teachers. In many respects, she is a typical teenager with a complex and varied social life. She keeps her Facebook page updated hourly through whatever technology she happens to be using at the moment—mobile phone, tablet, or computer— and luckily, these devices have spell-checker. Although Lydia is one of the top students in math, taking her math classes at the local university because she requires more advanced work than even the special school can provide, she cannot spell or write a simple paragraph. Lydia reads voraciously and is an articulate speaker. Her speeches for the debate club are always winners at competitions. She uses a speech adaptive program on her computer to compose her thoughts for her speeches.

Lydia works with an interventionist at Tier 3 for 30 minutes a day to provide her with practice in spelling and handwriting. New software helps her by predicting the word she wants to type and reading what she has written. During her RtI time, she works on the legibility of her handwriting and on spelling in the context of a linguistics course. Phonological awareness, decoding, spelling, grammar, and other language skills are taught in this course. Her teacher uses terminology such as "phoneme" and "morphemic structure." Lydia has made great progress with this approach, and her instructor now emphasizes morphemes—prefixes, roots, and suffixes. These activities help Lydia to spell more words correctly rather than guessing.

The ultimate goal of the Tier 3 intervention is to assist Lydia to gain facility in the spelling and writing skills she will need at the college level. Through intense intervention at Tier 3, Lydia is gaining the confidence she needs in spelling; she feels that the approach using the linguistic course has worked well for her because, "it isn't baby work like I used to have to do. Now I feel like the work is more respectful of me as a person. Before I came here I had to work with the little kids and that was so embarrassing!" Lydia continues, "Here I am taking a university math class, AP Physics, and AP Chemistry. I know I can't spell, and the linguistics course makes me feel like I am in another challenging class. Also, my teachers like everything word processed anyway, so my almost illegible writing isn't a problem, and they don't mind if I write ur [your or you are] or b/c [because] on a discussion post!"

Clearly Lydia is gaining confidence in her ability to write legibly and spell. Her outstanding work in math, in particular, has brought her to the attention of many high-ranking colleges and universities. Because of her positive experience with the RtI process in high school, she is looking for a university that will continue to accommodate her weakness while allowing her to advance as far as possible in her area of strength.

Conclusion

The characteristics and needs of 2e children are often overlooked because generally their area of weakness is noticed first. Sometimes their gifts and talents are masked and their adeptness at coping with a disability makes them appear to be solid students at or slightly below grade level. Using the RtI model may exacerbate this situation if only a universal screener is used to identify students who are at risk for a poor academic outcome. Gifted students who are not identified as such and do not receive services for their abilities do not have educational outcomes commensurate with their abilities; thus, they, too, have poor educational outcomes.

Teachers, specialists, students, and parents must become partners in the implementation of the RtI model. Like the seven blind men and the elephant, each one has a specific piece of information based on their own perspective. It is not until we put all those pieces together that we can form a more complete academic, social, and emotional picture of the 2e child.

References

Anderson, L. W., & Krathwohl, D. R. (Eds.). (2001). *A taxonomy for learning, teaching, and assessing: A revision of Bloom's taxonomy of educational objectives.* New York, NY: Longman.

Assouline, S. G., & Whiteman, C. S. (2011). Twice-exceptionality: Implications for school psychologists in the post-IDEA era. *Journal of Applied School Psychology, 27,* 380–402.

Baum, S. (1994). Meeting the needs of gifted/learning disabled students. How far have we come? *The Journal of Secondary Gifted Education, 5*(3), 6–22.

Baum, S. M., & Owen, S. V. (2004). *To be gifted and learning disabled.* Mansfield Center, CT: Creative Learning Press.

Bianco, M. (2010). Strength-based RtI: Conceptualizing a multi-tiered system for developing gifted potential. *Theory Into Practice, 49,* 323–330.

Bracamonte, M. (2010, March). Twice-exceptional students: Who are they and what do they need? *2e Twice-Exceptional Newsletter.* Retrieved from http://2enewsletter.com/arch_Bracamonte_2e_Students_pubarea_3-10.htm

Brody, L. E., & Mills, C. L. (1997). Gifted children with learning disabilities: A review of the issues. *Journal of Learning Disabilities, 30,* 282–297.

Coleman, M. R., Harradine, C., & King. E. W. (2005). Meeting the needs of students who are twice exceptional. *TEACHING Exceptional Children, 38*(1), 5–6.

Council for Exceptional Children. (2008). *CEC's position paper on Response to Intervention (RtI): The unique role of special education and special educators.* Retrieved from http://www.cec.sped.org/AM/Template.cfm?Section=CEC_Professional_Policies&Template=/CM/ContentDisplay.cfm&ContentID=11116

Dix, J., & Schafer, S. (1996). From paradox to performance: Practical strategies for identifying and teaching GLD students. *Gifted Child Today, 19*(1), 22–31.

Heitin, R. (2008). *New hope for twice exceptional students.* Retrieved from http://pdfbrief.com/new-hope-for-twice-exceptional-students.html

Hughes, C. E. (2011). Twice-exceptional children: Twice the challenges, twice the joys. In J. A. Castellano & A. D. Frazier (Eds.), *Special populations in gifted education: Understanding our most able students from diverse backgrounds* (pp. 153–173). Waco, TX: Prufrock Press.

Hughes, C. E., & Rollins, K. (2009). RtI for nurturing giftedness: Implications for the RtI school-based team. *Gifted Child Today, 32*(3), 31–39.

Individuals with Disabilities Education Improvement Act of 2004. Public Law 108-446, 108th Cong., 2nd sess. (December 3, 2004).

King, E. W., Coleman, M. R., & Miller, A. (2011). Response to Intervention: The changing role of school psychologists in relation to gifted students. *Journal of Applied School Psychology, 27,* 341–358.

Lerner, J., & Johns, B. (2009). *Learning disabilities and related mild disabilities.* Belmont, CA: Wadsworth.

Lovett, B. J., & Levandowski, L. J. (2006). Gifted students with learning disabilities: Who are they? *Journal of Learning Disabilities, 39,* 515–527.

McCoach, D. B., Kehle, T. J., Bray, M. A., & Siegle, D. (2001). Best practices in the identification of gifted students with learning disabilities. *Psychology in the Schools, 38,* 403–411.

McKenzie, R. G. (2010). The insufficiency of Response to Intervention in identifying gifted students with learning disabilities. *Learning Disabilities Research & Practice, 25,* 161–168.

National Association of State Directors of Special Education, & Council of Administrators of Special Education. (2006). *Response to Intervention: A joint paper.* Retrieved from http://www.casecec.org/pdf/rti/RtI%20An%20 Administrator's%20Perspective%201-061.pdf

National Center on Response to Intervention. (n.d.). *The essential components of RTI.* Retrieved from http://www.rti4success.org

National Joint Committee on Learning Disabilities. (2011). Learning disabilities: Implications for policy regarding research and practice. *Learning Disabilities Quarterly, 34,* 237–241.

Nielsen, M. E. (2002). Gifted students with learning disabilities: Recommendations for identification and programming. *Exceptionality, 10*(2), 93–111.

Nielsen, M. E., & Higgins, L. D. (2005). The eye of the storm: Services and programs for twice-exceptional learners. *TEACHING Exceptional Children, 38*(1), 8–15.

Pereles, D. A., Omdal, S. N., & Baldwin, L. (2009). Response to Intervention and twice-exceptional students: A promising fit. *Gifted Child Today, 32*(3), 40–51.

Rollins, K., Mursky, C. V., Shah-Coltrane, S., & Johnsen, S. K. (2009). RtI models for gifted children. *Gifted Child Today, 32*(3), 20–30.

Schiff, M., Kaufman, A., & Kaufman, N. (1981). Scatter analysis of WISC-R profiles of learning disabled students with superior intelligence. *Journal of Learning Disabilities, 14,* 400–404.

Schultz, E. K., & Stephens, T. L. (2008). *SLD identification: An analysis of state policies.* Retrieved from http://www.advocacyinstitute.org/resources/SLD. Identification.State.Policy.shtml

Silverman, L. K. (2009). The two-edged sword of compensation: How the gifted cope with learning disabilities. *Gifted Education International, 25,* 115–130.

Tannenbaum, A. I., & Baldwin, L. J. (1983). Giftedness and learning disability: A paradoxical combination. In L. H. Fox, L. Brody, & D. Tobin

(Eds.), *Learning-disabled/gifted children: Identification and programming* (pp. 11–36). Baltimore, MD: University Park Press.

Torrance, E. P. (1966). *Torrance Tests of Creative Thinking.* Bensenville, IL: Scholastic Testing Service.

Trail, B. A. (2011). *Twice-exceptional gifted children: Understanding, teaching, and counseling gifted students.* Waco, TX: Prufrock Press.

Warshaw, M. (2006). *Tips for parents: Meeting the needs of twice-exceptional children.* Retrieved from http://www.davidsongifted.org/db/Articles_id_10140.aspx

Weinfeld, R., Barnes-Robinson, L., Jeweler, S., & Shevitz, B. R. (2006). *Smart kids with learning difficulties.* Waco, TX: Prufrock Press.

Yssel, N., Prater, M., & Smith, D. (2010). How can such a smart kid not get it? Finding the right fit for twice-exceptional students in our schools. *Gifted Child Today, 33*(1), 54–61.

CHAPTER THIRTEEN

REMAINING CHALLENGES, LIMITATIONS, AND CONCERNS

Laurence J. Coleman and W. Thomas Southern

Readers of this book are likely to have a predisposition to implement Response to Intervention (RtI). Clearly, the preceding chapters have this orientation. However, we have reservations about implementation. This chapter lays out challenges and concerns about RtI and the education of gifted and talented children. The challenges have to do with implementing RtI, given the nature of schooling and children who are gifted and talented. The concerns have to do with conceptual and philosophical concepts implicit in the models underlying Response to Intervention and gifted education. We examine each. In addition, we attempt to delineate how the application of RtI from its roots in special education is a mistake for the field no matter which model for gifted education one adopts. Our critique is broad. It does not get into specific ways in which the primary aspects of RtI (e.g., a multi-tiered system of supports, use of data-driven decision making, progress monitoring, and assessments) might be altered to make models work better for gifted children. Picking at the particular primary aspects of the RtI implies that by tweaking the pieces we can fix the whole to be more efficacious for children who are gifted. We do not argue with the parts per se, because we favor many of them in isolation; but in the combination and interactions of those elements a hidden mindset operates that is antithetical to gifted education, undermines its core beliefs, and threatens its very existence.

A Philosophical Orientation

Supporting RtI is in our blood as special educators of children with disabilities and children who are gifted. We want the talents of all children to be recognized and developed further. National organizations such as The Association for the Gifted (TAG), a division of the Council of Exceptional Children (CEC), and the National Association for Gifted Children (NAGC) have made statements about inclusion and Response to Intervention that seem to echo those beliefs. We participated in many of those discussions and were generally supportive of them. As time has passed, however, we have come to doubt the melding of these approaches. Our rethinking has led us to contend that incompatibilities exist between education of disabled and gifted groups, theoretically and practically, which make their integration in the form of RtI initially marginally successful but ultimately destructive to the field of gifted education and to the development of talent in diverse groups. We have come to these conclusions both from a philosophical view about the nature of gifted education and a discomfort with the "goodness of fit" concerning the overall applicability of RtI to our field. We first will discuss the models that inform our philosophic unease.

Three models of education underlie discussions of the education of children who are gifted and talented and from diverse backgrounds and abilities. Two of the models, Gifted Talented Education (GTE) and Talent Development Education (TDE), are joined in this volume by a third model, Response to Intervention (RtI). An analysis of these models reveals the discontinuities among them in terms of conceptual underpinnings and practical implementation. This chapter provides such a review.

One element in the discussion is the claim of similarity between gifted and other exceptional learners. We believe such a claim minimizes significant differences that characterize human development and devalue the meaning of talent development. These differences should not be overlooked.

Analyzing/Dissecting the Models: RtI, GTE, and TDE

The analysis begins with commonalities among the models followed by a summary of each model. We continue by digging into the premises, goals, and operational means of the models to expose discontinuities among them.

The next section then examines of the root metaphors that are inherent in the models.

Summary of RtI, GTE, and TDE Characteristics

The models focus on children who are at risk in the general education classroom. They assert that educators should know their students, attend to individual differences, and modify instruction to meet the students' educational goals. They decry the one-size-fits-all way of thinking. Sensitivity to variations among students calls for thoughtful teachers, multiple teaching methods, and appropriate curriculum. A number of options should be available to provide an appropriate free public education.

The models also have implicit metaphors and notions on the goals of schooling, the role of schooling, student learning and development, and teacher and curriculum. These embedded differences raise questions as to their compatibility. This chapter reveals these differences. We begin by summarizing the models, look into the metaphors undergirding them, and then dissect more specific differences.

Response to Intervention summarized. The implicit goal of RtI is successful learning in the general education classroom. Independent functioning in the larger community is a special education goal, but we do not see it in RtI. Seeking the norm and attaining that level is desirable. The standards for success are essentially functioning at or meeting chronological age or grade norms. Students are expected to respond to interventions, which will enable them to override learning deficits and attitudinal barriers. When age norms are met, RtI steps away. A second implicit goal of fitting into the regular class is regulatory ideal because normal variation is minimized.

RtI is essentially a preidentification model with an instructional component. The intent is to reduce the numbers and cost of students in special education by implementing a scientific system attuned to the variations among students, which put them at risk for being successful in the school. Decisions are to be based on data and predetermined criteria so children may receive appropriate levels of service and resources. Interventions vary by intensity. The opening level is to determine the academic functioning of children in a regular classroom in which whole-class instruction is implemented. The heart of intervention is more direct, small-group instruction. The level of directness increases and the size of the treatment group decreases to one as the child does not learn as intended. The creativity, if there is any, of teachers is to devise ways to intervene in the lives of children who are unresponsive to the regular curriculum. Those who are unsuccessful at some predetermined level move on to future intervention.

Gifted Talented Education model summarized. The goal of GTE is to develop the abilities of students in order to maximize their potential. In most schools, this is evident in academics and sports and less so in artistic subjects. Gifted children exist in all groups and genders in proportion to the general population. Abilities are normally distributed. Identification involves assessing abilities and sometimes attitudes to find indication of potential and facility with learning. Identification can be effected using appropriate screening and identification procedures with attention to general ability, creativity, and achievement. Advanced learning is advocated as is maintaining child growth proportional to developmental and educational needs. Teaching is geared to broadening and developing those latent potentials as well as developing creativity and personal-social outcomes. Success is judged in terms of achievement, personal competency, and the relative balance among the abilities. Impediments are in the form of school structure, inadequate curriculum, and school policies. Unrealized potential manifested in underachievement is considered a serious problem. Education is most appropriate in classes with learners from diverse backgrounds, cognitive capabilities, and multicultural perspectives.

Talent Development Education model summarized. The goal of TDE is to promote development and excellence in a talent domain. In most schools, this means academic talent and less so other talents. Success is defined as moving to the most complex level possible in a domain. Identification is based on finding the most rapid learners in a domain and enabling their development. Teaching is directed to accelerating and broadening learning toward a goal that is defined fuzzily (indefinable), yet recognizable to experts in a domain as advancing development in that area. Students and teachers are expected to be engaged in the domain. The size of the treatment group gets progressively smaller as one masters the domain and creativity appears. Obstacles learners encounter may include the particular structure of the domain, their declining commitment to the domain, insufficient knowledge of the teacher, and lack of necessary resources. Exiting the domain would likely happen outside the school.

Our descriptive summaries of the models provide a peek into probable discontinuities among them, yet at this point do not seem to offer substantive points of conflict. In the next section, we begin to make the problems more apparent.

Metaphors and What They Tell Us About RtI, GTE, and TDE

Thinking is influenced by the hidden metaphors that people use to understand and interpret their world (Lakoff, 1992). Metaphors are abstractions and do not map on to the real world in a one-to-one perfect correspondence. In this sense, they are fuzzy constructs with less than sharply defined boundaries. Yet, they have the power to change completely our thinking about the world as we have seen in science in the works of Einstein (train: time and light), Piaget (digestion: accommodation and assimilation), and Freud (iceberg: unconscious).

Metaphors are the hidden controllers in the thinking of the proponents of the three models. We examine the root metaphors upon which the models are constructed and the nature of the narratives surrounding the models. The root metaphors can be understood also in terms of the professional roles associated with each model.

Root Metaphor for RtI: Technical Rationality (Exemplary Professional Role: Engineer)

At the heart of RtI is the belief in technical rationality. Schon (1983) has described it as "instrumental problem solving activity made rigorous by the application of scientific theory and techniques" (p. 21). The basic idea is that through systematic analysis, data gathering, and logic, solutions to problems will become evident and thus resolved. All of the literature on RtI reflects this orientation with assessment, protocol, monitoring, and so forth. The engineer is the profession that captures this model. In terms of general education, RtI is a remedial general education concerned with foundational (universal) domains and growth to the norm. The RtI model is a mix of administrative and instructional decisions in the sense that the child is treated primarily within the confines of the regular education program (Fuchs & Fuchs, 2006; Fuchs, Mock, Morgan, & Young, C., 2003).

Root Metaphor for GTE: Idealistic Reformer (Exemplary Professional Role: Teachers Such as Jaime Escalante)

Gifted Talented Education shares some ideas of both RtI and TDE and is a mixture of rationality and idealism. Proponents see potential in all children, work to find it, and encourage development in all areas. Open-endedness is valued in terms of academic and personal growth. Children of potential will realize that promise in the future, if we do the appropriate assessment, have the right curricula, and do the right teaching. Standardized measurement is a necessary tool for selecting and assessing children, although it is sometimes confining. GTE shares the belief that the issue of underrepresentation will be handled when we develop unbiased forms of measurement. In terms of general education, GTE strives to reform general education while maintaining balance in a child and growth proportional to universal development. The GTE model is a mix of administration and instruction in the sense that the person is treated primarily within the confines of the general education program (Gallagher & Gallagher, 1994; Renzulli, 1999).

Root Metaphor for TDE: Transform (Exemplary Professional Role: Creative Expert or Artist)

Talent Development Education shares some ideas with GTE and none with RtI. It is optimistic about future development and selective about students. The domain or talent area is the axis around which decisions are made about fostering development toward the limits of the domain. Persistent commitment is assumed on the part of learners and teachers. It is at the limits of a domain that excellence and transformation occur. Not all students are expected to progress in this model: Exiting is expected for most. Placement in a setting with like-minded children is typical. Special schools and mentors are needed. TDE is typically concerned with non-universal domains and attending to the development of talent. The TDE model is primarily an instructional model. The emphasis is on the individual's growth (Subotnik & Jarvin, 2005).

The expression of the root metaphors can be seen in the narrative surrounding the models. We have fashioned Table 13.1 to present terms that are associated with the models. Read the table from left to right. The clearest contrasts are between RtI and TDE. These terms are our interpretation of the narratives and are not necessarily found verbatim in those texts. Reading the terms from left to right makes it appear that a continuum exists across these models, and to some extent that is the case. But at a deeper level, it becomes apparent that we are not talking of a continuum but rather of increasing levels of irreconcilability. The reason these models do not work is that the metaphors limit what they will do and, like rubber bands, pull them back to irreconcilable places. Programs built on these models cannot work in the long term.

Following from the metaphors, we look more deeply into attributes or characteristics of the models in order to clarify subtle and significant differences. The discussion assumes an ideal version of the model in order to make

Table 13.1
Contrasting Terms Between RtI, GTE, and TDE

Response to Intervention (RtI)	Gifted Talented Education (GTE)	Talent Development Education (TDE)
Ameliorative	Constructive	Transformative
Technical	Journeyman	Craftsman/artistic
Remediation	Considered practice	Deliberative practice
Interested	Task commitment	Passion
Universal	Foundational/universal	Non-universal
Incremental	Episodic/periodic	Epiphany
Resilient	Supportive	Fragile
Average	Above average	Excellence
Convergent	Convergent/divergent	Divergent
Individual-group	Individual-subjects	Individual-domain
Age/grade	Age/grade/subjects	Domain
Steady	Rapid learning	Fast abstract/complex learning
All	All/some	Few
Reproduction	Little C creative	Big C creative

explicit the actual meanings. In practice, however, no implementation of a model is ideal. We believe by sharpening the differences, we can more readily see the educational problems facing children and educators when these models are combined.

Discontinuities of RtI, GTE, and TDE

The differences become more sharply focused when we look at them in greater detail. RtI, GTE, and TDE contain contrasting notions of education. Explications of the differences originated in previous analyses (Coleman, 1985, Coleman & Cross, 2005; Cross & Coleman, 2005) and are extended here. Others (Dai, 2010; Gagné, 2005) have covered some of the same ground in their interpretations of the field. Table 13.2 presents the discussion in a graphic form. We examine these attributes below.

Table 13.2
Differences Between RtI, GTE, and TDE

Attributes	Response to Intervention (RtI)	Gifted Talented Education (GTE)	Talent Development Education (TDE)
Long-term goals	Attain mastery of basic skills, reduce variance in grade	Maximize whole person, asynchrony minimized	Maximize talents of person, excellence
Developmental rate, learning rate	Normal age and grade progression, basic skills	Age and grade specific, fast, generally universal	Field specific, rapid, non-universal
Attitudes toward ability	Irrelevant, reactive, mastery of skills, narrow the range	Reactive, balanced, increase variance claimed	Proactive, mastery
Creative potential	Irrelevant, mastery of skills first	Normally distributed, emerges in most situations	Province of masters in field, increases with competence
Child's part in learning	Passive	Committed to tasks	Active, passionate
Timing of beginning instruction	Formal, school entrance, three R's first, group oriented	Formal, exploratory, primarily at school entrance, group oriented	Informal, explorative, early as possible, individually oriented
Teacher role and expectations of learners	Instructional manager-trainer, standardized protocols, reteach All must reach minimal level, otherwise refer, overlearning	Generalist, new teacher yearly, reteach as needed, small group Some will, some won't, mastery related to mental age	Expert, few teachers with multiyear contracts, reteach as needed, individual Child is committed, complete mastery, deliberative practice
Evaluation, lack of growth, resources	Frequent, age and grade related, mastery education's fault, targeted use to meet the standards	Infrequent; delayed; relative to age and grade and task; child, family, and prior teacher fault; education's fault; all that is possible	Frequent, encouraging, immediate, relative to task, teacher fault, all that is possible, sacrifice worth it

Long-Term Goal

The models start off with a different conception of where they are going. The starkest difference is between the gifted-oriented models (GTE and TDE) and Response to Intervention. The former want to maximize development and increase the variation among children; RtI is concerned with a narrower range of knowledge and skills, primarily reading and math, and with reducing the range of differences among students. However, what GTE and TDE aim to maximize is not exactly the same. Gifted Talented Education is focused on the whole child. Broad areas of education (i.e., academic, personal, social, and physical) are its concern. TDE strives to maximize the child's development within a talent domain with attention to other educational areas that accentuate that development. Asynchrony or imbalance is viewed dissimilarly. Talent Development Education embraces asynchrony as a certain concomitant of advanced development. GTE recognizes it and is discomforted by its presence.

Developmental Rate, Learning Rate

The models' orientation to rate of learning and development are controlled by whether development is tied to content (domain/field of interest) or age (chronological, mental, grade). Indicators of growth are judged according to relevant markers. All of the models support learning and development, but where they differ is in terms of the meaning of those broad terms. TDE is specific to growth within the field/domain. Learning precedes development. Not all children are expected to be able to learn quickly. The outcome of growth is the highest uncharted levels of the domain. GTE encourages faster learning, but development is presumed to be a prerequisite for advanced learning. Age and grade norms describe the expected level of growth. RtI wants learners to approach and meet normal age and grade indicators in basic skills. Concern is placed on those who are developing slower, rather than faster, than expected. Meeting age and grade indicators signals time to exit the system in RtI.

Attitudes Toward Ability

How ability is regarded separates out the models, too. RtI regards ability as relatively irrelevant to learning if instruction is appropriate. Narrowing the range of performance in a classroom by raising the lower performers to the age or class mean is the outcome. Gifted Talented Education seeks out high average general ability because it is considered crucial for future growth. For TDE, ability is more narrowly defined. The significance of any ability lies in its connection to domain-specific learning. General ability is less fundamental and less predictive to learning and development in the domain.

Creative Potential

Creativity has a place in the gifted-oriented models, but is of no concern for RtI. The difference between TDE and GTE is the source of creativity and its appearance in the learning and developmental process. Gifted Talented Education views creativity as present in all children in varying amounts, which is normally distributed. Creativity should be developed in most educational areas. The presence of creativity is judged in terms of the individual and peers. For Talent Development Education, creativity emerges relatively late in the learning process as one becomes conversant with the field. A person cannot be creative unless he or she has a deep understanding of the field or domain. Ordinary creativity is the province of GTE, and domain-specific creativity is implicit in TDE.

The Child's Part in Learning

None of the models sees the learner as simply a receiver of information and skill. Key terms are activity level, motivation, and attitude toward learning. Using these terms, in TDE the child has a highly active role in seeking out new learning and propelling him- or herself toward greater complexity and abstractness. Passion characterizes the motivations and expected attitude. For GTE, the child is active, not in an enthralled way, but rather in an earnest, absorbing manner. Helping children get excited about learning is advocated. Children who get too active and involved are considered problematic. For RtI, the child is less active as a learner, almost passive, needing to be drawn into learning and encouraged to be more engaged in the process. The activity level may change over time.

Timing of Beginning Instruction

When does instruction begin in the models? Two of the models tend to place their attention on the formality of school entrance as the start of instruction. When children show up for school, serious learning begins for GTE and RtI. GTE, like TDE, supports exploratory learning; RtI does not. For Talent Development Education, instruction is supported as early as it is recognized in the informal setting of the home or community.

Teacher Role and Expectation for Learners

The teacher role in each system can be summed up in three words: generalist (GTE), manager-trainer (RtI), and expert (TDE). The teacher in GTE is a generalist, usually replaced every year, who teaches the class group in multiple areas. The GTE teacher expects that most students will learn. Practice is encouraged and mastery is associated with students' mental or advanced cognitive age rather then grade norms. Reteaching occurs as needed. In RtI, standardized protocols are used for teaching basic skills. The RtI teacher, on the other hand, expects all children to reach the minimal appropriate age or grade level. Children are likely to be hesitant and uninterested in learning. Reteaching is expected until mastery is achieved. Exceptions require overlearning. In Talent Development Education, the child encounters relatively few teachers with multiyear contacts. The TDE teacher expects the child to be completely committed to learning in that field and willingly engages in deliberate practice to advance his or her mastery. It is inconceivable that a child would not be active in his or her own learning.

Evaluation, Lack of Growth, and Resources

How evaluation is carried out differs. Frequency of evaluation is high in RtI and TDE and less so in GTE, where it is often delayed. For RtI and TDE, evaluation is immediate, daily, encouraging, and closely monitored. The former tends to use standard measures; the latter the judgment of the teacher or performance. Lack of growth in GTE and RtI is regarded as primarily the teacher's responsibility. Resources to foster learning differ between TDE and RtI, too. The TDE model asserts that all that is possible should be done, and sacrifice is worth it if it advances development. When children are not learning as expected for the GTE model, it is others (the family, prior teachers, child) who are at fault. All of the resources that are available should be used to further learning.

Summarizing the Philosophical Issues

We have offered an analysis that points to serious discontinuities beneath the presumed commonalities among the models. These differing meanings suggest that melding the models in programs will create problems. In our view, these are points of potential conflict that cannot be reconciled. The metaphors act to pull proponents back to points where reconcilability might be possible. The specific attributes and assumptions point out in more detail where the problems lie and the torsion applied to these philosophical underpinnings.

Gifted Education as Special Education Metaphor

In one sense, it is understandable to borrow ideas and directions from special education. The genesis and direction of special education in general calls for a concentration on the individual, increasing the horizon of opportunities available to the student, and the advocacy for a neglected minority. Yet, the history of borrowings from special education seems checkered at best. In the most recent past, gifted education has borrowed the concepts of resource rooms, hemispheric specialization instruction, process instruction, and inclusion—among others. We would argue that might also be true of Response to Intervention.

For example, inclusion was touted within special education as a means to several ends and couched in terms of civil rights and the separate but unequal implications thus accruing. It, however, militated against offering unique and individualized programs that would maximize students' talents, and it allowed a social imprimatur for denying these services.

Although inclusion as a concept for the education of the gifted may have been one more thrust upon the field than enthusiastically adopted, it has caused problems in its application. The same may be said for adoption of RtI. There have been a number of clarion calls for adoption of the methods of RtI for gifted students, certainly more than one saw for inclusion or some of the other metaphoric acquisitions one has seen in the past. A closer examination of the origins of RtI and the assumptions underlying the model might be illustrative, paying particular attention to the implication of each assumption for gifted students.

The Genesis and Assumptions Underlying RtI

Overidentification. Certainly, much of the impetus for Response to Intervention in special education arose from the assumption that the population of students identified with disabilities was skyrocketing. A widely held assumption was that students were being identified as having special learning needs solely to escape rigorous accountability (Yell, 2005). Overidentification has severe impacts on the economic resources of school districts. A relatively small part of the expense of special education falls to the federal or state governments. The largest portion of the mandates falls to individual school districts. Identification of students requires service, and service is rather stringently defined in terms of resources and caseloads. Hence, overidentification has a real impact on the district.

Arrayed against this assumption, however, are marked differences for the students with gifts and talents. Unlike other populations of exceptional learners, identification of the gifted and talented is not mandated in most states. Nor in most states does it incur mandated extraordinary expenditures. Convincing districts to identify students at all for special provisions is one of the major tasks we face in the field. Given that, the greatest additional problem associated with identification has been underidentification of students from diverse populations. This has consumed a huge share of the research and advocacy efforts in the field and was the focus of every major federal research initiative in the last 20 years. Secondly, identification of students as gifted does not seem to impose a similar social stigma. Although some researchers have posited some negative stereotypes surrounding an identification of gifted students, this has not proven to be as serious as one might think (Gross, 2006). Thus, there is no further disincentive to identification for gifted students. Or, at least, the negative pressure for identifying gifted students does not arise primarily from concerns over social or cultural implications. The problems we face in gifted education are not identifying too many students. Rather, it is whom we identify when we manage to convince districts to do so at all. For our field, the impetus to employ RtI for economic or social reasons simply does not apply. There are no real incentives for districts to employ what we may decide are best practices for it.

Students with disabilities are overidentified because of inadequate instruction. The assumption appears to be that given appropriate or adequate instruction, these students would not eventually be identified for special education services. Hence, schools would be eager to adopt a framework for service provision like RtI that structures timely intervention with effective interventions to reduce the numbers of exceptional learners. Schools would thus reduce the economic impact of such services, improve their performance on high-stakes accountability measures, and generally improve public perception.

But for gifted students, this assumption seems particularly inappropriate. These students may receive poor or inadequate instruction, but they may be much better able to maximize its effectiveness. Moreover, schools have little to no incentive to insist that gifted students reach their potential. In most cases, the ceiling on accountability measures is far below the potential performance levels of these students. There is no reward for maximizing potential in the kind of outcomes targeted by politicians and the public. There are certain markers for prestige accorded schools that identify gifted students. However, those achievements pale in comparison to the censurable reports accruing to poor performance on widely reported accountability tests. Especially in times of diminishing resources, these markers of prestige may not be deemed worth the effort and expenditure to maximize.

To the extent we can maximize instructional effectiveness, special education will wane in numbers and expense. The assumptions here suppose that effective "evidence-based" instruction can provide cheaper interventions than those mandated by special education. It is also supposed that here exist appropriate programmatic instructional models that will assist most students to perform. Finally, it assumes that there is a canon of such practices approved with general consensus for addressing and/or remediating most if not all types and categories of deficits.

For the gifted, such assumptions seem even more problematic. There is a dearth of agreement concerning a canon of such practices to meet the needs of students identified across multiple academic and performance areas. Acceleration, one of the most researched and recommended practices, can't achieve that kind of unanimity of approbation.

Attempts to apply some sort of RtI version to gifted students, even those with educational disadvantage, might prove futile given the range and scope of the talents we can observe. Furthermore, successful application of good instructional techniques would result in greater, not smaller, deficits from the general population. RtI will increase the number of students and the observed achievement differential.

Learning can be connected to a criterion that makes the student's performance typical. The assumptions underlying RtI include one that presupposes that students' performance can be described as normal or typical of age peers. This is sort of the obverse of the notion that special needs learners fall behind their peers in academic achievement and that special assistance will remediate the differences.

In the case of the gifted, such an assumption simply does not apply. Any criteria adopted for the gifted would presumably be based on how the student maximizes an already demonstrated capacity for learning. Students may achieve some thresholds of performance earlier than other students, but what would signify that they have reached potential? Normative approaches are ill suited to judge high-achieving students or even potentially high-achieving students because the demands of assessing gifted students quickly outstrip the type and capacity of the norms developed for RtI in regular education. Even supposing that we might target RtI approaches that would serve to recognize and reward increasing student achievement variance, two problems ensue. Common goals that are instituted for gifted programs include many that simply have no well-developed criteria that one might measure to determine the degree of deviation. These include things like creativity, analytical thinking, and knowledge production rather than consumption, to provide only a few examples. Secondly, schools do not have a strong financial or societal incentive to do this. Even if one presumes such criteria might be developed, what district would adopt such goals and provide support for interventions that would serve to meet these new criteria while struggling to meet those already imposed? There is a benefit to declaring a child no longer in danger of qualification for special education. But an analogous one for the gifted does not currently exist.

Instruction can be provided that is competent and faithful to the treatment deemed effective. This assumption that also underlies much of the RtI initiative supposes that teachers can perform the instruction or intervention sufficiently well to be effective. For gifted students, however, there is a lack of well-defined interventions, and those competent to deliver instruction are often not available for gifted students. In fact, as gifted students diverge from peers in achievement, and as they do so at earlier ages, the likelihood is that they will not have access to persons qualified to provide appropriate instruction. At further issue is the question of time allotment for intervention. When one targets achievement of prescribed norms, it likely that some idea of the average and appropriate amount of time to attainment can be calculated. It is one of the ways that concerns about potential disabilities are generated. Falling behind is perhaps the first bit of evidence of an at-risk status. With gifted students, such a notion is not precisely analogous. How far ahead should they be? How long should advanced instruction be provided before concluding it is not effective or that the student is gifted? How serious are missing instructional skills when a broad level of high achievement is observed? These questions are difficult to answer, leaving the notion of what constitutes fidelity of treatment for the gifted undefined.

Good practice will improve instruction overall. This assumption is largely an intuitive one that proponents of RtI hold forth to others. With gifted students, the transfer of benefit from appropriate and effective instruction seems less applicable. As gifted students' achievement discrepancy widens, the direct effect on other students becomes more attenuated. Even where more generally applicable instruction for the gifted is concerned, like creativity and analytical skills training, the opportunities for other students to benefit from and apply these skills become fewer and fewer. Acceleration and advanced training in alternate settings such as concurrent enrollment make generalization of beneficial practices less applicable. Moreover, schools have not traditionally seen the benefits accruing to gifted education in the past. As students proceed through the grades, the impact of their learning on the school community becomes less and less overt. Without any evidence or intuitive assumption, it is unlikely that schools will invest in the benefit of this type instruction.

It is possible to make a case for the need for some species of RtI for the gifted as a form of superior educational practice. Schools will do it because they are convinced that this is the best practice for students who are twice-exceptional or who come from diverse and underserved backgrounds. Although the underlying assumptions of RtI itself may not be supportive of school efforts, state-of-the-art educational practices would be. This is probably supportable, but it would seem that it would have to carry the full burden of all the other assumptions and presumptions of RtI. So why would we do so?

In summary, the assumptions and presumptions of RtI pose some serious potential practical difficulties:

➢ The financial incentives are not present for schools to employ RtI techniques for gifted students to actually *improve* and *increase* the numbers of gifted students even from diverse and twice-exceptional populations.

➢ The mechanisms to do so are useful in identifying students failing to meet some normative goals. They are not attuned to finding underperforming gifted students.

➢ Schools do not generally view potentially talented students as a resource in these times, particularly when identifying them would increase already heavy financial burdens.

➢ The instruments and curricular options available to districts inhibit best practices in applying RtI to the gifted.

Crafting New Assumptions

One might view the entire discussion above and say either that the field of gifted should craft its own RtI assumptions or should limit discussion of RtI to those students who are either twice-exceptional or who are educationally disadvantaged. The assumptions described above might not precisely fit for gifted students, but can't they be adapted, especially for those in the above-mentioned categories? Two problems surface. The first is that schools have an incentive to identify fewer special education students. They do not have a similar impetus to identify more gifted students. The model of RtI, at least that part of it that is based on presumptions of misidentification of special needs learners, has very poor mechanisms to seek out and provide additional services for those who are functioning at or above the norm. Students who are gifted but also have a disability may be found through the normative criteria, but the interventions selected will more likely address only the disability.

Secondly, the triggers for more intensive intervention will likely miss most of the students from diverse populations. Exposure to appropriate, effective instruction might result in better, even extraordinary performances and achievement. However, it seems unlikely that schools will do so without the external incentive provided by the supposed benefits of RtI.

Why Has the Field Moved Toward RtI?

It would seem that some of the underlying assumptions of RtI do not lend themselves organically to gifted education. Why, then, borrow at all? Perhaps one reason to do so is to tie, at least at one level, gifted education to the legislative and litigious strength of federal and state mandates for special education. RtI became a part of federal initiatives almost concurrently with the concerted effort to add twice-exceptional learners into IDEA. Consequently, there is a natural desire to look at entrees into the law as potentially beneficial to the field of gifted education. Moreover, the spread of the concept of RtI has been rapid and encompasses a great deal more than one would have predicted. Professionals in a variety of fields have embraced the concept (e.g., school psychology). The strength of this notion makes it seem more an imperative than perhaps it is. Nonetheless, it is becoming more and more recognizable as a movement in education. We also believe that it is impossible to adopt a title's and a strategy's good parts without subsuming any of its negative connotations. Schools will not look at RtI for the gifted as a pristine and unalloyed creation. It will come bearing all of the gifts and curses accruing to its older namesake. Many of us recall that the field toyed for a while with IEPs for the gifted. Most of us also recall that that those three letters were so fraught with the original's baggage that we reluctantly abandoned the effort for the most part. RtI as it is practiced in special education arouses some major resistance among regular and special educators. Using the term for those practices in identification and intervention, we may well jeopardize those practices through association.

There are practices that are readily and quite clearly supported under the auspices of RtI that are appropriate for some children. At the same time implicit in RtI are ideas that do not map well on to either Gifted Talented Education or Talent Development Education. This lack of congruence foreshadows problems as RtI goes forward. From our vantage point, the metaphors implicit in the models and current special education practices suggest where problems are likely to surface. Our warning to practitioners and to the field in general is to be aware of these points of potential conflict and anticipate appropriate responses. The intention of RtI is to make education more attuned to individuals. Our worry is that the discontinuities among the models may endanger the enterprise of education for gifted and talented children.

References

Coleman, L. J. (1985). *Schooling the gifted.* Palo Alto, CA: Addison-Wesley.

Coleman, L. J., & Cross, T. L. (2005.) *Being gifted in schools: Issues of development, guidance, and teaching* (2nd ed.). Waco, TX: Prufrock Press.

Cross, T., & Coleman, L. (2005). School-based conception of giftedness. In R. Sternberg & J. Davidson (Eds.), *Conceptions of giftedness* (2nd ed., pp. 52–63). New York, NY: Cambridge University Press.

Dai, D. (2010). *The nature and nurture of giftedness: A new framework for understanding gifted education.* New York, NY: Teachers College Press.

Fuchs, D., & Fuchs, L. (2006). Introduction to Response to Intervention: What, why and how valid is it? *Reading Research Quarterly, 41,* 93–99.

Fuchs, D., Mock, D., Morgan, P., & Young, C. (2003). Responsiveness-to-Intervention: Definitions, evidence, and implications for the learning disabilities construct. *Learning Disabilities Research & Practice, 18,* 157–171.

Gagné, F. (2005). From gifted to talents: The DMGT as a developmental model. In R. Sternberg & J. Davidson (Eds.), *Conceptions of giftedness* (2nd ed., pp. 98–119). New York, NY: Cambridge University Press.

Gallagher, J., & Gallagher, S. (1994). Teaching the gifted child (4th ed.). Boston, MA: Allyn and Bacon.

Gross, M. U. M. (2006). Exceptionally gifted children: Long-term outcomes of academic acceleration and nonacceleration. *Journal for the Education of the Gifted, 29,* 404–429.

Lakoff, G. (1992). *The contemporary theory of metaphor.* Retrieved from http://www.ocf.berkeley.edu/~katclark/coganthrodecal/lakoff.pdf

Renzulli, J. (1999). What is this thing called giftedness, and how do we develop it? A 25-year perspective. *Journal for the Education of the Gifted, 23,* 3–54.

Schon, D. (1983). *The reflective practitioner: How professionals think in action.* New York, NY: Basic Books.

Subotnik, R., & Jarvin, L. (2005). Beyond expertise: Conceptions of giftedness as great performance. In R. Sternberg & J. Davidson (Eds.), *Conceptions of giftedness* (2nd ed., pp. 343–357). New York, NY: Cambridge University Press.

Yell, M. L. (2005). *The law and special education* (3rd ed.). Upper Saddle River, NJ: Pearson.

CHAPTER FOURTEEN

FUTURE DIRECTIONS AND OPPORTUNITIES

Susan K. Johnsen and Mary Ruth Coleman

This book has examined Response to Intervention (RtI)—its components, gifted education models that might fit within a tiered framework, and related issues and concerns. RtI has its proponents and critics, but most would agree that a multi-tiered system of supports and services is needed to address the range of strengths and needs of today's students. The concept of progressive services versus labeling students might, however, encompass more than our initial expectations of the model. This chapter will summarize what we have learned about RtI for students with gifts and talents, opportunities that this approach offers, and future directions for consideration.

Effective Response to Intervention Frameworks for Gifted Students

RtI is a schoolwide process that integrates curriculum and instruction with ongoing assessment and intervention (Johnson, Mellard, Fuchs, & McKnight, 2006). It is intended to match appropriate interventions to the needs of students so that students will attain higher levels of development as they progress through a set of multi-tiered supports and services. For RtI to be effective with gifted students, the classroom curriculum needs to be driven by high academic standards, be above grade level, be challenging and meaningful, and support each student's strengths and interests within a talent domain. For students who have already met or exceeded the expected benchmarks, research-based interventions should occur, including acceleration, compacting, enrichment, and other forms of targeted support. These services will often involve professionals, parents, and community members acting as mentors. All of these interventions need to be examined for their effectiveness with a diverse group of gifted students using balanced assessments that incorporate formative, benchmark, and summative measures and that discriminate among students who are advanced or gifted in a particular domain. Assessments therefore need to be differentiated, minimize bias, be above grade level, and provide enough ceiling so that students can show what they know. Practitioners who are implementing RtI with gifted students need to be supported by professional development and policies that permit the inclusion of gifted students such as flexibility of the curriculum, above-grade-level benchmarking, and accelerated options. If these characteristics are present, academically advanced and gifted students are more likely to be recognized and served (Hughes, Rollins, & Coleman, 2011). If the premise of RtI is that it is meant to help all students reach success, then it is essential that the needs of students with gifts and talents be included.

Gifted Education Models That Nurture Potential Within an RtI Framework

Gifted education is already familiar with multiple types of services that provide support for emerging potential. This book has described a few models that might be effective for serving gifted students within an RtI framework. These models all share progressively intensive levels of support that target a student's strengths. These services may be offered within and/or outside the general education class setting.

For example, the Schoolwide Enrichment Model (SEM) focuses on a response to talent approach, in which the educator provides enrichment and gifted education pedagogy within or beyond the general education curriculum. In Chapter 7, Reis, Gelbar, and Renzulli described parallels between Tiers 1, 2, and 3 within the RtI service delivery model and Types I, II, and III Enrichment in the SEM model. Just as in Tier 1, Type I Enrichment provides an enriching curriculum that enhances all students potential; Tier 2 or Type II Enrichment is more targeted toward the specific needs of the student; and Tier 3 or Type III

Enrichment is more intense one-on-one with gifted students involved in self-selected studies. Just as with RtI, the focus is on developing gifted and creative behaviors instead of labeling students.

Another model is the Autonomous Learner Model (ALM). This model uses a multi-tiered framework that focuses on the learners' development with intensity of support determined by the needs and potential of the individual learner. Although Betts and Carey (Chapter 8) viewed some of the activities within the ALM as appropriate for all tiers, responses of learners determine the degree of engagement at a higher level and the need for scaffolding. For example, at Tier 1, all students engage in Orientation and Individual Development; at Tier 2, the Enrichment Dimension might target specific learning opportunities. At Tier 3, the Seminar and In-Depth Study Dimensions provide opportunities for the most intensive programming.

As discussed in Chapter 9, VanTassel-Baska's Integrated Curriculum Model (ICM) also includes features that would fit within an RtI framework. For example, creative and critical thinking that results in high-level products might be appropriate for all students and be used at Tier 1. Tier 2, on the other hand, would include activities that might be accessible to only those students who are advanced or above grade level in a particular domain. Tier 3 would be reserved for students who are engaged in individual learning projects, which would explore deeper issues, themes, and topics related to the unit.

The final model, U-STARS~PLUS (Coleman & Shah-Coltrane, 2010), which was described in Chapter 10, is centered in the K–3 regular education classroom and helps teachers nurture, recognize, and respond to their students' strengths. With an emphasis on hands-on science, U-STARS~PLUS teachers are better able to recognize high potential in students from culturally/linguistically diverse and/or economically disadvantaged families (Coleman, Shah-Coltrane, & Harrison, 2010). Professional development modules focus on strategies to address student strengths across the three tiers. Tier 1 emphasizes whole-class observations for students with potential, differentiated instruction, and family engagement. Tier 2 includes individual observations of students, targeted enhancements for students with specific interests and strengths and additional collaboration with families. Tier 3 includes a body-of-evidence approach to identifying students with gifts and talents in combination with more intensive enhancement and parental involvement in collaborative planning.

Other gifted education models also include tiered approaches to providing services such as the Levels of Service approach (Treffinger, Young, Nassab, & Wittig, 2003) and the Purdue Three-Stage Enrichment Model (Feldhusen &

Kolloff, 1986). It is clear that there are ample models to consider when implementing RtI with gifted and talented students. This foundation provides guidance for those educators who are interested in building more inclusive systems that respond to the full range of abilities.

Opportunities

When effective models in gifted education are integrated with effective Response to Intervention models, occasions for the enhancement of gifts and talents are multiplied. This combination creates the following opportunities for gifted educators and their students.

> *To create a new problem-solving culture in schools.* The inclusion of students with gifts and talents within an RtI framework provides opportunities for the development of a problem-solving culture that encompasses the educational needs of all students. Using a problem-solving approach, teams of educators are more likely to be focused on ways to be responsive to student performance and examine possible modifications, support, or enhancements to the general education curriculum. As Pereles and Omdal suggested in Chapter 4, a problem-solving orientation supports school improvement and develops effective, safe, and trusting learning environments for all students.

> *To focus on talent development.* Response to Intervention supports a more developmental approach, which is consistent with the current theories and models of giftedness. For example, Gagné's (2005) model explains that natural abilities need to be developed into talents through the learning, training, and practicing of skills that are relevant to a particular domain. This developmental focus may require an expansion of the RtI terminology. Reis, Gelbar, and Renzulli suggested a response to talent framework to ensure that assessments include students' strengths and interests and match challenging enrichment opportunities. Pereles and Omdal encouraged the use of multi-tiered systems of support because the term intervention often connotes a more deficit-driven approach, and Coleman and Shah-Coltrane discussed nurturing potential. In any case, the ultimate goal is the development of services that benefit all students and focus on making schools places for talent development for all young people.

➤ *To focus on services rather than labels.* Paralleling the approach toward talent development within RtI is the focus on services rather than labeling students. Attention to services shifts the emphasis away from identifying who is and is not gifted to concerns about ways of developing students' strengths and talents. Formal identification, primarily at the Tier 3 level, is used primarily to access services such as specialized schools and programs, rather than to apply a label. In this way, gifted educators are able to serve students at an earlier point in their talent trajectory instead of waiting until they are formally identified.

➤ *To provide better services to traditionally underrepresented groups in gifted education.* In Chapter 11, Ford and Scott argued that RtI has much to offer the field of gifted education, particularly with populations who are underrepresented. Students from low-income groups or those from diverse backgrounds who are frequently overlooked by traditional assessments may begin receiving supports earlier within a responsive environment and consequently have more opportunities for services. If RtI is also culturally responsive, then it will be more effective with students who are culturally and linguistically different (e.g., African Americans and Hispanic Americans). For these students, a focus on assets rather than deficits is critical for their talent development. Models like U-STARS~PLUS have shown that teachers can recognize, nurture, and respond to children with high-potential across the tiers, providing young children with the supports needed to meet with success.

➤ *To provide better services for twice-exceptional students.* Of particular relevance to the RtI model is the recognition of children who are twice-exceptional. If both academic strengths and weaknesses are the focus of interventions, then students with both disabilities and gifts and talents will more likely be served. However, this service is dependent on the quality of assessments and the students' ability to access a challenging and accelerated curriculum in their areas of strength and interests while at the same time receiving supports in their areas of weakness. Adams, Yssel, and Anwiler pointed out in Chapter 12 that flawed or incomplete assessments may increase the likelihood that students with specific learning disabilities would be excluded from special education and gifted education services. Therefore, in the case of twice-exceptional students, multiple sources of information need to be included within all tiers.

> *To enhance the general education curriculum.* In Chapter 1, Johnsen, Coleman, and Hughes pointed out that access to key resources such as qualified teachers and relevant and rigorous standards-based curricula need to exist for gifts and talents to emerge. Many of the authors described ways that the general education curriculum needs to be differentiated across all tiers. Reis, Gelbar, and Renzulli suggested incorporating elements of gifted pedagogy into the general education curriculum, such as curriculum compacting and enrichment; VanTassel-Baska proposed including acceleration, higher level problem solving, complex products, and interdisciplinary concepts; Betts and Carey recommended a learner-based differentiated curriculum; Davis and Coleman and Shah-Coltrane addressed early engagement in families to support the child's academic success; and Ford and Scott argued for a culturally responsive analytical model of teaching. In all cases, RtI provides gifted educators with an opportunity for enhancing the general education curriculum so that all students' talents become apparent and can be developed.

> *To create a more personalized and individualized accountability system.* In Chapter 5, Coleman and Job looked at the emphasis within RtI on more direct and frequent samples of student performance and the use of data for decision making. Because assessment occurs before, during, and after instruction, it provides more information and is therefore more personalized and individualized than traditional forms of identification. Data can be used to assess a student's talent development within different domains and help students qualify for more intensive gifted education services. Assessments do need, as Johnsen and Sulak (Chapter 2) pointed out, to have sufficient ceilings so that gifted students are able to show above-grade-level performances. Johnsen and Sulak elaborated on how we can use data to support and monitor students' continuous progress across tiers of services to help them engage them in higher levels of enrichment and talent development opportunities.

> *To identify more evidence-based strategies in gifted education.* In Chapter 6, Robinson and Stein identified research-based strategies, including encouraging creativity, higher level thinking, and inquiry-based learning and teaching; compacting the curriculum; using flexible grouping and various forms of acceleration; using primary sources in history; and offering career exploration and guidance for students who are on

career trajectories that involve more than a decade of postsecondary study. With the requirement of continuous monitoring, RtI provides an opportunity for gifted educators to assess whether or not specific curricula and instructional strategies are effective with gifted learners. Similar to special education, individual case-based research can be used to build a bank of evidence-based practices.

➢ *To develop collaborative partnerships.* Pereles and Omdal suggested that gifted education can become an equal partner with general and special educators in developing services that are appropriate for each student. Working as a team, gifted educators can influence the focus of the RtI process and encourage more interventions that focus on students' strengths. RtI also provides more opportunities for parents to be involved, as shown by Coleman and Shah-Coltrane's model for family engagement across all tiers. In Chapter 3, Davis discussed developing collaborative partnerships with parents and communities that enable school personnel to become more familiar with the traditions, values, and strengths of their students' families and communities, which in turn impacts student success and strengthens the cultural competencies of school personnel.

➢ *To build responsive educational systems.* VanTassel-Baska, Coleman and Shah-Coltrane, and Betts and Carey all pointed out that effective implementation of an innovation requires teachers' commitment to positive change in their classrooms, professional development that provides a deep knowledge and understanding of the innovation, and strong leadership. Johnsen, Coleman, and Hughes reminded us that setting high-level standards for programs and learning is important when planning for gifted students. And all indicate that with respect to professional development, teachers need to have systematic training that models desired practices and follow-up support in their classrooms in the form of observation and coaching. Leadership then needs to provide the teacher with time and the necessary resources to make the needed changes. With professional preparation, Robinson and Stein found that trained teachers were more sensitive to the needs and interests of talented learners and had more strategies to meet their needs. RtI provides an avenue for gifted educators to become involved in professional development and to build more responsive educational systems.

Future Directions

Some of the authors indicated that RtI's theoretical underpinnings and purposes are different from those in gifted education (e.g., Coleman & Southern; Reis, Gelbar, & Renzulli). RtI was originally designed (and often operates) as a preventive, early intervention approach to remediate learning difficulties in core subject areas—specifically reading and math. RtI approached in this way is intended to improve instruction in the general education classroom with evidence-based practices to reduce the number of students who might need more intensive special education services. The goal of the intervention is for the student to perform at grade level.

On the other hand, with gifted students, RtI should be designed as an early response to talent, which focuses on recognizing and nurturing a student's strengths. Given the range of possible areas of strength within the gifted and talented population, a broader array of domains beyond the core subject areas would need to be provided. Similar to the traditional RtI model, the RtI model that includes gifted students is intended to improve instruction in the general education classroom so that the potential in *all* children is apparent and developed. The goal, however, is not simply to attain on-level performance but rather to allow for above-level performance and acceleration within a talent domain.

A critical look at how RtI evolved and is still evolving provides important directions for future research on its implementation with gifted students. What are well-defined interventions that develop talents? What would signify that individual students needed more intensive services? How does the collaborative problem-solving process work for children with gifts and talents? What assessments might be used to monitor progress and show complex learning outcomes? When would educators know that a student had reached his or her potential and how should formal identification take place? These are just a few questions among many that need to be answered for RtI to be effective with gifted and talented students.

Robinson and Stein have noted that there are no large-scale studies applying RtI to students with gifts and talents; however, we do have research that supports components of the service delivery approach as noted by the authors in this book. RtI provides a framework within which evidence-based strategies can be placed. This multi-tiered framework organizes access to supports and services based on each student's strengths and needs. The supports and services themselves should have an evidence base showing their effectiveness. Although few studies have been done showing the efficacy of the overall framework itself, studies have shown the efficacy of the strategies used to support the development of a child's potential, gifts, and talents. A large-scale study of RtI's implementation with gifted learners would make a substantial contribution to the field's understanding of the pros and cons of multi-tiered frameworks for this population.

Although the field of gifted education is just beginning to explore this service delivery approach, the door is open for implementing practices that would benefit students with potential who are in the general education classroom and who have not yet been identified as gifted and talented. We recommend that those who are involved in RtI with gifted students begin to pool their accumulated data to examine talent trajectories and effective general education curriculum and instruction, interventions and talent development activities, assessments, and data used in making decisions about progress. In this way, RtI may be improved not only for gifted and talented students but also for all students needing enrichment and acceleration opportunities.

References

Coleman, M. R., & Shah-Coltrane, S. (2010). *U-STARS~PLUS professional development kit.* Arlington, VA: Council for Exceptional Children.

Coleman, M. R., Shah-Coltrane, S., & Harrison, A. (2010). *Teacher's observation of potential in students: Whole class form.* Arlington, VA: Council for Exceptional Children.

Feldhusen, J. F., & Kolloff, P. B. (1986). The Purdue Three-Stage Enrichment Model for gifted education at the elementary level. In J. Renzulli (Ed.), *Systems and models for developing programs for the gifted and talented* (pp. 126–152). Mansfield Center, CT: Creative Learning Press.

Gagné, F. (2005). From gifts to talents: The DMGT as a developmental model. In R. Sternberg & J. Davidson (Eds.), *Conceptions of giftedness* (2nd ed., pp. 98–119). New York, NY: Cambridge University Press.

Hughes, C. E., Rollins, K., & Coleman, M. R. (2011). Response to Intervention for gifted learners. In M. R. Coleman & S. K. Johnsen (Eds.), *RtI for gifted students* (pp. 1–20). Waco, TX: Prufrock Press.

Johnson, E., Mellard, D. F., Fuchs, D., & McKnight, M. A. (2006). *Responsiveness to Intervention (RtI): How to do it.* Lawrence, KS: National Research Center.

Treffinger, D. J., Young, G. C., Nassab, C. A., & Wittig, C. V. (2003). *Programming for talent development: The Levels of Service approach.* Waco, TX: Prufrock Press.

ABOUT THE EDITORS

Mary Ruth Coleman, Ph.D., is a Senior Scientist at the FPG Child Development Institute at the University of North Carolina at Chapel Hill. She directs Project U-STARS~PLUS (Using Science, Talents and Abilities to Recognize Students~Promoting Learning for Underrepresented Students). Her projects have included: ACCESS (Achievement in Content and Curriculum for Every Student's Success), a National Significance Project funded by OSEP, and applications of RtI for young children through the Recognition and Response Project sponsored by the Emily Hall Tremaine Foundation. Dr. Coleman has numerous publications including the 13th edition of the seminal textbook, *Educating Exceptional Children*, by Samuel Kirk, James J. Gallagher, Mary Ruth Coleman, and Nicholas J. Anastasiow (2011). She has served three terms (9 years) on the Board of Directors for The Association for Gifted (TAG), one of which she was President; three terms (9 years) on the Board of the National Association for Gifted Children (NAGC); and two terms (6 years) on the Board of Directors for the Council for Exceptional Children (CEC). She was president of CEC in 2007.

Susan K. Johnsen, Ph.D., is a professor in the Department of Educational Psychology at Baylor University in Waco, TX, where she directs the Ph.D. program and programs related to gifted and talented education. She is editor of *Gifted Child Today*; editor and coauthor of *Identifying Gifted Students: A Practical Guide*; coauthor of the *Independent Study Program, Using the National Gifted Education Standards for University Teacher Preparation Programs,* and *Using the National Gifted Education Standards for PreK–12 Professional Development*; coeditor of *RTI for Gifted Students*; and author of more than 200 articles, monographs, technical reports, and other books related to gifted education. She has written three tests used in identifying gifted students: Test of Mathematical Abilities for Gifted Students (TOMAGS), Test of Nonverbal Intelligence (TONI-4), and Screening Assessment for Gifted Elementary and Middle School Students (SAGES-2). She serves on the Board of Examiners of the National Council for Accreditation of Teacher Education and is a reviewer and auditor of programs in gifted education. She is past president of The Association for the Gifted (TAG), a division of the Council for Exceptional Children (CEC), and past president of the Texas Association for the Gifted and Talented (TAGT).

ABOUT THE CONTRIBUTORS

Cheryll M. Adams, Ph.D., is Director Emerita of the Center for Gifted Studies and Talent Development at Ball State University. She has coauthored three successful Jacob K. Javits Gifted Programming Grants and serves on the editorial review boards for *Roeper Review*, *Gifted Child Quarterly*, and *Journal for the Education of the Gifted*.

Heidi Anwiler is a graduate student at the Center for Gifted Studies and Talent Development at Ball State University.

George T. Betts, Ed.D., is a professor of gifted education in the School of Special Education at the University of Northern Colorado. He founded and has been the director of the Summer Enrichment Program for the past 35 years. His major research areas are the social and emotional needs of gifted, talented, creative learners and the Autonomous Learner Model.

Robin Carey, Ph.D., received her doctoral degree in educational administration and policy studies from the University of Denver with her doctoral dissertation, "Examining the Utility of the Response to Intervention Framework in Meeting the Needs of All Learners." Robin holds a master's degree in gifted education from the University of Northern Colorado, and a bachelor's degree in music education from Concordia College, Moorhead, MN.

Laurence J. Coleman, Ph.D., is the Daso Herb Professor of Gifted Education at the University of Toledo. He is past editor of the *Journal for the Education of the Gifted* and has received the Distinguished Scholar Award from the National Association for Gifted Children and the Outstanding Service Award from The Association for the Gifted, a division of the Council for Exceptional Children.

Joy Lawson Davis, Ed.D., is the director of the Center for Gifted Education at the University of Louisiana at Lafayette. She has served as chair of the Diversity and Equity Committee of the National Association for Gifted Children. Dr. Davis also worked as the Virginia state gifted education K–12 specialist for 5 years. She is the author of *Bright, Talented, and Black: A Guide for Families of African American Gifted Learners* (Great Potential Press).

Donna Y. Ford, Ph.D., is a professor of education and human development at Vanderbilt University. She has served as a researcher for the National Research Center on the Gifted and Talented and has authored more than 150 publications, including *Reversing Underachievement Among Gifted Black Students* (Prufrock Press).

James J. Gallagher, Ph.D., is Senior Scientist Emeritus and former director of the FPG Child Development Institute. He was instrumental in founding the North Carolina School for Science and Mathematics and has influenced gifted education policy for more than 50 years.

Nicholas W. Gelbar is a doctoral student in school psychology and gifted and talented education at the University of Connecticut. His research interests are interventions for students with learning disabilities, particularly twice-exceptional students, postsecondary education and transition for students with disabilities, and effective online education.

Claire E. Hughes, Ph.D., is an associate professor of special education at the College of Coastal Georgia. She is the chair of the Special Populations Network of the National Association for Gifted Children. Her areas of interest include twice-exceptional students, teacher preparation, and high-functioning autism.

Jennifer Job is a doctoral candidate in curriculum studies at the University of North Carolina at Chapel Hill. She has had articles published in *Gifted Child Today*, *The National Teacher Education Journal*, and *The High School Journal*.

Stuart Omdal, Ph.D., is a professor of gifted education at the University of Northern Colorado. His work has been featured in, among other publications, the *Journal of Advanced Academics* and *Inquiry: Critical Thinking Across the Disciplines*.

Daphne Pereles is the executive director for the Learning Supports Unit at the Colorado Department of Education. Over the course of her career, Daphne has been a teacher in gifted, special, and general education, and her work has focused on twice-exceptional students for more than 15 years. She currently directs state efforts to assist districts and schools to create educational systems that support increased student achievement for all. She has published articles in *Gifted Child Today*.

Sally M. Reis, Ph.D., is Vice Provost for Academic Affairs and a Board of Trustees Distinguished Professor at the University of Connecticut. She was a teacher for 15 years, 11 of which were spent working with gifted students at the elementary, junior high, and high school levels, and is a well-known researcher in the field, having authored or coauthored more than 250 articles, books, book chapters, monographs, and technical reports.

Joseph S. Renzulli, Ph.D., is a professor of educational psychology at the University of Connecticut, where he also has served as the director of The National Research Center on the Gifted and Talented for the past 21 years. His research has focused on strength-based assessment, the identification and development of creativity and giftedness in young people through personalized learning strategies, and curricular and organizational models for differentiated learning environments that contribute to total school improvement for all learners.

Ann Robinson, Ph.D., is a professor of educational psychology and the founding director of the Jodie Mahony Center for Gifted Education at the University of Arkansas at Little Rock, where she coordinates the personnel preparation programs in gifted education. She is the Immediate Past President of the National Association for Gifted Children and a former editor of *Gifted*

Child Quarterly and has focused on intervention studies with talented learners and their teachers.

Michelle Trotman Scott, Ph.D., is an assistant professor of special education at the University of West Georgia. Her publications have appeared in multiple journals. She also has authored a chapter in *Studying Diversity in Teacher Education* (Rowman & Littlefield) and is a co-editor of *Gifted and Advanced Black Students in School: An Anthology of Critical Works* (Prufrock Press).

Sneha Shah-Coltrane is the academically and intellectually gifted consultant for the North Carolina Department of Public Instruction. She is coauthor of the U-STARS~PLUS materials with Mary Ruth Coleman.

W. Thomas Southern, Ph.D., is professor and director of gifted programs at Bowling Green State University. He is co-director of the Center for Evaluation Services at Bowling Green and coauthor of *The Academic Acceleration of Gifted Children* (Teachers College Press).

Mary Kathryn Stein has worked with gifted students as a parent, teacher, administrator, and education service cooperative gifted and talented specialist and is currently the gifted programs coordinator for the Arkansas Department of Education. She is working on her doctorate in gifted education at the University of Arkansas at Little Rock.

Tracey N. Sulak, Ph.D., received her doctorate in educational psychology at Baylor University. She has an M.Ed. in curriculum and instruction with an emphasis in gifted and talented education.

Joyce VanTassel-Baska, Ed.D., is the Smith Professor Emerita at The College of William and Mary in Virginia where she developed a graduate program and research center in gifted education. Formerly, she initiated and directed the Center for Talent Development at Northwestern University. She has published widely, including 27 books and more than 500 refereed journal articles, book chapters, and scholarly reports.

Nina Yssel, Ph.D., is an associate professor of special education at Ball State University. Her research interests include twice-exceptional students and teacher education.